Postman Pat

Letters on Ice

Story by **John Cunliffe**
Pictures by **Celia Berridge**

from the original Television designs by Ivor Wood

Scholastic Children's Books,
7-9 Pratt Street, London NW1 OAE UK
A division of Scholastic Publications Ltd
London - New York - Toronto - Sydney - Auckland

First published in hardback by André Deutsch Limited, 1985
This edition published in the UK by Scholastic Publications Ltd, 1995

ISBN 0 590 13250 4

Printed in Italy by Amadeus S.p.A. – Rome

Typeset by Rapid

10 9 8 7 6 5 4 3 2 1

Greendale was having a hard winter, and there had been a lot of snow in the night. It was icy as well.

Postman Pat was out on his rounds as usual, but he had to go very carefully.

Sam Waldron was out, too, with his mobile shop.
"Hello, Pat!" called Sam. "Rough weather!"
"Hello, Sam. How's it going?"

"Well... I don't think I'll be able to get up to Granny Dryden's with her groceries," said Sam. "I got stuck up there yesterday."
"I'll take them with the letters," said Pat. "My van's good in snow."
"Oh, thanks, Pat. Mind how you go."

Sam handed Pat a box full of groceries: packets of tea, biscuits, butter, bread, flour, bacon, sausages, and a big tin of humbugs.

"That'll keep her going for a while," said Pat.
"Thanks," said Sam. "Cheerio!"

And Pat was on his way.

The van skidded and slithered along the steep road to Granny Dryden's house.

She was very glad to see him, specially when she saw he had her groceries, as well as a letter. Pat called out cheerfully, as he came in, "Good morning!"

"Oh, thank you, Pat, that's lovely," said Granny Dryden. "This letter will be from that lass of mine, in London. I cannot find my reading glasses anywhere – would you tell me what she says, Pat?"

"Certainly. Now... let's see..."

Pat tore the envelope open, and read aloud. "She says... 'Dear Mum,
just a line to let you know...'"

"Speak up, please, Pat," said Granny Dryden, "I can't hear you."

Pat went on... "'We'll be able to come up to Greendale to see you for your birthday. Jim started school this week, and Dad's bought a new car. We're all well, and hoping you are, too. All our love, Sally and family.'"

"Ee, that's good news. Thanks, Pat. Have a cup of tea?"

"Thank you, Mrs Dryden. It's just the thing, this cold weather."

Pat enjoyed his cup of strong hot tea. "Well, I'll be on my way, before it starts snowing again. Goodbye!"

"Bye, Pat!"

14

Pat's next stop was at Ted Glen's workshop.

"Morning, Ted!"

"Hello, Pat!"

Pat went to warm himself by Ted's stove. "That's a grand stove you've got there," he said. "I could do with that in my van. Ooooooh...it's lovely."

He had a letter for Ted. "Here's someone writing from a warm place – Australia!"

"It'll be our Bert," said Ted. "It's ages since he's written. That reminds me... I found Bert's old skates this morning. I reckon they'll be just about your size, Pat. Do you fancy trying them? They say the tarn's frozen hard."

Pat looked at the skates. "Well... I don't know," he said. "I'd love to have a go. Is it safe?"

"Aye, it's all right," said Ted. "Miss Hubbard tested the ice this morning. You never know when skates might come in handy."

"Thanks, Ted. Cheerio!"

Pat was off again, along the snowy roads. The wind was blowing the snow into drifts, deeper and deeper. Soon, he had to stop. The road was blocked with a huge drift of snow. Pat thought he would never get through with his letters now.

Then he looked across to the lake, and saw George Lancaster on the ice. That gave Pat an idea. "It's worth trying, Jess. I can take a short cut across the ice."

"Come on, Pat," George shouted, "it's lovely."

"You stay here, Jess, and mind the van," said Pat. "I'll just put these skates on."

Pat laced the skates up firmly, got his bag of letters, and walked carefully out on to the ice.

"Here we go!"

What a time Pat had! He toppled and teetered, and nearly fell over,
many a time; he went whirling round in circles; he just missed a tree,
then had to grab a branch to stop himself.

Somehow, he skated across the ice. Charlie Pringle looked over the
wall, and spotted him.

"Hello, Pat," he called. He was very surprised to see Pat arriving
on skates, instead of in his van.

"Hello, Charlie," said Pat. "Special ice-delivery today."

He handed the letters over the wall.

"Thank you," said Charlie. "Good skating!"

Pat whizzed off again. George was still on the ice. He did get a surprise when Pat shot by with a letter for him. Mrs Thompson was out for a spin, too.

When Pat tried to spin round on the ice, he fell down with a bump.

"Hello, Pat," said Mrs Thompson, "are you all right? What are you doing down there?"

"Just out for a spin," said Pat, and gave her some letters.

"Look at Jess," said Mrs Thompson.

Jess had come to try his paws at skating. His paws went in all
directions at once.

"Come on, Jess," said Pat, "that's enough skating for today. We'll
go home on wheels."

Pat backed his van out of the snow drift, and went on his way.

When Pat arrived at the school, there was no one there: they were all snowed up at home. But they had left a snowman to wait for Pat. Pat had an old envelope in his pocket, so he addressed it to the snowman – Mr Snowman, The Drift, Greendale School – and tucked it under the snowman's arm. Then the school door opened; it wasn't empty after all!

"Hello!" said Pat.

It was Ted Glen and Miss Hubbard.

"Hello, Pat," said Miss Hubbard, "have you seen my bike?"

"It'll be somewhere under this snow," said Pat.

They all searched in the deep snow. Pat thought he saw a handlebar sticking out of the snow, but it was only an old kettle. They found the bike at last.

"Just in time for choir practice," said Miss Hubbard. "I'll be off now."

Pat opened the gate for her.

"Thank you, Pat. Goodbye!"

"Bye, Miss Hubbard!"

"Nothing stops her, does it?" said Ted.

"See you in church on Sunday," called Miss Hubbard, as she wobbled off along the snowy road.

Pat could hear miaowing from the van. How Jess hated the cold! "Cheer up, Jess," said Pat, "I'm coming, now! It's time to go home; and this snow can't last forever."

HOW TO WRITE A COMPUTER MANUAL
A Handbook of Software Documentation

Price

Group
ter, Inc.

000071

The Benjamin/Cummings Publishing Company
California • Reading, Massachusetts
London • Amsterdam
Don Mills, Ontario • Sydney

For Lisa

Sponsoring Editor: Alan Apt

Production Editor: Wendy Earl

Copyeditor: Holly Wunder

Text and Cover Design: Gary Head

Composition: Typothetae

Library of Congress Cataloging in Publication Data

Price, Jonathan, 1941–
    How to write a computer manual.

    Bibliography: p.
    1. Electronic data processing documentation.   2. Technical writing.   I. Apple Computer, Inc. Apple II Division. User Education Group.   II. Title.
QA76.9.D6P75 1984   808'.066001   84-18425
ISBN 0-8053-6870-1
    EFGHIJ-AL-898

The Benjamin/Cummings Publishing Company, Inc.
2727 Sand Hill Road
Menlo Park, CA 94025

Introduction

You may wonder who this book is for, what it's about, how to use it.

IS THIS BOOK FOR YOU?

This book addresses several different audiences: experienced writers, beginners, students—and a few programmers.

If you're just learning technical writing, this book will introduce you to a small but important part of the computer world—writing manuals for the people who will actually use a program. You do not have to know programming to use this book. You do not have to own a computer, either. You do have to enjoy writing, though. And, in general, you need to be curious, flexible enough to work as a member of a team, and patient enough to make corrections to your golden prose. If you have these characteristics, this book will help you get started on your first manual.

If you're an experienced writer, this book will serve as a checklist, reminding you of many ideas you've already mulled over. You'll also find the book helpful in overcoming management's fondness for the old-fashioned style of documentation, which frequently produced user-hostile manuals.

You may be a programmer with an exciting new product. If so, this book will show you how to document your program. You may already have done some writing. This book will show you how to produce user documentation for your program.

WHAT THIS BOOK IS ABOUT

This book assumes that you want to write a manual for ordinary folk, not programmers, not engineers, not computer experts. I focus on manuals for people who are about to use application programs such as word-processing packages.

This book does not explore the writing of technical manuals, those aimed at an audience of experts, such as manuals about electronic circuit boards written for repair people. And the book does not discuss reference material aimed only at advanced programmers, such as the people who have to maintain and update a series of interconnected programs providing inventory, payroll, and billing for the phone company.

A QUICK OUTLINE

This book has five main sections: Introducing the Big Idea, Getting Started, Writing the Manual, Revising the Manual, and Helping Other People Write.

Introducing the Big Idea

The big idea is friendliness. This section gives an overview of what makes some manuals helpful, informative, easy to use, and other manuals terrible. You'll get an idea of how the computer world started producing ugly and unreadable "documentation." And you'll get a glimpse of what I mean by "a friendly manual."

Getting Started

This section offers a survey of the whole process of producing a manual, from your first notes to the printed copy. That's to give you a general idea of the context. Then you get started. You figure out who you're talking to, start gathering information, and make rough outlines of the manual.

Writing the Manual

Here's how to write the beginning, middle, and end of your manual. Special sections focus on the two most common ways of presenting the information: in a very specific step-by-step tutorial, and a general reference section. You also learn about tutorials that do not use paper at all—these are known as computer-assisted instruction.

Revising the Manual

Alas, you'll probably have to rewrite. In this section, you'll find out how to get people to read your draft, to test it, and to verify every fact. Then you have to sit down and make a thousand little changes, throughout.

Helping Other People Write

Once you've written a few manuals, you'll be ready to help other people write. This section tells you how. I review the best ways to review someone else's manual. I also tell you how to improve the writing in the computer program.

HOW TO USE THIS BOOK

If you're just starting to do technical writing, read straight through. If you've been writing for a while, feel free to browse, dipping into any topic you'd like some tips on.

To help you make your way through the book when you want to look something up, I've included these features:

1. *A table of contents.* This lists all the main sections; it appears at the beginning of the book. Plus, at the start of each chapter, there is another table of contents for your convenience.

2. *Lots of headlines.* You can use these to skip to the part of the book you want.

3. *Checklists of key points.* I put these at the end of every chapter. All of them are collected in the back of the book in the Giant Checklist. You can remove the Giant Checklist to use for quick reference.

4. *A glossary.* This has definitions of many of the terms I mention. It's in the back of the book.

5. *An index.* This covers all the important topics, giving you the pages they show up on. This is at the very end of the book.

HOW THIS BOOK GOT STARTED

This book began at Apple Computer as a guide to new employees and freelance writers working for the User Education group in the division that produces the Apple II family of computers. To start, I went around and talked with about fifty of the writers, editors, and supervisors in User Education. In a sense, this book is a report on the way they go about planning, writing, revising, editing, and producing manuals.

But they read manuals by other companies, too. And they see themselves as part of a trend toward user-friendly documentation—manuals that do not frighten, intimidate, or torture the reader. In the computer world of the 1980's, this is still a new idea. (I'll explore the idea more in the first chapter.) So you'll find examples from other companies' manuals here.

Using these ideas, I've taught courses at the University of California, Berkeley, and I've learned a lot from my students' questions, comments, and writing. They'll glimpse flashes of our conversations throughout this book.

Acknowledgements

It's not just my idea. Here are some of the people who have worked together at Apple to develop and refine the strategies I'm summarizing in this book.

Al Agrella	Brad Hacker	Raoul Reed
Lorraine Anderson	Nancy Hecht	Laurel Rezeau
Loretta Barnard	Steve Hix	Rod Riggenbach
Cheryl Bartley	John Huber	Lyn Sims
Meg Beeler	Scot Kamins	Darcy Skarada
Ernie Beernink	Chris Kelly	Martha Steffen
Kathleen Bennett	Heather Kelly	Kelly Stirn
Jon Butah	Jody Larson	Rob Swigart
Toni Calavas	Dick Leeman	Jon Thompson
Jenean Campos	Leslie Liedtka	Bruce Tognazzini
Steve Chernicoff	Connie Mantis	Paul Trueblood
Marilyn Clauder	Susan Meade	Molly Tyson
Rani Cochran	Joe Meyers	Jeff Vasek
Carol Cook	Peggy Miller	Dirk van Nouhuys
Linda Curry	Daunna Minnich	Allen Watson
Amy Davidson	Sherri Morningstar	Elizabeth Weal
Mary Dieli	Kris Olsen	Kathy Williams
J.D. Eisenberg	Dorothy Pearson	Konrad Yoes
Chris Espinosa	Linda Preston	Geri Younggren
Sue Espinosa	Roy Rasmussen	
Judith Friedlander	Don Reed	

And here are just a few of the people—outside of Apple—who have helped me understand and articulate the techniques for writing friendly manuals:

Alan Apt	Nancy Dannenberg	Joe Esposito
Nick Bakalar	Martha Downey	Dirk Gifford
Maureen Baron	Wendy Earl	Barbara Hodgdon

Gerry Howard

Sonya Johnson

Jack Jorgens

Van R. Kane

E. Ann Kaplan

Henry Korman

Bill Lipsky

Elizabeth McKee

Mark Merker

Lisa Price

Bob Roberts

Carlene Schnabel

Tracy Smith

Linda Urban

Amanda Vail

Mitra Varza

Chris Williams

John Woods

Holly Wunder

John Zussman

Jonathan Price, who is a senior technical writer at Apple Computer, Inc., developed the book in collaboration with other members of the User Education Group in the division that makes the Apple II$^+$, Apple IIe, and Apple IIc personal computers. He has taught at the University of California, Berkeley, Rutgers University, and New York University. His other books include *30 Days to More Powerful Writing* and *Put It In Writing!*

Contents

PART I   **INTRODUCING THE BIG IDEA 1**

1   THE BIG IDEA **3**

Don't Beat Up the Reader 5
Where Bad Manuals Come From 6
   Schedules 6
   Lack of Audience Definition 6
   Poor Design 6
   Downright Disdain 6
A New Idea 6
Thinking About Your Readers 8
   Recognize They're Different 8
   Assume They Want to Learn and Grow 8
   Stick With 'Em 8
What a Reader Wants from You 8
A Quick Review 9

PART II   **GETTING STARTED 11**

2   DEVELOPING—AND REVISING—YOUR SCHEDULE **13**

A Typical Project Schedule 15
   Request 15
   Design 15
   Implementation 15
   Maintenance 17
   Update 17
   Migrate 18
But What About Your Own Schedule? 18
   An Antidote to Optimism 18
   Some Other Rules of Thumb for Scheduling 19
   Giving and Taking 19
Taking Other Projects Into Account 20

What You Do at Each Stage 20
  Document Design 20
  Alpha Draft 21
  Beta Draft 22
  Final Draft 22
  Edited Draft 23
  Typeset Versions 23
  Printed Version 23
Memo-ing the Team 24
And When the Schedule Dissolves 25
How Your Schedule Affects Other People 26
A Quick Review 27

3   UNDERSTANDING YOUR AUDIENCE **29**

Get Specific 31
Distinguish Between Audiences 32
Keep the Focus on Their Goals—Not Yours 32
Remember They're Smart 32
Organize Around What They Want 33
Imagine Their Questions 33
Conduct Research—On the Spot 34
A Quick Review 35

4   GATHERING INFORMATION ABOUT THE PROGRAM **37**

Ask Questions 39
Talk, Talk, Talk 40
Become a Member of the Team 41
  Talk With the Team Leader First 42
  Say What You're Going to Do 42
  Keep Everybody Informed 42
  Learn the Lingo—Fast 42
  Don't Make Them Repeat 42
  Recognize That They Are Creative 42
  Be Prepared 42
  Advertise 42
  Write Down Your Suggestions 43
Read Whatever 43

Dissect the Specs 43
   Configuration Section 43
   Implementation Procedures 43
   Data Dictionary 44
   Input 44
   Processing Operations 44
   Secret Formulas 44
   Files 44
   Decision Tables 44
   Security 44
Write to Find Out What You Don't Know 45
Participate in Developing the Program 46
Grow Slow 47
A Quick Review 47

5   ORGANIZING THE MANUAL **49**

Follow the Reader 51
Speed Up Access 52
Distinguish Between Tutorial and Reference 53
   Tutorials: On Paper or on the Computer 55
   Reference: On-line or on Paper 56
Figure Out the Minimum 56
Make a Series of Manuals Look Like One 57
A Quick Review 58

PART III   **WRITING THE MANUAL 61**

6   BEGINNING EVERY MANUAL—AND EVERY CHAPTER **63**

Make Your Tables of Contents Helpful 65
Show Your Readers How to Use the Manual 67
Make a General Introduction, Too 69
Add Detail to the Table of Contents for Each Chapter 71
Provide an Overview of Every Section 72
And Now . . . A Quick Review of Beginnings 73

7   CREATING A STEP-BY-STEP TUTORIAL **75**

Organization Is Crucial 78
Think Like a Teacher 78
Tell 'Em How and Where 79
Introduce Each Section 80
Divide Your Material Into Short Steps 82
Show People How to Get Out 83

Separate What to Do from What It Means 84
Put In Lots of Displays 85
Define Your Terms 85
Put In Pictures 86
Anticipate Variations 88
Summarize 89
Give People a Break 91
Allow Yourself Some Asides 91
Allay Anxiety 91
Restore Your Sample Files 92
Test It. Revise It. Test It Again. 92
Tell People Where to Go Next 93
A Quick Review 95

8   CREATING COMPUTER-ASSISTED INSTRUCTION **97**

The Main Benefits 99
The Disadvantages 100
A New Way of Writing 101
Focus on Basics 101
Flash a Menu 101
Explain What You're Going to Do 102
Make Every Segment Short 102
Keep It Light 103
Play Foreground Off Against Background 103
Keep a Rhythm Going 104
Encourage Guessing 105
Catch Those Errors 105
Do the Boring Stuff 106
Give People Some Free Play 106
Sum It Up 106
Tell People Where to Go Next 107
A Quick Review 107

9   SETTING UP REFERENCE SECTIONS **109**

What To Include 111
Adopt a Familiar Order 113
A Typical Function 113
Show How to Do Some Sample Tasks 114
Don't Forget to Summarize 115
When in Doubt, Make a Table 117
Provide Some Forms, Too 119
Report the Reports 120
Translate the Messages 122

Define New Terms 123
And, for Further Reading 125
Make a Handy Reference Card 125
A Quick Review 128

10   DRAWING UP YOUR INDEX **133**

Making Up Entries 136
    Multiple References 136
    Detail 136
    Subdivisions 137
    The Same Idea 137
    See Also 137
    Synonyms 138
    Singular or Plural 138
Including References 138
Punctuating 139
Sorting 139
Revising 140
A Quick Review 140

11   REFINING YOUR STYLE **143**

Noun Clump 145
Before the Before 146
Runt 146
Whazzat 147
Passive Nobody 147
Its Its 148
The Dead Hand 148
Long Words 149
Cliches 150
Trailing Off 150
Parallels That Aren't 151
Half a Contrast 151
Mechanicalness 152
Miss Krinkow's Rules 153
    Dumb Rule #1: Never Start a Sentence with *Because* 153
    Dumb Rule #2: Never Say *I* 154
    Dumb Rule #3: Watch Out for *May* and *Might* 154
    Dumb Rule #4: Never Use *About* 154
    Dumb Rule #5: Don't Use *Then* so Often 155
False Good Cheer 155
Bloodless Writing 155
A Quick Review 156

12   INDULGING IN HUMOR **157**

Understand the Reversal 159
Allow Yourself Some Admissions 160
Make Your Wordplay Accessible 161
Keep It Informal 162
Show Your Sympathy 162
A Quick Review 163

13   DESIGNING YOUR IMAGES **165**

Creating a Look 167
Laying Out the Elements 168
Dreaming Up Images 170
What Might Make an Image? 171
  Where Is It? 171
  What Is It? 171
  How Does It Work? 172
  Why? 172
  What's on That Level? 172
  And Below That? 172
  But What's the Big Picture? 175
  What Are the Steps Involved? 175
And If You Don't Feel Comfortable Sketching 186
  Think of What the Artists Need 186
A Quick Review 187

PART IV   REVISING 191

14   REWRITING **193**

Ask for Comments from the Team 195
Listen Hard 196
Call a Meeting 196
Take the Long View First 198
Check Back—But Not too Often 198
Plan for Updates and Revisions 199
Deciding When to Update or Revise 201
Call an Update an Update 201
Read What the Readers Say 203
Talk to Anyone Who Can Help 204
Recognize When Rewriting Means Writing It all New 204
A Quick Review 205

15   TESTING YOUR MANUAL **207**

Get Started Early 210
Decide What You Want to Test 210
Estimate Your Time 210
Recruit Real Users 211
Figure Out How Many 211
Relax 212
Start with a Lecture 212
Set a Problem—for Reference Manuals 213
Watch Carefully 214
Ask, But Don't Argue 214
Make Notes as You Go 215
Discuss It Afterward 216
Congratulate Yourself 216
And Repeat 216
A Quick Review 216

PART V   HELPING OTHER PEOPLE WRITE 219

16   REVIEWING SOMEONE ELSE'S MANUAL **221**

Your Aims 223
What to Watch For 224
Preserve the Manual's Consistency 225
Maintain Your Innocence—and Sympathy 226
Communicate with the Writer 226
A Quick Review 227

17   SOFTENING UP THE SOFTWARE **231**

Keep Track of the Irritations 233
Do Less, Not More 234
Help Users Guess 234
Don't Lead Users Astray 235
Don't Make Users Feel Stupid 235
Block Any Jargon 236
Help Users as They Go 236
Make All the Menus Look the Same 237
Group Activities the Way Users Think of Them 238
Provide Some Examples 238
Give People a Way Out 239
A Quick Review 240

APPENDIXES 241

A SAMPLE STYLE SHEET 243

FOR FURTHER READING 265

GLOSSARY 267

INDEX 277

THE GIANT CHECKLIST

HOW TO WRITE
A COMPUTER MANUAL
A Handbook of Software Documentation

PART ONE

Introducing the Big Idea

Chapter 1: The Big Idea

1

The Big Idea

Don't Beat Up the Reader
Where Bad Manuals Come From
Schedules
Lack of Audience Definition
Poor Design
Downright Disdain
A New Idea
Thinking About Your Readers
Recognize They're Different
Assume They Want to Learn and Grow
Stick With 'Em
What a Reader Wants from You
A Quick Review

The Big Idea

The Big Idea? You can make your manual friendly.

DON'T BEAT UP THE READER

I'm sure you don't want your manual to act like a bully:

- Bombarding people with techno-babble
- Leaving out key ideas
- Droning on and on
- Never explaining, never defining
- Omitting cross-references and the index
- Filling the pages with solid text

Instead, you probably would like your manual to be:

- Accurate
- Bright
- Clean-cut
- Encouraging
- Friendly
- Full of information
- Kind
- Quick to help
- Trustworthy
- Well-organized

No writer wants to turn out an unhelpful, inaccurate, noncommunicative manual. But it happens.

WHERE BAD MANUALS COME FROM

In many areas of the computer world, an unfriendly tone is almost traditional. The mixture of contempt and indifference, snobbery and laziness tends to accumulate for many reasons.

Schedules

The writer is given almost no time to document a complex system, then is deprived of contact with the designers because "they have important work to do." To speed up the schedule, the writer is told to stop working on the manual before the product has reached its final state. Accuracy, completeness, corrections, warnings, errata sheets, and updates are all considered unimportant. "The key thing is we'll have a manual out there."

Then management decides to cut production costs by using a dot matrix printer that can send small type almost to the edge of the page, and reproducing the pages on a copying machine set to "Light." (This saves toner.) Now no one can read the inaccuracies.

Lack of Audience Definition

The team designing the program takes the attitude that the user is a nuisance. The writer, who has never seen a real user, writes to please the team. In turn, the team treats the writer as a glorified secretary who is supposed to pretty up their prose. The writer begins to resent the team and takes it out on the reader.

Poor Design

The team itself disagrees on what the product should do. The inconsistencies emerge in the manual, baffling the innocent reader.

Downright Disdain

The team takes the attitude that only professionals will use this program— and all professionals like challenges. Anything written in ordinary English is viewed as talking down. Jargon is equated with professional dignity, complexity with membership in the elite. As one team manager put it, "If they don't understand this, they're not qualified to read it."

A NEW IDEA

Attitudes like these have been so common in the industry that most manuals have puzzled and panicked ordinary users. A few of the braver readers actually got angry. Their protests, generally, were ignored until companies like Apple Computer started selling personal computers.

Now a manual could help clinch a sale. The people who make personal computers found that without a good manual customers came storming back to ask for a refund. And the customers complained to their neighbors.

Slowly, throughout the computer business, management, marketing, and even design teams became interested in a new concept—user friendliness. The phrase itself, of course, is a tacit admission that most earlier manuals were user-hostile.

At the same time, the data-processing group in many large corporations started getting a lot of calls from confused users. In some data-processing groups, 30% of the programmers' time went to answering these questions—most of which would have been taken care of by a good manual. Management began to cast about for ways to reduce the expense of answering these calls. Clear, understandable manuals began to seem more attractive.

In addition, companies of all sizes were paying millions of dollars for computer programs that were so poorly documented that the users never got around to using more than half the functions. Management had paid for dozens of capabilities that no one could figure out. Again, an appealing manual began to seem like a good way to show people how to invoke these advanced—and expensive—functions.

So in the early eighties, a new idea began to inspire the computer world. The phrase *user friendliness* started cropping up in conversations in the cubicles of data processing people in large banks, in the garages where programmers were patching together new products, and in the offices of magazines that feed on the boom in personal computers.

A few companies began to release friendly manuals. And, sure enough, they found that friendly manuals sell products, expand users' understanding of the extra features, and save everyone's time.

But there are more personal reasons for you to write a friendly manual. You help people to use the program without suffering too much anxiety. And you have the satisfaction of making them feel competent.

You learn a lot about writing, too, producing one of these manuals. Easy reading usually comes from hard writing. That means more rewriting, testing, and editing than was done on traditional manuals. You'll find out what works and what doesn't, and you'll get a chance to grow.

But *user friendly* is such an ugly phrase that people who use it a lot don't really know what it could mean. So, even with magazine pages full of ads about how friendly the new computers are, and how easy their programs are to learn, you may still be pushed to produce an incomplete, inaccurate, uninformative, and unhelpful manual.

This book aims to help you make your writing friendly, despite the pressures.

THINKING ABOUT YOUR READERS

To make your manual friendly, begin by considering the readers.

Recognize They're Different
You may be writing for several different audiences at once. Make a list of the ways they differ from you and from each other—in their tastes, interests, and levels of experience. Respect those differences.

Assume They Want to Learn and Grow
For instance, learning means going step-by-step, starting at the real beginning, not somewhere in the middle of the whole process. You're a teacher, in a way, and you must think through what they need. Don't set booby traps and ambushes in their path.

Stick With 'Em
A lot of manuals mention the readers in the first paragraph, then dismiss them forever. Instead, you could imagine yourself talking to them throughout the manual, full of advice and alert to their changes in mood and understanding. In each paragraph, take an active interest in what they think and feel. When you think they might start to feel insecure, chat with them. When they just want the facts, speak neutrally. Adapt, as they learn.

WHAT A READER WANTS FROM YOU

Here are some things an ordinary reader wants when you write a manual:

- Tell me the truth. Don't turn a bug into a feature. Admit difficulties. Honesty improves your style.

- Follow me. Organize by what I want to do—the tasks I want to accomplish—not by what some programmer or engineer thinks. Remember who you're talking to. And don't make me jump all around the manual just to find one fact.

- Make it clear. Make the manual easy for me to understand. Accurate. Sharp. Cut through the false dignity. Define whatever jargon you have to use and drop the rest.

- Take the long view. Give me an overview at the start—of a manual and of a chapter. Tell me what's coming up and why I should read it.

- Teach me. Take me through the basic functions, step by step. Tell me what to do and what I should see on the screen each moment.

- Speed up access. Help me to find facts quickly. At least give me a summary, a glossary, and an index. Use active verbs, too, so I know who does what without having to figure it out.

- Update. Include the latest changes. Don't let me find them out later as a big surprise.

- Be complete. Include every detail I might want or need. But put all the technical data in a reference section. Show me how to move from one manual in a series to another.

- Check it again and again and again. Have experts check your facts. And test the manual on real readers. Get their reactions. Then rewrite, rewrite, rewrite.

A QUICK REVIEW

To make your manual friendly, then:

☐ Recognize that readers are different—from you and from each other.

☐ Assume that readers want to learn and grow. Your job is to help them.

☐ Tell the truth.

☐ Follow the readers' changing moods and growing understanding.

☐ Write clearly.

☐ Take the long view, so readers get a good perspective.

☐ Teach, don't lecture.

☐ Speed up access.

☐ Keep up to date.

☐ Be complete.

☐ Check it again and again and again.

PART TWO

Getting Started

Chapter 2: Developing and Revising Your Schedule
Chapter 3: Understanding Your Audience
Chapter 4: Gathering Information About the Program
Chapter 5: Organizing the Manual

2

Developing and Revising Your Schedule

A Typical Project Schedule

Request

Design

Implementation

Maintenance

Update

Migrate

But What About Your Own Schedule?

An Antidote to Optimism

Some Other Rules of Thumb for Scheduling

Giving and Taking

Taking Other Projects Into Account

What You Do at Each Stage

Document Design

Alpha Draft

Beta Draft

Final Draft

Edited Draft

Typeset Versions

Printed Version

Memo-ing the Team

And When the Schedule Dissolves . . .

How Your Schedule Affects Other People

A Quick Review

Developing and Revising
Your Schedule

That's the way other people sometimes think of writers. Sprawled out for a nap. Staring into space. Dreaming. Occasionally scribbling a line or two before turning back to lunch. A wonderful schedule.

Scheduling is where every manual seems to start. In fact, on most projects, a schedule is often the first thing you write.

This chapter outlines the usual stages a programming project goes through, indicating where your writing fits in. Experienced writers will look at this outline and laugh, because it states the ideal. Few projects follow such an orderly progression, but most writers dream of it.

An important element for success is estimating your own time without being pressured into accepting totally unrealistic deadlines. Of course, when you start scheduling your writing, you may get so exhausted just thinking of all the work you have to do in almost no time that you may want to go off to the country for the rest of the day.

A TYPICAL PROJECT SCHEDULE

In general, a programming project goes through these phases: Request, Design, Implementation, Maintenance, Update, and Migrate. The first three phases may cover anywhere from one to four years. The last three have been known to go on for twenty years.

Request
Someone asks for a program, spelling out what it should do. This someone could be a manager who wants to computerize some work, or it could be a marketing person who wants a new product to sell.

Design
A team of programmers, often led by a systems analyst, analyze what the program will have to do. They come up with a detailed plan specifying the functions people will be able to use and the techniques of programming needed to make that possible.

Implementation
An even larger team goes to work building the actual program. Once this

kind of money has been committed, management may think of the need for a manual. You are asked for an outline and description, known as a document design.

You become a member of the team—sometimes sooner, sometimes later, occasionally never. Usually you get to meet the key programmers.

Other members join the team: marketing people, if this will be a product to be sold; or representatives of the users, if the product is being developed for in-house use.

Gathered around a table, the team may look something like this:

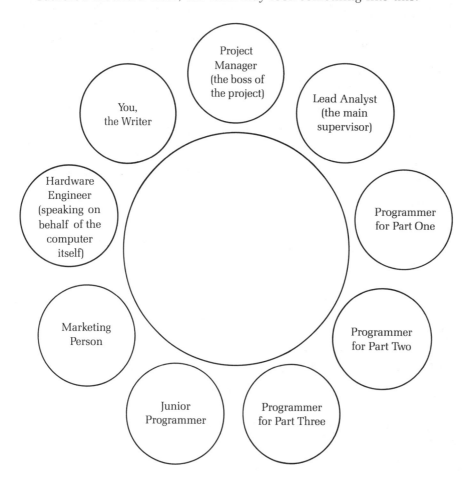

The developing program goes through the following phases. I'll discuss them in greater detail later in this chapter.

1. *Alpha Software.* The team believes that it has put every function any-one ever asked for into this program. Many people on the team think most of the program works right.

Now you can complete your first draft of the manual, often known as the alpha draft. You finally have enough to write about without feeling that you are creating science fiction.

This is the first time that potential users get to see the program. They will ask for some design changes—add this function, modify that one. So what you write in the manual will also have to be revised later.

2. *Beta software.* Now the team really believes that the whole—slightly modified—program works. Testers may still find little bugs here and there, but there will be no more design changes. Well, probably not.

You produce your beta draft of the manual. It's significantly different from your alpha draft, since you had to add and subtract whole topics and possibly rearrange the organization. You are very close to a final draft.

3. *Final software.* The program now has all its functions—and they all work right.

You produce your final draft of the manual, reflecting all the most recent changes to the program, plus a few thousand wording changes requested by a half dozen reviewers.

Your final draft may now be edited, typeset, and printed. Or it may just be photocopied and distributed.

The final software gets duplicated and distributed.

Maintenance

A much smaller team now fine-tunes the software to keep it running. They make small adjustments to speed it up and minor modifications to accomodate new twists in the business. But mostly, they just keep it running. This can go on for years. You might think that the program would just run itself. But circumstances change, and that means someone has to make adjustments to the program.

Occasionally these changes affect users, and you have to rewrite all or part of the manual. In addition, you discover mistakes in your own manual, and you have to send out errata sheets, or change pages. Sometimes there are so many changes to the program that you actually have to revise a chapter or two and issue an updated version of the manual.

Update

Now management wants a wholesale revision of the software. That usually means completely rewriting the manual. You are starting from scratch again— but at least you're familiar with the way the program works, so it won't take you as long to learn the new version as it did to learn the first version.

Migrate

Sometimes the computer itself gets outdated. Management, however, doesn't want to waste the money spent developing the program, so they assemble a team to "port" (as in "transport") the program onto a new— faster, smarter, smaller, more powerful—machine. The boss announces, "Let's migrate that program."

Even though the program will do the same work as before, users will probably have to learn a new keyboard or a new set of procedures. Depending on how much time has passed, you may rewrite the old manual or start a brand-new one.

BUT WHAT ABOUT
YOUR OWN SCHEDULE?

You often have to concoct a schedule before you know very much about the program. If you're in luck, someone else in your company knows how long it took to write a similar manual in the past. In fact, there may be an old manual for a similar program lying around. That may give you an idea of length and complexity of your proposed manual—and hence, a vague idea of how long it will take to write.

Under near-impossible conditions, people do turn out manuals. Despite pressure from some people to move up the schedule, and opposite pressure from others who keep putting off giving you the necessary information, you have to tell all of them when you're going to deliver. You want to please. And at the beginning of a project you don't really know how difficult the manual will be to write. You can only guess.

That's why Dirk van Nouhuys, who has supervised dozens of writers, says, "Scheduling is normally overoptimistic." An overoptimistic scheduler ignores the fact that there will probably be delays in getting the software running, that beta testing may take longer than it should, and that some reviewers will wait until the last minute to insist on tons of changes.

An Antidote to Optimism

Before you set a schedule, make up a fairly detailed table of contents and figure out about how many pages you're talking about. This is where similar manuals from the past can be a big help. If you can't find any, add up all the functions, all the reports, and all the important ways to tinker with the inner workings of the program. Multiply that number by three to get a (very rough) estimate of the number of reference pages you'll need. Then add about a page for every minute of step-by-step instruction you intend to offer.

Then multiply your page count by the number of hours you need to take a single page from scratch to print. A common industry figure is four hours per page. If you're just doing the writing and delivering it to the editors to carry through to print, two hours per page might be enough.

Whatever number you use, you'll come out with an amazing figure. Far more hours than you think you need. But don't start trimming it quite yet.

Now look at your average week. Start with the number of hours you normally work, then subtract the time you have to spend on other tasks—going to meetings, writing status reports, interviewing job applicants, answering the phone. Then—and this is optimistic, too—assume you could spend all the rest of your time working on the manual. Thus, if you usually work 40 hours per week, but spend four hours on meetings, you'd have 36 hours left to devote to the manual.

This gives you a very rough idea of the number of weeks involved. To write a 230-page manual might take 920 hours, and if you could, you'd like to have at least 25 weeks to complete that. Of course, due to a crisis, you'll probably be asked to get it out in ten.

Some Other Rules of Thumb for Scheduling
The first draft of the material takes the longest. Allocate at least three times as much time for the alpha draft as for the beta draft or final draft.

Figuring that you're going to have to have people read your drafts to critique them, and that they may take their time getting back to you, it's reasonable to leave yourself at least a month between the due dates for your alpha and beta drafts, and another month between the due dates for your beta and final drafts. (Ideally.)

Also, the longer the manual, the longer the turnaround time for reviewers; and the more reviewers you have, the longer your revising will take.

Giving and Taking
Now that you have an idea of about how long it will take you to write the manual, find out if you're going to be allowed that much time. If you think it will take you six months to write the manual, and the team expects to ship the product in four, you've got a problem. Perhaps you'll have to trim your outline, perhaps the software schedule will slip enough to give you all the time you need—and more.

So talk with the team to get a sense of when the product will be functioning well enough to describe it. Their estimates are almost always overoptimistic. Look at their schedule for alpha, beta and final software, and then pick dates at least a week or so later for your alpha, beta, and final drafts. (You can usually make some educated guesses about the software before it's delivered, but you have to see the actual alpha software to be sure you've described it accurately.)

When the software schedule slips, yours will too. You'll have to negotiate the changes in your own schedule—with your supervisor, with the programming team, and anyone else involved. Sometimes it can be as simple as sending a memo with your new schedule; sometimes it involves a week of informal discussions.

Your schedule, then, emerges from a complex form of give-and-take. You figure how much time you need; you get pressured into planning less time than that; you adjust the length and complexity of the manual to match the time available; and finally, you agree to a series of deadlines—all this before you've written enough to know if the deadlines are realistic. You can bet they aren't.

TAKING OTHER PROJECTS INTO ACCOUNT

Another factor to consider: other projects. Since you're likely to have several projects at any given time, you might try estimating the hours and weeks for each of them, and see if they add up to more hours than you have available. If they do, that's when you need to talk with your supervisor. Which is the most important? Which can be postponed? Which is most likely to slip its schedule, letting you off the hook?

This conversation will help you confirm your schedule for this manual. You're almost ready to write it up for the team.

Incidentally, you and your supervisor should agree on a plan for your work over the next few months, but count on revising it every week as the situation changes. Having this long-range schedule in hand will help your supervisor explain why you can only take on three extra manuals at the same time.

WHAT YOU DO AT EACH STAGE

As you can see, scheduling is a social process. You want to emerge with something written down, so you can circulate it to people on the project team. You are asserting a contract, insisting that they give you some information by a certain date, and promising that you will deliver a draft of the manual to them a week or so later.

To add some details to the schedule, you need to spell out the various stages your manual will go through—and what you will need from other people to meet each of your due dates. You might include condensed versions of the following definitions of document design, alpha draft, beta draft, and final draft, so people know what you mean by them.

Document Design
Before you can write the document design, you need a detailed description of what the program will do for users (known as the functional specifications), a prototype of the product, or, at least, a glowing advertisement from the team leader.

Your document design will include:

1. *Table of contents.* Shows an introduction, a tutorial, a reference section covering each function, a glossary, and an index.

2. *Audience definition.* Discusses the different audiences and the way you will satisfy their various needs.

3. *Level and approach.* Describes the tone you will adopt and how it is appropriate for your various audiences' levels of experience and expectations.

4. *What you need, and when.* Details the information you have to have from the team before you can write.

How long will it take to write these few pages? It depends on how much information you get and how reliable it is. If you're given a lot, and it's reliable, the design should only take a week or so.

Alpha Draft

To get started on your alpha draft, you need anyone's old notes on the design and specifications on how the functions will work and what they will do. Over time, you'll get to see some parts of the program working, so you can write about them, then record their growth and change. Before you can finish this draft, however, you'll need an alpha version of the program.

Here is what your alpha draft does:

- Describes the alpha software accurately. No mistakes. Every keystroke right. Nothing left out.

- Fulfills the document design. It's complete, covers all the functions, has an organization that meets the needs of people who will be learning the program or looking up material, and is written in English. It includes all sections, plus a draft table of contents, appendixes, a glossary, and an index without page numbers, since this is just a draft.

- Includes preliminary drawings for all planned illustrations.

- Meets current standards of usage and format.

The amount of time it will take you to write the alpha draft varies enormously. If the program is brand-new and you start just when the programmers start implementing the design, you could spend two years writing a series of incomplete drafts working up to your alpha draft. You are learning the program and learning what users will do with it—two different things. You are trying out several approaches. At least half of the time available for writing the manual should be devoted to the alpha draft. The cleaner it is, the faster your beta and final drafts can be produced.

Beta Draft

Before you can write the beta draft, you need comments from people who reviewed the alpha draft and a copy of beta software. This means that the team has agreed that there will be no more changes in the design. They swear that, at the least, any further changes will be invisible to users, so you won't have to document them in the manual. Only bugs remain to be changed.

Your beta draft does all this:

- Incorporates all wording changes suggested by reviewers of the alpha draft. Some of these involve technical inaccuracies. Some affect style. Some force you to rethink your organization. Keep the reviewed drafts and mark off the changes as you make them. You may even want to write memos to the key reviewers, pointing out which of their suggestions you have and have not accepted.

- Documents all changes to the program since the alpha draft.

- Corrects all problems you've noticed in usage, design, grammar, and spelling.

Your beta draft should be so good that you are willing to have it tested by experts, who can verify its accuracy, and typical users, who can see if it helps them learn to use the program.

Writing the beta draft doesn't take nearly as long as writing the alpha draft did. But you will probably feel as if you are juggling a few thousand balls at the same time. You have a lot of little knots to untangle. Timing also depends on how much the product changed, how many comments you got, and how long your alpha draft was. For a 100-page manual, you might take three or four weeks to produce the beta draft. Then again, you might have to fix it in a week.

Final Draft

Before you can write the final draft, you need comments from people who have reviewed the beta draft—at least two weeks before the final draft is due; and you need confirmation that all bugs in the software have been fixed and that there have been absolutely no changes that will affect the users.

Here's what the final draft does:

- Incorporates all changes suggested by reviewers of the beta draft and all last-minute enhancements in the program—at least, ones that affect what the user sees.

- Corrects grammar, spelling, usage, and formatting so that you consider this manual perfect, or nearly so.

It will usually take you about as long to produce the final draft as it did to produce the beta draft.

Edited Draft

An editor or supervisor combs through your final draft to make sure that you have organized it clearly, written it so the audience can understand it, obeyed company conventions, and prepared the manuscript so it can be typeset correctly.

You may have to answer hundreds of questions, reach a mutually acceptable compromise on some issues, and bow to pressure to meet some standard you had ignored.

The time this takes depends on the length of manuscript and the amount of editing done at alpha and beta stages. For a 300-page manuscript, not seen before, an editor might need three or four weeks.

Typeset Versions

If your company typesets manuals, you'll have to proof them. Typeset copy emerges in many stages. You may see galleys (yard-long sheets of type for you to check for typos), first page proofs (at last it looks like a real manual), second page proofs (have they fixed all the errors you caught earlier?), and camera-ready copy (the printer can now take a picture of the pages, make plates, and print).

During this process you should not tinker with style. Fix typos, yes, but don't give the typesetter a chance to introduce new errors. This means that you should not do any new writing, unless absolutely necessary to correct those errors that could trash the program, the data, or the user.

The time it takes to finish the proof stages depends on the length of manuscript, the number of absolutely-the-last changes in the program, and the quality of the typesetter. If your company has not really worked out a book design, you're in trouble; you can count on this process keeping you up all night. You can get an estimate from the typesetter or a production coordinator if your company has one. Anywhere from a few days to a six weeks.

Printed Version

You don't have to do much now. You will get some samples to look over—a lot if your manual's going to be in color. When you say "Go," the printer starts the presses rolling. And, for once, you just sit around waiting. (Of course, by now, you've been assigned to another project.)

Again, the time involved depends on the number of desperate last-minute changes in the program and the number of manuals to be printed. You can get an estimate from the production coordinator. A month or two.

MEMO-ING THE TEAM

Now that you have a rough idea of your manual and schedule, send a memo to everyone on the team with the whole schedule and highlight the dates you will need information from them if you are to meet this schedule. You have to make it clear that the schedule depends on them: if they don't meet their schedule, or if they don't provide you with the information you need, you can't meet your deadlines.

If you think you need to explain the whole process to them, to show why you depend on them to meet the schedule they've boasted about, use a chart showing the *critical path* of the project. That makes it clear that you can't test your beta draft before you receive beta software—despite the fact that some people wish it were so. Part of the chart might look like the chart shown here:

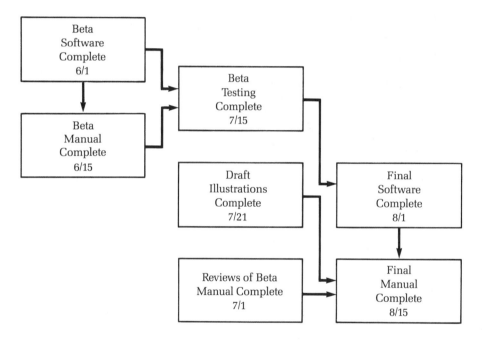

You could translate it this way: "I have to have the beta software in my hands for at least two weeks before I can turn out the beta manual. I need the results of beta testing (with an indication of which changes you'll be making), plus the reviews of the beta draft and absolutely final software for at least two weeks before I can hand you the final draft of the manual."

By spelling out what you need up front, you cover yourself in case software isn't ready but everyone expects a manual anyway. You also lay the groundwork for revising the schedule.

AND WHEN THE
SCHEDULE DISSOLVES . . .

For all your planning, priorities will shift on high, and you'll find that you won't see anything close to beta software for two more months. The temptation is to stop work on the project and wait for news.

"The worst aspect of all this," Dirk van Nouhuys says, "is that you don't do the work you should do. For instance, when a project begins to slip, you tend to jump to another crash project." Then when you come back to the original project, you don't have time to do more than a quick fix. "So you have six consecutive quick fixes, instead of one or two fundamental changes."

Schedules get even mushier when the project is large. The more parts in the program, the longer it all will take. But no one can predict which parts will come in on time. So your first schedule assumes everybody's making accurate forecasts. Many people assure each other that they will all meet the release date. And to meet that date, they will steal some time for themselves—from your schedule.

And that's why Dirk van Nouhuys says, "No one wants to hear a realistic schedule. They don't believe you. They just ask, 'Why can't you write it quicker and have a manual that's not quite as good?'"

Poor manuals are the biggest complaint of customers. It is true that you can slap together an inaccurate, infuriatingly incomplete manual in a few weeks. Why bother to make it accurate, helpful, thoughtful, complete, and useful? If you don't care about word-of-mouth reputation, if you don't think ahead of the initial sale, and if you don't care what users think of you, give them a lousy manual.

The problem is that the real delays don't come from some last-minute addition of excellence. Often the delays stem from the very people who complain the most bitterly about the schedule: marketing people who change the design late in the project; engineers who enhance and enlarge and perfect the product, tinkering long after the agreed-upon day for the product to be finalized; users who think of new functions after seeing the final software; supervisors who decide that you should change the entire format of the manual the day before you should go to press. If the form and content keep changing, how can you possibly finish the manual on time?

You may not be able to. But you can change the schedule and explain why. Every time some slippage occurs in the project you have to reevaluate your original plan. As John Huber, author of several manuals about programming languages, says:

> I tend to be overoptimistic when I'm asked for a date, because I want to please. "Sure I can have it by such and such a time." I'm just too eager to show off, give somebody the impression that I can work wonders.

And of course things happen to prevent it, to make things last longer than I thought they would. If the changes affect 40% of my pages, I'd say, "Well OK, it's going to take a lot longer. It's not my fault."

But if it was only 5 or 10% of my pages, I'd start looking at my calendar and thinking of ways I could work later and weekends I could give up, just to get it done.

If you decide that you've got to have a new schedule, do a few things:

- Write a memo to the entire team. Say what the new schedule is and why you've had to revise it. Give them new dates when you expect them to provide you with functioning product and the dates when you will deliver drafts.

- Talk with your supervisor. Ask for help in carrying the message to the other team members involved.

- Show your critical-path chart to anyone who complains about the manual's schedule slipping. Explain why publication takes time. Talk about what you've done to speed things up.

- Negotiate. Offer alternate possibilities and identify tasks you could accomplish while waiting for what you've been promised.

HOW YOUR SCHEDULE
AFFECTS OTHER PEOPLE

Here's another reason for keeping your schedule up to date: there may be half a dozen other schedules resting on yours. For instance, the supervisors may have a grand schedule of all work flowing through the department. It may show your manual as one line with information such as its title; type (new manual, developer handbook, errata sheet, revision, addendum, update); your best guess of the due dates for the document design, alpha draft, beta draft, final draft, edited version, camera-ready copy, and printed version; along with your name, your supervisor's name, and any internal code number for your manual. Every time you change your schedule, the whole department schedule may ripple to reflect the new data.

If you have editors, they have another schedule, showing when your manual will hit their desk. The program itself probably shows up on another list for the engineers. Marketing may also have its own list of products, with release dates. And the operations team has another list showing when they have to get the software up and running. If your company sells the program, then manufacturing wants to know when they'll get every part of the final box—your manual, oh, and the program, plus items such as tape, shrink wrap, thermoform tray, sleeve, and pop-top box. Your organization may have even more groups waiting for news about your manual's schedule.

As a writer, you probably won't have to read all these lists. In fact, if you're lucky, you won't see most of them. But take pity on the poor people who have to correlate them and keep them up to data. It's enough to put a writer to sleep.

A QUICK REVIEW

Here's how to develop your schedule:

☐ Recognize that most schedules—including your own—exaggerate.

☐ Figure out how many pages your manual may have and multiply that by the number of hours it takes to do a page (two to four, on average).

☐ See if you have that many hours between now and the date the boss would like the manual. If so, proceed. If not, you and your supervisor better have a discussion. Take into account your other projects and the (probably exaggerated) schedule for the program.

☐ Carve up the available time, setting deadlines for document design; alpha, beta, and final drafts; and edited, typeset, and printed versions. Figure the alpha draft will take at least three times as long as the beta or final drafts.

☐ Figure out what you need when—and tell the other members of the project team.

☐ If needed, create a critical-path chart showing what you're depending on to finish on time.

Understanding Your Audience

Get Specific
Distinguish Between Audiences
Keep the Focus on Their Goals—Not Yours
Remember They're Smart
Organize Around What They Want
Imagine Their Questions
Conduct Research—On the Spot
A Quick Review

Understanding
Your Audience

When you begin to work on a manual, the biggest question you face is: Who will be reading what you write? Your answers will suggest an appropriate style and structure.

The more you know about your audiences (yes, there are probably several), the more you can shape your prose so they understand you, and the easier it will be for you to organize your information so they can find what they need.

Unfortunately, most writers begin with only a hazy sketch of their true audience. A label, perhaps. A phrase—"Oh, this product's aimed at middle managers."

If you don't know exactly who's listening, you may make your audience angry at your complexity, wary of your oversimplifications, puzzled by your assumptions about what they do, or frustrated in their efforts to learn.

GET SPECIFIC

To avoid baffling your audiences, you need more specifics about them. For instance, what kind of managers are you talking to? How old are they? How many years of high school, college, or graduate school have they had? How long have they worked with similar products? Do they have computers at work and at home? Are they the people who made the purchase decision? Or is this product being forced on them?

What's the main reason people will be buying or using the program? What kind of business people—or families—will be using it? The answers will suggest what kind of examples to use and what topics to include or exclude.

And—very important—how do they expect to learn? By classes? Through computer-assisted instruction? With only a reference volume? Or through a series of graduated lessons? How much time can different people be expected to devote to learning?

DISTINGUISH BETWEEN AUDIENCES

As you ponder your audience, avoid the tendency to think of them as all one type of person. Perhaps they have different positions in life—small-business proprietors, teachers, scientists, students, and clerks. Imagine different users complaining—in their own ways—about earlier manuals. What bothers one group more than another?

What do they want? For instance, some people want the manual to be short—otherwise they get frightened. Others just want a list of technical details—no lead-in, no training, no orientation. Others want a little training at the beginning.

KEEP THE FOCUS ON THEIR GOALS— NOT YOURS

Having warned you not to generalize too quickly, I'll make a few generalizations about the audiences you're likely to be writing for. In general, you'll be talking to people who want to get a job done using a computer. These people see the computer and your particular product as an appliance, not an opportunity for 18 hours of tinkering, troubleshooting, and debugging.

You will usually not be talking to programmers or experienced users who know a lot about hard disk drives, asynchronous communications, and baud rates. Sure, you may have some hobbyists and even pros on your mailing lists, and you want to help them out; but they're not the major audience for most of your documentation.

REMEMBER THEY'RE SMART

Most of the people you'll be writing for know a lot—about their own work and the world. They are not naive. You can figure that some read private newsletters, professional and trade journals, *Business Week*, *Fortune*, *Time*, *Wall Street Journal*.

Within their own businesses, most users can stand gobbledygook. But they don't know, and don't want to be browbeaten with, phrases like these:

- Load boot diskette.

- I/O Error. Reboot.

- Invalid parameters.

ORGANIZE AROUND
WHAT THEY WANT

Most audiences are not interested in learning how the operating system works. They think in terms of their wants, their problems, their solutions. So they're puzzled when a manual gets organized in terms of parts of a program:

- Equipment Needed
- Input
- Output
- Errors

They want you to organize the manual around what they do—tasks they bought the program to perform. For instance, they expect an organization that looks like this:

- How to put your inventory on the system.
- How to keep your inventory up to date.
- What to do if something goes wrong.
- Using the inventory system for taxes.

Basically, organizing a manual for your many audiences means rethinking the program in terms of the needs and wishes of the various people who buy it. Sometimes these are immediately obvious. Often they are not.

IMAGINE THEIR QUESTIONS

You might draw up a list of questions you think these people would like to ask before using the program for the first time:

- How easy will it be for me to learn this program? How many hours do I have to put into getting it going?
- Is it really easy to use on a day-to-day basis?
- How flexible is it? If I change my methods, will I be able to change the system? Or will I have to go out and buy a different one and spend months changing my records?
- Exactly what is this going to do for me that my secretary can't already do?

They have anxieties about the job they're asking the computer to do. Their business poses special problems, requires unique formats, and demands recurrent changes in method. You can find out how much you actually know about *their* business by writing down the questions they have to answer every day at work.

CONDUCT RESEARCH—ON THE SPOT

Yes, you can find out more about your audiences. Market research can help quantify their tastes, interests, fears. Reading trade journals can give you a taste of their business.

   If your company is going to be selling the program, be sure to talk with the people who will be marketing it. But recognize that marketing people, too, inhabit a different world. Kris Olson, who has handled the marketing of half a dozen programs for Apple, says:

> Understand the marketeer's world. It's really moving fast. I'm handling 19 things at once. My attention is really fragmented. I think intuitively and associatively, jumping around a lot, but I'm not irrational or illogical. So I want to see that you're really concerned about the user's needs. I want you to work with me cooperatively on figuring out who the users are, going on field trips, watching them at work.

The best way to understand the people in your audience is to meet them. Talk to any representative users you can find. Ask the systems analysts where to locate some. Go out to visit people who are already using similar programs. Talk with them informally. You might act as a reporter, asking them leading questions like these:

- What are the biggest headaches in your business—and how do you expect this program to cure them?

- What annoys you about similar programs?

- What worries you about the idea of using a computer to do this part of your job?

- Are you being forced to use this computer? How does that make you feel about the program?

- How much time have people spent training you on this computer? How much time will they spend teaching you this program?

- What do you use the computer for now?

- Have you read any of those books that came with the computer?

- How much do you want to know about the insides of the program—how it works?

You need to know how people are going to fit the program into their daily routine. If you can show readers that you understand their problems—in detail—you may be able to convince them to try the program out, rather than raging at the computer, at the program, and at you. To do this, you'll need to include topics they want and leave out what bores them. You'll need to think of helpful hints to add along the way. And you'll need to speak their language. In a way, you'll be getting more personal.

A QUICK REVIEW

In summary, when you are thinking about your audiences:

☐ Get specific.

☐ Distinguish between audiences.

☐ Keep the focus on their goals—not yours.

☐ Remember they're smart.

☐ Organize around what they want to know.

☐ Imagine their questions and figure out how to answer them.

☐ Conduct research—on the spot.

4

Gathering Information About the Program

Ask Questions
Talk, Talk, Talk
Become a Member of the Team
Talk With the Team Leader First
Say What You're Going to Do
Keep Everybody Informed
Learn the Lingo—Fast
Don't Make Them Repeat
Recognize That They Are Creative
Be Prepared
Advertise
Write Down Your Suggestions
Read Whatever
Dissect the Specs
Configuration Section
Implementation Procedures
Data Dictionary
Input
Processing Operations
Secret Formulas
Files
Decision Tables
Security
Write to Find Out What You Don't Know
Participate in Developing the Program
Grow Slow
A Quick Review

Gathering Information About the Program

Gathering information about a program is like opening up a giant fish, discovering a dozen smaller fish inside, cutting those open, only to find hundreds more, each with its mouth around two tinier fish. In fact, the process of collecting facts never stops—even when you've got the manual printed, you'll hear of mistakes to correct in the next edition.

You collect information from the beginning to the end of the project. At first, when creating your document design, you're just looking for crude approximations—the gist of what you'll have to cover. As you write each draft, you'll get to know the program better, particularly in these areas:

- What it does.

- How ordinary users can make it do all those wonderful things.

- What goes on behind the scenes, in the program, while it's doing something.

- Key facts users need to know to get started or avoid disaster.

Let's say you've already begun to get to know your audience. In this chapter, I'll show you how to explore your subject.

ASK QUESTIONS

At first, you may be almost as inexperienced as beginning users. That's fine. In fact, it's a help, because you can ask exactly the questions users might ask:

- What does this program do? More important, what are the benefits of using the program?

- How is it different from similar programs?

- How complicated is it to learn? To use?

- Can people use a small part of it to do real work, right from the start, and put off learning the trickier functions?

- What's the minimum users have to learn to begin using the program?

- What problems can users expect to run into?

- Does this program really save time, money, energy? Or is this just a form of entertainment, something to pass the time with?

As you learn about the product, you'll find times when you feel confident that you understand it all. Those are the times to ask these questions again. You may find new answers and new meanings behind old ones. Of course, in a few more days, you'll discover further mysteries, smaller puzzles, or a few changes in the basic design, so you'll be launched on another series of questions.

For most products, you'll need to ask questions like these:

- What can users do with this product? Really?

- What do users need to know before using it?

- What commands are available? What do they do? What are their rules?

- How can things go wrong? How can users set them right?

- What information do users have to enter? What should its format be?

- How do users have to prepare the program?

- What's optional? What's required?

- How can users move from one part of the program to another?

- What steps do users have to go through to save information? Retrieve it? Alter it?

- How much information can the program handle at once?

- What reports, calculations, or graphics does the program generate? How do users ask for those? And what do they mean?

- What other little facts will users have to know to get this system to work?

- Does the program work with other programs? Does it receive information from other programs? How?

TALK, TALK, TALK

Talking's the best way to find the answers. If the product is designed to be used by some group within your organization, go talk with the people who requested the program. If the product is going to be sold, talk with the marketing people. Sit in on any roundtable discussions or *focus groups* (potential users who are led through a discussion focussed on the kind of program they would like). These folks can give you a good general idea of the product—who it's for, what it should do, how much users already know about this kind of program, what kind of training they need.

In one sense, you are a reporter, trying to get a quick overview of the product. But you're not writing in general. You're writing for users, so you're also figuring out how to tailor your manual to their needs. Most writers find these conversations inspiring—and educational.

For the fine details, arrange to have scheduled—and unscheduled—conversations with the programmers and analysts. If your project involves some modifications of hardware, visit with the engineers. At first, of course, you may find their personality very different from your own. Allen Watson, a writer who has worked closely with both programmers and hardware engineers for years, asks:

> How do you form an intense relationship with someone whose background is radically different from yours, whose style of expression is different from yours, whose prejudices about the product and the company are radically different from yours, whose work habits are so different from yours that you never see him?
>
> Programmers and engineers talk in shorthand. The elements of the shorthand are jargon words used in a heavily loaded way. It's almost impossible to describe to a programmer or hardware person the narrowness of his view of the product, because he has no vocabulary in which you can describe such a thing. From his point of view, he fully understands the product. He designed it, he made it. It is his.... Unfortunately, his point of view is radically different from the point of view of most people who will be using it.

Don Reed, who has written manuals for programmers who want to know more about operating systems, says:

> Programmers tend to be more precise about the things that have to be understood perfectly in order to get the program to run correctly. But they are less precise about names—they often call the same thing by different names in different places.

So Reed pleads with programmers to write notes. "Sometimes I've had to corner a programmer, and sit down and take dictation at the keyboard. They'll say, 'Well, what you say here isn't quite right,' and I'll say, 'What would you say?' And I type that in."

BECOME A MEMBER OF THE TEAM

Many programmers and engineers appreciate your work. They understand that a good manual will encourage people to use the product and cut down the number of calls on the hot line.

So work together with other team members. Here are a few ideas on how to do that.

Talk with the Team Leader First

Get the team leader to ask the team members to cooperate with you. Make it clear that the manual depends on information from the team. And if you're not getting cooperation, point that out and give the team leader an estimate of how many months this will add to the schedule.

Say What You're Going to Do

Let everyone know what you're going to do. And deliver. When people know that you do what you say you're going to, they don't feel they're wasting their time talking to you.

Keep Everybody Informed

Even the people you don't think need to know. (They may.) When the project begins to miss its deadlines, revise your own schedule and explain, so no one expects you to meet the deadlines you set up earlier. When you tell people what you're up to, they don't mind letting you know what they've just done. Stay up to date.

Learn the Lingo—Fast

As soon as anyone on the team drops a new term, ask what it means. When you do understand it, use it to reassure them that you are following their conversation.

Don't Make Them Repeat

Once you've learned something, don't make team members repeat it. But if you don't get it, ask again and again until you do.

Recognize That They Are Creative

Programmers are creators, even writers. You actually have more in common with them than either of you imagines. Show you've really explored the program they're creating.

Be Prepared

Do your homework. Take an organized list of questions to each meeting.

Advertise

Make it clear why your work will help justify the product, sell it, simplify what users have to do, cut down on hot line calls, and postpone users' demands for drastic overhauls. Remind them that manuals are products, and that good manuals sell hardware and software—within your organization and outside it.

Write Down Your Suggestions

If you think something in the program should be changed, fine, write your ideas down. Offer well-thought-out reasons for your suggestion; don't rely on emotional appeals.

READ WHATEVER

Don't overlook written material, if there's any lying around:

- The original request for the program that outlines what it should do and why.

- Diagrams that show how information flows through the program (flowcharts). These are very helpful if current.

- Detailed descriptions of how users can get the program to perform its functions (functional specifications).

- Actual computer programs, if you can read these.

- Memos, reports, proposals, cover letters—anything that might give you an idea what this product's for and how it should work, eventually.

- Manuals for similar projects, including internal documentation for the maintenance programmers.

DISSECT THE SPECS

Of all this written material, the report describing how each function will actually be performed by users—the functional specifications—*may be* the most useful. At first glance, each section gives you all kinds of information, answering questions you need to pose.

Configuration Section

The *configuration* is the equipment needed. What's required? What's optional? What else will work—for sure? What printers can handle the information coming from this program? What communications protocols (conventions for communicating with other computers) are built in? What communications packages (programs that allow your computer to talk to another) can be added? What modifications will a purchaser have to make to the program to customize it for a particular installation?

Implementation Procedures

Implementation procedures tell how to get the program up and running on a particular computer. If the program will be a real bear to get running, what should users plan for? Do purchasers have to reformat some files? Redo three rooms and lay cable to forty terminals?

Data Dictionary

A data dictionary lists every *type* of information the program deals with, along with information about the way it should be formatted. For instance, "Then we have the abbreviation for the state, if known. This must be two letters. No numbers, please." In the data dictionary you can find out what kind of information the program must have to work. You may also find out where that information comes from. What kind of ranges and limits are imposed on it? What does the system call each data item? And what in the world does that mean?

Input and Output

Input is the information that users must—or may—put into the program for processing. What are the rules for entering data? How do users edit an entry? Delete it? Save it? Lock it? What kind of messages will appear prompting users to enter something? Will there be screens with helpful information available (possibly duplicating your manual)? Error messages when users goof? Reports popping out at the end? Totals?

Processing Operations

What operations does the program perform on all that information? Essentially, what can someone do with this program? What are the restrictions and rules? What does the program do then? What kind of results come out at the other end?

Secret Formulas

What equations are used, behind the scenes? What are the unknowns, the constants—and what do those mean?

Files

Just as in a filing cabinet, your program keeps folders of information, with labels like "Employees" or "Memos to the Boss." What kind of files does the program create? How are they distinguished from each other?

Decision Tables

Decision tables indicate how the program actually makes some decisions. What's the logic behind all of them? Under which conditions will x, y, and z occur?

Security

What's the password? How many levels of access will there be, and what can I do at each one? Who gets to go to every level, and how?

Similarly, program specifications (showing programmers how all this will actually be done by the program) will show you how the designer has carved up these tasks and assigned them to different modules, how one module flows into another, and where the system depends on some other system.

From designer to designer, from year to year, specifications vary enormously in format and detail. But one thing's usually true about them: They're no longer valid. They've been outdistanced by events.

By the time you read them, most specifications have become a mild form of fiction. Susan Meade, who was writing a tutorial for a complex data base program, says, "Generally, you'd learn about a product by the specifications. But the specifications I got were so outdated that the product I was looking at didn't match." So read the specifications, but don't believe them too readily, or you may end up having to unlearn them.

WRITE TO FIND OUT
WHAT YOU DON'T KNOW

The process of writing—rough outlines, notes, drafts of chapters—will also bring you face-to-face with what you don't know. For instance, as you write your document design, you may try a series of outlines: first, just the chapters; then the main sections in each chapter; then the subheadings within those sections. You'll quickly come up with a list of fuzzy subjects to clarify.

And as you write, keep notes on such unimportant things as your first impressions. You may not know exactly why a particular function makes you frightened, but recognize that it does, and make a note. Later you can bring it up with the programmer to see if some improvements can be made. If not, you'll know to make a special effort to calm readers down when you introduce that function.

Pay attention to your own doubts, anger, uncertainty. You'll probably notice a fair number of inconsistencies, too. Probe those. Try to figure out if there's a valid reason behind them—or just whimsy.

Keep looking for softly mentioned ideas and topics to add. You'll never be complete, but you can keep getting closer if you remember that it's impossible to be sure you haven't left something out. After doing a series of detailed reference manuals, Allen Watson says:

> The one thing that you cannot get from the technical reviewers is detection of errors of omission. There were several glaring omissions in one book I did, and that thing went around in any number of drafts, went past lots of technical people, and we had many meetings about it, and I saw their marks all over the pages. But the omissions were not detected.

You have to keep asking about topics you've never heard of. Know that you're ignorant, then, but keep trying to learn. For instance, when you're designing your document, stuff your table of contents with more than you think really belongs there. In designing the owner's manual for the Apple IIe, Joe Meyers did that because "people are more likely to see something that doesn't belong than think of something that's missing."

As you write, you'll encounter passages that just don't go. You try it one way, you try it another. Every way you write the passage, it comes out tangled. When this happens, take a break, and think about the subject. Probably you're trying to make sense out of something illogical, inconsistent, or downright bananas. If so, go to the programming team and ask them to straighten things out—for the sake of users and you.

PARTICIPATE IN DEVELOPING THE PROGRAM

Get involved in developing the product, where you can. When Susan Meade joined the data base team, she says:

> They were talking about every word that was seen on screen, wondering whether that was the right word. For instance, whether we were going to call the place where you enter a certain type of information a *field*. Field is a term that comes from old-fashioned data bases, but we also have an Apple product called Quick File™, which was supposed to be friendlier, and Quick File uses *category*.
>
> And so there were arguments between marketeers who wanted something that would look like Quick File, but be bigger, and engineers who wanted their product to be looked at as a real data base, with *fields*, not some little fly-by-night little thing with *categories*. It took forever to decide what terminology to use.

In that case, *fields* won. But in other terminology debates, Meade's suggestions helped make the program easier to understand. Clearly, in debates like this, a writer has a lot to contribute. And by participating, you refine your conception of the product.

For instance, Meade also rewrote the information designed to help users who have gotten confused:

> I rewrote those help screens because the engineers had written rough ones 16 lines long. They had tried to put in as much information as they could.
>
> So I looked at those screens and looked at the product and figured out what the programmers were really saying. And then I wrote up a draft of all the help screens, and went over them with the engineers, and if there were technical inaccuracies, or if they really hated something, then we changed that. At one point I thought the screens were pretty final. Then the software changed again. But that's how I learned

a lot about the product. The programmers were surprisingly open about having the screens rewritten, and they helped by reading and commenting.

As the product moves forward, you may also find you're at the center of it with different technical people working on parts of it, and no one really knowing what the others are doing. You can see how the pieces fit together—and yell when they don't. That's a way of learning, too. Meade recalls:

> I knew more about how the whole program worked than the individual programmers did, because they never really looked at the other person's stuff until it was time to integrate the programs. I pointed out that the terms one programmer used didn't match what the others were using, that there were three different ways of doing the same thing, and I asked them to settle on one way, throughout.

Just checking to make sure that something's really inconsistent lets you confirm your somewhat shaky knowledge of the program.

GROW SLOW

You don't learn the product all at once, then write. You write, ask for opinions, make corrections, try that out on your team, rewrite, improve, change the program, write a new draft—learning all the way. If you dream that any one draft is final, you set yourself up for disappointment and cancel future learning. Instead, think of the process as continuous.

A QUICK REVIEW

In gathering information about the product, make sure that you:

☐ Ask all the questions real users might have—plus plenty of your own.

☐ Talk with everyone—potential users, marketing people, programmers.

☐ Become a member of the team.

☐ Read whatever you can get ahold of, particularly the specifications.

☐ Write to find out what you don't know. Then find out.

☐ Participate in developing the program.

5

Organizing the Manual

Follow the Reader
Speed Up Access
Distinguish Between Tutorial and Reference
Tutorials: On Paper or on the Computer
Reference: On-line or on Paper
Figure Out the Minimum
Make a Series of Manuals Look Like One
A Quick Review

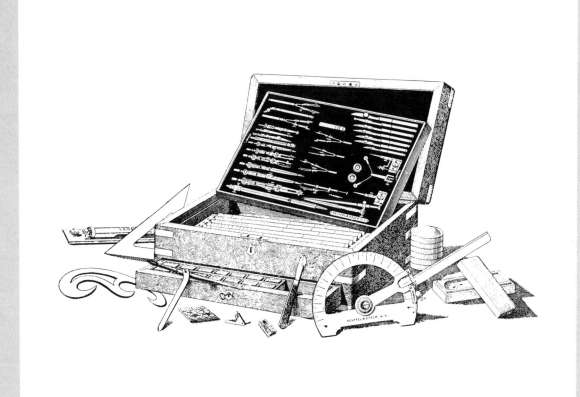

Organizing the Manual

As you learn more about your audience and your subject, you'll probably revise your table of contents several times before you start to write. That's good. You can save yourself a lot of rewriting later by making some smart decisions now.

As you refine the organization of your manual, here are some objectives to keep in mind:

- Follow readers' thought processes—not programmers'.

- Speed up readers' access to the information.

- Distinguish clearly between tutorial and reference material; between paper tutorials and computer-assisted instruction.

- If you've only got time for a minimal manual, figure out what you can—and can't—manage.

- Make a series of books look like one.

In the rest of this chapter, I'll discuss what I mean by these objectives.

FOLLOW THE READER

You can make your manual easier to use if you arrange your table of contents the way readers look at the subject. That way, readers can look up an idea they think of and get going quickly. Avoid organizing the manual the way systems analysts might sort out the program, with sections titled Input, Errors, and Output.

Who would want to do something called input? Why bother? And what good is all that output? What readers want to know is: What can they do with the program, and how can they get started?

In order to follow readers' interests, you need to organize in two stages:

1. You need to think through the program the way the systems analyst does to make sure you understand every facet of it.

2. You have to put all that aside and think about what purchasers may want to do with that program—the business functions, the applications, the rules of the game.

So when you're gathering information, look through the specifications and try to understand the system from the designer's point of view. To the designer, the program probably looks like this:

- Equipment needed

- Setup procedures

- Input

- Processing

- Output

But users just want to balance the accounts or write reports. So once you've collected all this information—it may just squeeze into a 4-inch binder—you're ready to rearrange it. (You may be in a similar situation if you're rewriting an old-fashioned manual that was set up this way.)

Now is when knowledge of your audience pays off. What do they want to do with the program? What problems will the program solve? What needs does the program answer? What impulses does it encourage? What fantasies does it help entertain?

Organize by motives. What are the main things users will want this program to do? Those activities should be the subjects for sections of your manual. Maybe a chapter each. Maybe just a key part of a chapter. Somehow they'll provide the most important blocks in the book you're building.

You are downplaying, but not discarding, the programmer's point of view. You may want to move a lot of this material into the reference sections, rather than surrounding readers with it right off—and losing them. Thus, the back of the book comes to resemble a map of the whole forest, complete with elevations, labels, numbers, and cautions. The front of the book acts as a true guide.

SPEED UP ACCESS

Few people dream of reading a manual straight through. They get stuck in the middle of a job, then turn to the manual. They want help fast.

But different folks look for help in different ways. Some turn to the table of contents, others flip through the book looking for summaries or tables, still others patiently go through the index. In a way, your job is to open up these paths through the material, so that whatever route they choose, they'll find their way to the single fact that lets them get back to work.

For instance, you could provide a guide to the manual. This page points to the sections in which you answer the main questions people might bring to your manual. Instead of the usual "In Chapter 17, we discuss input rules," you could begin with what users want to do, then tell them where to find it. (How many people really start out wanting to know what is in Chapter 17?)

Your table of contents, too, can be helpful and quick or cryptic and slow. Ironically, longer sometimes means faster. In the main table of contents, then, offer enough information so that users can locate minor sections within major ones. And in front of each chapter, provide an even more detailed table of contents, so that once readers find the general area, they can pin down the exact location of the topics they are looking for.

Overviews at the beginning of chapters and summaries at the end of chapters help readers figure out if they have found the right chapter. Remember, you're performing a service to readers when your overview at the start of a chapter makes clear that this isn't what they're after. You save them time.

Some people always start at the back of the book. Make sure you include an index. To estimate how many pages the index will be, figure that you want to include every topic you discuss, plus synonyms. That way, even readers who don't know your terms can find the subjects they're after.

Back among the appendixes, you could include a lot of tables. Arranging data in rows and columns helps people locate the information they want without reading a lot of irrelevant paragraphs. And a quick-reference card could sum up the most important tables and lists; that way, users can have key facts at their fingertips without even opening the book.

Plan to make a thorough glossary, so that if all users want is a definition, they can find it without having to hunt through every reference in the index.

You may come to view the organization of your manual as an open forest with thousands of paths through it. Sadly, you can't force people to read the manual from page 1 to page 200. They'll miss many of your finest turns of phrase. But by carving out the paths, you can help them on their way, so at least they can find the facts they need when they need them—not an hour later.

DISTINGUISH BETWEEN TUTORIAL AND REFERENCE

This is really important! A tutorial offers step-by-step training focused on a particular activity. You guide readers through every keystroke. Reference material is more general: it offers procedures that users can apply in many different circumstances, giving exceptions, warnings, asides, and extra data.

The distinction may not seem very significant. But if you attempt to save paper by mixing the two types of information, you'll confuse or delay your readers. For instance, if they are proceeding step by step, nervously checking to make sure they've gotten the right results, and suddenly come across five pages of reference material that you included just in case they might want it later, they may plunge into the reference stuff and forget what step they were on and what the point was. It would be little wonder if they just closed the book.

Then, later, when they really just want to look something up, they'll stumble on all these irritating step-by-step instructions designed to teach something.

By separating the two types of presentation, you make each simpler, easier to use. In the tutorial, introduce readers to a sampling of the basic functions—enough to get a taste of what the program offers. Usually, you won't plod through every option of every menu. A tutorial gets people used to the program, gives them confidence, shows them how things work, and makes them ready to go forward on their own. For instance, here's the table of contents for the *QuickStart*™ *Course* on VisiWord™, from VisiCorp:

Introduction	4
The QuickStart™ Course	5
The Keyboard	6
References to the Keyboard and the Screen	6
Loading the VisiWord Program	8
Initializing Your Document Disk	9
Using the VisiWord Program	11
Creating a Document	12
Entering and Formatting a Document	13
Editing Your Document	17
Saving the Document	18
Printing the Document	19
Where to Go From Here	20
Leaving the VisiWord Program	21
Summary	22

Remember: a tutorial should not wear readers out. Do not plan to cover everything. Leave advanced features for the reference sections. (Sure, you can mention them, but don't plan to cover them all in your tutorial.)

In reference sections give full explanations of all options, most possibilities, many situations. Yes, that means repeating the information you provided about a few of these functions in the tutorial. But your purpose is different and your manner of presentation is more complete and compact. For instance, here's part of the table of contents for the *VisiWord User's Guide* for the IBM Personal Computer:

Chapter 4 Editing Documents

Unit 1 Moving the Cursor Within Documents 4-3

Unit 2 Entering Text. 4-6
      Text Wraparound 4-6
      Required Returns 4-6
      Insert and Over-Type. 4-7

Unit 3 Deleting and Restoring Text. 4-9
      Delete Keys 4-9
      Deleting Text and Columns 4-11
      Restoring Text. 4-13

Unit 4 Copying Text and Columns 4-14

Unit 5 Moving Text and Columns 4-16

Unit 6 Looking for Characters, Words, or Phrases 4-19
      Doing Repeated Searches 4-20

Unit 7 Replacing Characters, Words, or Phrases. 4-21
      Replacing One String at a Time 4-21
      Replacing all Occurrences 4-22

Unit 8 Splitting the Screen into Two Parts. 4-23
      Creating Windows. 4-23
      Moving the Cursor From One Window to Another. 4-24
      Moving or Copying Text Between Windows 4-25
      Loading a Document Into a Window. 4-27
      Clearing a Document From a Window 4-27
      Closing a Window. 4-28

Here's one way to think of the distinction between tutorials and reference sections: When I want to study, I like a gradual progression. When I'm in the middle of printing a report and get some incomprehensible error message, I just want to find out what it means, fix the problem, and finish my report. Nothing gradual. I want to be able to zoom in, find the fact, and drop the manual.

Once you've figured what you want to tutor people in, you may want to do some of that tutoring on paper and some with computer-assisted instruction. How can you tell what material should go where?

Tutorials: On Paper or on the Computer

People like to get their hands on the keyboard right away. Computer-assisted instruction helps them learn about the program while actually using the computer and a simulation of the program. This way of learning is so easy that many people fear that they will not recall what they've learned once they start to use the actual program.

So, if you have the opportunity, and do not worry much about people recalling every single command you teach, by all means create a tutorial that can run on the computer. But, if you want people to feel confident that they know every command you teach, and if you want them to be able to look up those commands later, use a paper tutorial. A book allows people to study in a way they're familiar with and to come back later for a quick lookup.

Reference: On-Line or on Paper

You face a similar choice with reference material: What should go in the book and what should go in the program itself?

If your program allows help screens or another form of on-line reference (where users don't have to leave the program to look something up), you'll probably be called on to design the text. Think short. Just the gist of procedures. If you can, include a glossary with definitions of all the terms used in the program so that users can scroll through it. Make sure that once people have found a fact they can return to their work with nothing changed.

Paper allows you more room. Even if your program has room for hundreds of pages of information, I'd suggest you keep the on-line references short, using the paper version for exceptions, additional comments, and further details.

FIGURE OUT THE MINIMUM

Sometimes you'll be assigned to write a manual—or revise one—in a few weeks. You don't have time for a complete reference section. You won't be able to tell users about every little exception. You will probably make some serious mistakes.

So what should you include if you have so little time? Here's what an experienced writer, Van R. Kane, suggests:

1. *Overviews and summaries.* These paragraphs help readers get oriented—even if what follows is a bit hectic.

2. *A quick course.* A tutorial on the simplest functions—maybe only twenty minutes long. Any introduction is better than none.

3. *An index.* You can make up for the disorganization brought about by haste if you include an accurate index.

4. *A table of contents and lots of headings.* These help readers browse and skim when they're looking something up.

MAKE A SERIES OF MANUALS
LOOK LIKE ONE

Sometimes you have such a complicated program, aimed at several levels of expertise in several audiences, that you decide you're going to have to produce more than one manual. You're not sure what to include and what to leave out of each manual.

Start with a list of all the tasks your audience might use the program to do. Sort these into piles, like this:

- Beginners must know.

- Only experts will care.

- Leave for the technicians and developers.

- Necessary for beginners, but should go only after an introductory tutorial.

- Should be included in the tutorial.

- Can be left for reference sections.

- Helpful for beginners who want to learn to use the product like an expert—it's a bridge to expertise.

You'll find a few piles are so small they have to be merged with others. Some topple over so you have to divide them into sections. But after a while, you've got an outline—from the users' point of view. Whether that means two manuals or ten, you've now got a few more challenges ahead of you:

1. *Cross-reference.* You don't want to keep telling readers, "Go somewhere else for that information." On the other hand, you don't want too much crammed in each section.

2. *Guidance.* Include a guide to the series in the front of each manual, so that no matter which one readers pick up first, they can find their way to the others.

3. *Audience.* Make clear which manual is for which audience—in the title, introduction, overview, and guide to each manual.

4. *Tasks.* Put all the information needed to complete each task—and nothing irrelevant—into the reference sections. If that means repeating yourself, then repeat yourself.

5. *Standards.* Establish a common terminology and design and use it throughout.

6. *Length.* Don't make any one book too long (usually no more than 300 pages) or too short (no less than 30).

7. *Titles.* Make all your titles consistent, with information about the program's name, the name of the tasks described, the level of audience addressed, and whether this is a tutorial, general overview, or reference.

Keep in mind that you're helping readers to understand an entire system, not a bunch of isolated tasks. Think of the suite of manuals as a small library.

A QUICK REVIEW

Here's a summary of points to remember when you're organizing your manual:

☐ Follow the readers' interest, not the programmers'.

☐ Include sections that will speed up readers' access to information.

☐ Distinguish between tutorial and reference; and between what should be done on paper and what should be done on the computer.

☐ Figure out the minimum.

☐ Make a series look consistent in these areas: cross-reference, guidance, audience, tasks, standards, length, and titles.

PART THREE

Writing the Manual

Chapter 6: Beginning Every Manual—and Every Chapter
Chapter 7: Creating a Step-by-Step Tutorial
Chapter 8: Creating Computer-Assisted Instruction
Chapter 9: Setting Up Reference Sections
Chapter 10: Drawing Up Your Index
Chapter 11: Refining Your Style
Chapter 12: Indulging in Humor
Chapter 13: Designing Your Images

Beginning Every Manual and Every Chapter

Make Your Tables of Contents Helpful

Show Your Readers How to Use the Manual

Make a General Introduction, Too

Add Detail to the Table of Contents for Each Chapter

Provide an Overview of Every Section

And Now . . . A Quick Review of Beginnings

Beginning Every Manual
and Every Chapter

Few people start your manual on page 1. Some flip through the whole book looking at headings. Others skim the table of contents. Still others read the first paragraphs in a chapter, wondering whether to bother with the rest. A few settle down and read your introduction.

Your job is to create all of these potential beginnings. You might think of them as a series of advertisements inviting people in.

Let's say your table of contents actually gives readers an idea what's in each chapter. Your introduction to the manual answers some of their initial questions. And, at the beginning of each section, the overview helps readers decide whether or not the section will offer the material they're after, so they can skip until they find the right one. If all that's true, then people will begin to think your manual is easy to use.

MAKE YOUR TABLES OF CONTENTS HELPFUL

No matter how short your manual is, people count on your table of contents as an outline of the material, as an indication of what you consider the major and minor topics, and as a map leading them to the information they need. At a minimum, then, your main table of contents should include chapter titles and the first level of headings from each chapter, along with page numbers.

All chapter titles should make sense to a beginner. First-level headings should, too. (Below that, you may be forced into using jargon.) The titles of your chapters may be rather broad: Introduction, Tutorial, Reference. But when you're creating the headings within your chapters, get specific.

Use verbs when you can. They suggest the reader can actually do something with the program. Do not use a bunch of nouns, which look like a list of topics to study:

The Delete Function	The Move Function
The Copy Function	The Search Function

A series of verb phrases would liven this up, suggesting that your manual will help readers do real work, not just learn about a series of functions. A function should do something; if it does, say what. Here's the previous table of contents rewritten with verbs:

Deleting Words and Phrases   Moving Text from Here to There

Copying   Searching Through Your Text

Be consistent. For instance, once you've started using *ing* phrases, keep it up, unless you hit something that refuses to be squashed into that form. You might recast a series of headings from: "Unpacking, Setting Up, Planning, Data Security," to: "Unpacking, Setting Up, Planning, Safeguarding Your Data."

Questions make interesting headings, too, as long as you don't ask too many. They don't all have to end with a question mark, either. Often you'll have an introductory section, explaining the ideas behind the topic you're about to detail. This justifies headings like these:

Why Device Drivers?

How to Decide Which Driver to Use

Why It's Called a Handshake

Avoid headings which consist solely of key words. Who wants to find out what *ACK*, *STAT*, *REN*, and *PIP* mean? If you feel that some people will be looking commands up in the table of contents, then include them—but as an afterthought. First use English, then append the acronym. Here, for instance, is part of the table of contents for a BASIC manual:

What a Subroutine Is   85

Branching to a Subroutine (GOSUB)   87

Coming Back from a Subroutine (RETURN)   90

Tracing Your Program as It Runs (TRACE)   92

That way the table of contents doubles as a quick-reference card—but only if you do this for every single command and function.

In general, keep titles short enough to scan. Short titles and heads look better on the page. They let readers understand what you mean at one glance—not three or four. Avoid titles that take up a full line.

To make your table of contents indicate which sections are more important than others, indent the less important headings. If your main headings are in uppercase letters, put the smaller headings in uppercase and lowercase letters. Don't let your table of contents look like this:

The Distinction Between Logical and Physical Devices
under this Operating System   54

Requesting Ownership of the Printer—the LST Command   56

Some Simple Uses of the LST Command   58

Illustrations of Advanced Uses of the LST Command   64

Make it look more like this:

USING LOGICAL AND PHYSICAL DEVICES   54

    Printing—with the LST Command   56

    Simple Uses   58

    Advanced Uses   64

SHOW YOUR READERS HOW TO USE THE MANUAL

Take a page or so to indicate which parts of the manual readers may want to read. Don't just go through a list of chapters indicating what's in each one. Who cares? Have you ever had anyone ask you, "What's in that seventh chapter, anyway?"

Instead, start out with the main reasons someone might open the manual:

TO DO THIS	*TURN TO THIS SECTION*
Get a Quick Overview of the Program	Introduction, Page 11
Learn the Basics	Tutorial, Page 21
Customize the Program for You	Customizing, Page 101

TO DO THIS	TURN TO THIS SECTION
Solve Problems	Troubleshooting, Page 121
Find a Command	Quick Reference, Page 131

In this way, you advertise the different ways to use your manual and the different entry points. After each *if*, give readers the *then*—where to turn for the information. Include chapter, section, and page numbers, so they can turn there immediately.

Not a lot of talk. More a table than a chapter. You might even provide a diagram. Figure 6.1 shows one from VisiCorp's *VisiWord User's Guide* for the IBM Personal Computer:

Figure 6.1

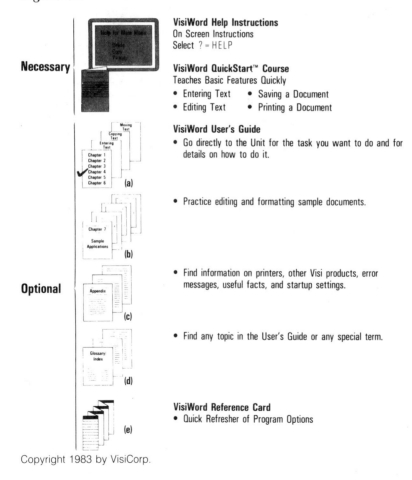

Necessary

VisiWord Help Instructions
On Screen Instructions
Select ? = HELP

VisiWord QuickStart™ Course
Teaches Basic Features Quickly
- Entering Text
- Editing Text
- Saving a Document
- Printing a Document

VisiWord User's Guide
- Go directly to the Unit for the task you want to do and for details on how to do it.

(a)

- Practice editing and formatting sample documents.

(b)

Optional

- Find information on printers, other Visi products, error messages, useful facts, and startup settings.

(c)

- Find any topic in the User's Guide or any special term.

(d)

VisiWord Reference Card
- Quick Refresher of Program Options

(e)

Copyright 1983 by VisiCorp.

MAKE A GENERAL
INTRODUCTION, TOO

Introduce the product—then the manual. Point out the benefits of the product, what it can do for the reader, how it works, and what kind of preparations purchasers must make to use it. Only then will anyone want to hear how you've organized the manual.

Right off, tell people what the program can do for them. You'd be amazed how many writers forget to do this. Maybe they figure the readers bought the program, so they must know what it's good for. Not necessarily so. Remember that the boss may buy the program and turn it over to someone else who has no idea what it's for. Anyway, knowing what a program can do may make people more interested in your tutorial.

Here's an example of a high-speed, condensed, general introduction, from the Software Guild's manual on The Sensible Speller™:

> Spelling problems? Tired of trying to proof your document files by hand? Having trouble analyzing your use of the English language? The Sensible Speller is an easy-to-use program designed to help you overcome these difficulties. It will locate spelling errors and "typos," and then give you a count of the number of times you used each word in a document. As an added feature, you can tailor the Sensible Speller's dictionaries to suit your specific needs. Or you can create as many different dictionaries as you wish and use them all to proofread a document.
>
> Copyright 1982 by the Software Guild, Inc.

That's the whole overview. But then, the manual itself is only 44 pages, a triumph of condensation.

Here's how a somewhat more leisurely writer advertised the benefits of a business graphics package at the start of a training manual:

> **WITH BUSINESS GRAPHICS YOU CAN:**
>
> - Edit data
> - Show files as
>   bar graphs
>   scatter-plots
>   pie charts
>   data points
> - Use vertical and horizontal titles
> - Create titles and put them anywhere on the graph
> - Print your graphs

Another question to answer quickly: How does it work? Just a thumbnail sketch of how the program works—a few paragraphs, or a few pages. Here's an example from a tutorial manual on VisiCalc™ III:

How Does It Work?

VisiCalc provides you with an enormous "electronic sheet of paper" 63 columns by 254 rows giving a total of 16,002 cells into which you can enter data.

The video monitor serves as a "window" through which you can look at a portion of this "electronic worksheet." With a few simple keystrokes, you can scroll the worksheet left and right or up and down. You can even "fold" the electronic sheet to look at two widely separated parts of it at the same time.

People also want to make sure that this is the right program and manual for them. You might single out these things in your introduction:

- Each group who'll be reading the manual (for instance, first-time computer users, old hands, people who know the application well but hate computers). Then indicate what each group ought to read or ignore.

- What you expect readers to know before beginning. (For instance, common accounting procedures or COBOL.) That way you'll warn the unprepared.

- What other manuals on similar or related subjects the users should read before starting your manual.

Many users worry that they may not have the right equipment. So include that information in the introduction, like this:

What Equipment Do You Need?

Before you start using Quick File, make sure you have the following:

- A 128K Apple III Computer with a second disk drive.
- The Quick File Boot Disk.
- The Quick File Program Disk.
- The Quick File Sample Files Disk.
- A printer (optional).

Since people are impatient, you might tell them what they should do first. (Make backup disks, for instance.) Then tell them how to get started, even if you go over that in the tutorial. You might consider explaining how errors are handled and how people can escape from the program.

If the program can't handle some things that readers might expect, say so here, so they don't look all around the manual for them. If readers can customize the program for different purposes and different arrangements of software and hardware, this is the time to say so. Indicate where the manual explains how to make the changes.

If you think your manual's complicated, you might outline it now so readers will get a sense of its organization. Try to avoid the simpleminded recitation of chapters and contents. If possible, organize this outline around the reasons users might open your manual in the first place. Even though this may be the first item on your agenda, it belongs at the end of the introduction.

ADD DETAIL TO THE TABLE OF CONTENTS FOR EACH CHAPTER

In a complicated chapter, you should offer readers a table of contents so they can zip to the section they want. For a reference section, for instance, which you know nobody wants to read from beginning to end, you can offer readers help by putting this kind of outline at the start.

Another reason for a chapter table of contents is to provide an extra level of detail, one not found in the manual's main table of contents. The question to ask yourself is: Would people be looking up these topics? If so, include them in the chapter table of contents.

For instance, here's what the main table of contents said about some functions of the Pascal Editor for the Apple III:

115	Text Changing Commands
115	Insert
121	Delete
125	Zap
126	Copy
129	Exchange

And here's how the chapter table of contents covered the same ground:

115	Text Changing Commands
115	Insert
117	Text Formats
117	Inserting in Programming Mode
119	Inserting in Document Mode

Continued

120	Inserting with Auto-indent and Filling Both True
120	Inserting with Auto-indent and Filling Both False
121	Delete
125	Zap
126	Copy
126	Copying from a File
128	Copying from the Copy Buffer
129	Exchange

PROVIDE AN OVERVIEW OF EVERY SECTION

Start off every chapter—and every large section of your manual—with a brief overview. An overview helps casual readers, who glance at it, recognize that this isn't the chapter they're after.

If this chapter does deal with the topic readers are after, an overview will answer most of their initial questions about the topic, at least in a general way. Put the most important ideas first—why people should read this chapter and what this part of the program will do for them. Start, then, with principles, and only later get into the details.

Introduce each chapter, explaining such things as these:

- What readers have learned so far, and what they will learn in this section. And how this chapter grows out of the ones before it and leads to the next ones.

- What the chapter will and will not discuss.

- The gist of the subject you'll be dealing with in the chapter.

- How different users can best approach the chapter. For instance, which sections could be skipped by someone familiar with computers.

- Where else to turn for information on the subject (other chapters, other manuals, data banks).

Don't be afraid to use diagrams and definitions as part of your overviews. As you get farther into your manual, your definitions can become more functional—they can define by what the users can do with the program. For instance, here's a chapter overview from Apple's *Quick File Sampler*:

> Creating a Report
>
> By now you know how to move the cursor through a Quick File file, how to change information in the file, and how to change record layouts. Now you will learn how to create a simple report, which is usually a printed version of information from your file.
>
> To create a report, you must specify a report format. A report format consists of instructions to Quick File about what to include in the report: which categories, for example, or which records. And it tells Quick File how the report should look: what information should go where and how it should be printed.
>
> Quick File lets you design report formats using all of the information in the file; or you can use only the information that suits your needs at any time. You can use a report format only once, or you can save it and use it whenever you want.
>
> This chapter explains some of the basics of reporting. It tells how to:
>
> - Choose a report style
>
> - Begin reporting
>
> - Create a format for your report
>
> - Print the report
>
> - Save the format of your report

A useful overview advertises the features you are about to discuss. Remember that some people will pick up your manual and start right here— even though it's the overview to the fourth chapter. So be especially careful of jargon. If you must use it, make it clear what it means and indicate where you discussed the topic earlier. (You can always hope that a few readers will turn back there if they don't understand.)

If one chapter has five or six subsections, include an overview for each. You'll feel like you're repeating yourself. Fine. Few people will read through all the sections in order as if they were literature. Again, remember the poor soul who looks up something in the table of contents, turns to the section, and wonders, "Is this the right section or not?"

Don't treat an overview as the place to discuss exceptions, obscure qualifications, warnings, or frightening jargon. Keep in mind that you're offering readers a chance to look over the broad landscape before they go down into the twisting streets full of detail. It's a beginning, not an afterthought.

AND NOW . . . A QUICK REVIEW OF BEGINNINGS

Here's a brief review of beginnings.

Your tables of contents should:

☐ Offer enough information so readers can find major and minor sections using the main table of contents.

☐ Appear at the front of complicated chapters, so readers can find out what is in the minor sections.

☐ Use active verbs, not abstract nouns.

☐ Arrange material in the order readers think about it— not in the order programmers think about it.

☐ Use consistent phrasing.

Your guide to the manual should:

☐ Anticipate the main reasons readers might want to open the manual and direct them to the right spot for each.

☐ Not talk too long.

☐ Highlight major sections. (A quick outline of the manual from the users' point of view.)

☐ Offer page numbers or chapter numbers, so readers can turn to them quickly.

Your overviews should:

☐ Answer most initial questions about the topic—at least in a general way.

☐ Promise further information—and announce what subjects you will discuss in the rest of the chapter.

☐ Establish general principles before discussing details.

☐ Put the most important ideas first—why readers should read the chapter, what this part of the product will do.

☐ Start positively.

☐ Show how this chapter flows out of the last one and leads into the next one.

Creating a Step-by-Step Tutorial

Organization Is Crucial
Think Like a Teacher
Tell 'Em How and Where
Introduce Each Section
Divide Your Material Into Short Steps
Show People How to Get Out
Separate What to Do from What it Means
Put In Lots of Displays
Define Your Terms
Put In Pictures
Anticipate Variations
Summarize
Give People a Break
Allow Yourself Some Asides
Allay Anxiety
Restore Your Sample Files
Test It. Revise It. Test It Again.
Tell People Where to Go Next
A Quick Review

Creating a Step-by-Step Tutorial

A tutorial offers nervous novices a series of exercises that put the program to work. You quickly get people up and running on the program—within an hour.

People like that. Your tutorial helps them feel comfortable with the product, because they can now do the basics. You show them that the program may actually work the way the dealer said it would. Why, it may even help them do their jobs.

Without a tutorial readers may never use the program. Or they may only use a few parts of it. They may end up hating the whole thing.

In a tutorial you take your readers through the fundamentals of the program, step by step. Some tutorials just introduce the basics—topics such as these:

- Starting up

- Creating a file from scratch

- Changing a file

- Saving a file

- Loading a file

- Leaving the program

Other tutorials proceed to advanced functions, particularly those functions that make this program more useful than others. Some tutorials come with a disk full of sample data, so users don't have to create any before learning to use the program. Some fill about a dozen pages, others fill more than a hundred.

I call them all tutorials, because you act as the tutor:

- Guide the users step by step.

- Point out what the screen shows.

- Anticipate confusion.

- Remind gently.

- Explain the significance of each step.

- Get the users out of trouble.

ORGANIZATION IS CRUCIAL

Often, you're creating a plot—an imaginary story. "You're going to write a letter to an insurance company." "You're going to set up a budget to see if you can afford a new car." Sue Espinosa, who has supervised the development of dozens of tutorials, stresses, "Things to do, not functions to memorize. If a single story line can carry through the entire tutorial, so much the better."

The story line sets up a real-life context, so people have an aim before they make a keystroke. That makes clear the *why* before the *how*—and makes the *how* easier to learn.

You may find it helpful to *storyboard* the whole tutorial. A storyboard divides your tutorial into a series of frames, like a movie. Assign a frame to each keystroke. Then test your storyboard. You've probably left out a few steps. Moving a few frames aside, you can insert those and go on. You can see whether your plot justifies all the actions you're insisting on.

Throughout, says Espinosa:

> Cultivate a sense of coherent architecture and forward momentum. The end should be visible from the beginning. One activity should follow another naturally and logically. Keep to the point. Don't digress into asides and extras that result in information overload.

Too many tutorials just jump from one little skill to another, without showing readers why one leads to the next.

Be selective when deciding which functions to include. Espinosa says, "Don't present six ways of doing the same thing. The new user remembers part of one, part of another, and then flubs up with the live software. Save alternatives for asides or the reference manual. From a family of functions, teach just one function."

Above all, resist covering every function. Sure, it's tempting. But it's a mistake. "Your motive may be golden," says Espinosa. "But the result will be leaden—a 250-page opus that is exhaustive and—for the user—exhausting. People don't usually have the time or the energy to sit through more than an hour of material. They want to use the software fast."

THINK LIKE A TEACHER

As you write the tutorial, keep in mind all the possible confusions readers may suffer:

- Anticipate readers' every move. This includes goofs. What happens on the screen if users press ESCAPE at this point? How can users recover? What if users select an option that isn't offered?

- Be alert to anything that might puzzle users. It's helpful to keep notes on your own first experiences with the program. What confused you?

- Remember that you are writing for two levels of readers. One may know other programs and expect certain familiar routines. Tell those readers whenever this program violates those expectations. The other readers think that *booting a program* means kicking in the video display.

- Separate the basic from the advanced functions. In fact, give users a break in between.

- Take it easy. Don't rush your readers through. Pause to observe the scenery and let your readers catch a breath.

TELL 'EM HOW AND WHERE

You can start readers out on the right track if you explain how they can use the tutorial. For instance, you might tell them:

- What they will learn from the tutorial.

- What the major sections of the tutorial are.

- What parts of the tutorial to read if they already know how to use the product—and what to read if they don't.

- What parts of the tutorial to read if they already know the business function this program helps them with—and what to read if they don't.

- What equipment, disks, and supplies they need to use the tutorial.

- What is not covered in the tutorial. (Advertise the owner's manual or reference material.)

If you have a tutorial with more than half a dozen sections, include an outline in the form of a table of contents. That helps people to pick and choose, to anticipate what they will learn, and to return later for a quick refresher. For the titles of each section, use terms that will help readers when they come back later to look up a particular function. Not "Some Other Functions," but "Deleting and Wiping Out."

You may find that a picture can help show how to use your tutorial. For instance, writer Peggy Miller wanted to show that users could enter one

Figure 7.1

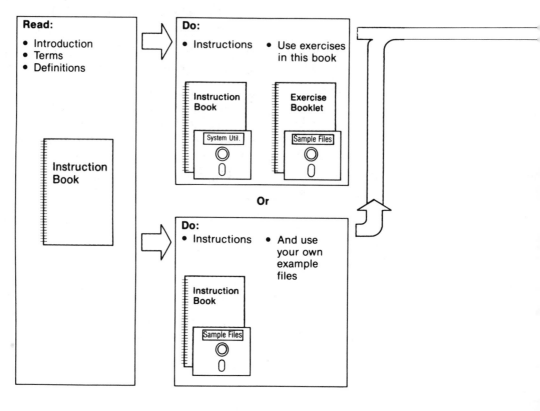

tutorial (on some system utilities) at several places: the introduction, the description of the main menu, or the explanation of one of the options on the main menu. In addition, readers could use the book of exercises and the disk of sample data or work on their own. To make these choices clear, and to outline the whole tutorial, Peggy Miller made up the sketch shown in Figure 7.1.

INTRODUCE EACH SECTION

Say what they're going to learn in each section—right at the beginning. When readers know what's relevant and what's not, they won't get distracted as easily; knowing what you're working towards, they'll begin to see how your argument develops and why you're making the asides you are. It's a general rule: When people know what they're going to learn, they learn more.

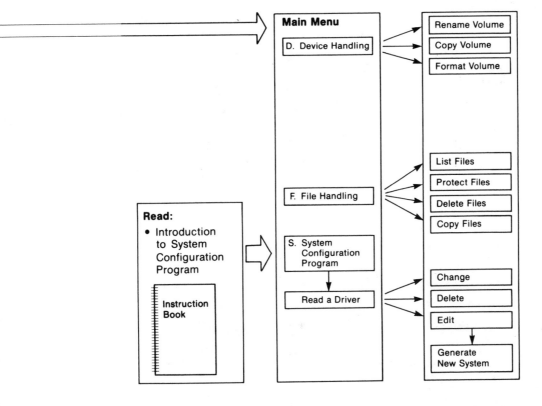

Here's an example from the *Quick File Sampler:*

> This section explains more Quick File basics. But instead of just moving the cursor, as you did in the last chapter, you'll actually be changing information in a file. You'll be using Sue's Business Cards again.
>
> Section 3 tells you how to
>
> - Change an entry
>
> - Find records in a file
>
> - Insert a record
>
> - Arrange records
>
> - Save changes

If you're encouraging people to jump into your tutorial at any point, you may need to define the key words for this section at the start. That way, someone who's already learned a word in an earlier section can skip the definition. But someone who's starting here can pick up the terminology before plunging into the tutorial itself.

Also, if different sections require different disks or different amounts of hardware, you'll want to add an introductory note about that.

Here's an example of a lengthy—but necessary—introduction to a section of Peggy Miller's tutorial on system utilities:

FORMAT A VOLUME

Formatting a volume prepares a volume to receive and store files that you create. It also erases all information previously stored on that volume.

A volume need only be formatted once but all must be formatted. The number of files you store on the volume depends on the capacity of the volume and the length of the files. You can mix different types of files (Apple Writer, VisiCalc, computer programs, etc.) on the same volume.

What you will need to format a volume:

- System Utilities disk

- The volume you wish to format

- The Exercise booklet (if you wish to practice)

Key words to know:

Volume—A volume is a disk on which computer files are stored.

Device —A device is any piece of computer hardware, other than the computer itself. Disk drives and printers are examples of devices. Devices may be built-in or external.

.d1   —This the device name used to represent the internal (built-in) disk drive (drive 1).

.d2   —This is the device name used to represent the first external drive (drive 2).

DIVIDE YOUR MATERIAL
INTO SHORT STEPS

Figure that a section should take no more than five minutes for the user to complete. This probably means six or seven steps, each about as long as a short paragraph.

Number each step so readers can find their place when they come back from the keyboard and the screen. Tests show that just by adding numbers you help people move much faster, because they don't have to retrace their steps as often. Here, for instance, is the VisiCorp tutorial on initializing a document disk, in the *QuickStart Course* for VisiWord:

A flexible disk must be *initialized* (prepared for use) before it can store VisiWord documents. If you have formatted a disk using the IBM DOS Format command, you do not have to initialize the disk over again. If you have not, follow these instructions to initialize a document disk.

1. Select Create by typing C or pressing ENTER. The screen clears and is replaced by the VisiWord editing screen. You will learn more about this later.

2. Press ESC to use the Main menu.

3. Select Storage. The editing screen disappears, and the screen now displays the storage screen. This tells you what drive (Drive B) the program expects to contain your document disk, and what the current document is.

4. Select Maintenance.

5. Select Initialize. You are asked where the document disk will be.

6. Type b: ENTER.

7. Insert the document disk into drive B and type Y.

The initialization process begins. Drive B whirs and the light goes on. When the disk is initialized, the screen displays the Maintenance menu again.

SHOW PEOPLE HOW TO GET OUT

Very early in your tutorial, show users how to escape from tangles and how to go back to the main menu. You can't imagine how many ways users can get lost if you don't tell them this on the first page.

Keep telling them how to recover from errors. You might have running feet that tell what page to go to for advice. Users don't want to have to remember that while they're doing OK, but as soon as they foul up, they want help. That's when they appreciate that you keep saying where to go. For instance, one tutorial has a box like this at the bottom of every page:

TYPING ERROR?   Turn to page 39 for corrections.

This doesn't condemn readers. It doesn't leave them pounding the keyboard in frustration, wondering how to get back to the tutorial. And it keeps reminding readers that there is help available.

SEPARATE WHAT TO DO
FROM WHAT IT MEANS

In a two-column format, put what readers should do on the left and the results—plus what they mean—on the right. Spread general information and warnings that everyone should read across the two columns.

Some people like to skim through a tutorial, entering all the commands and seeing what happens. They get the general idea and don't want to get bogged down in descriptions. They can read down the left column.

Other people get nervous. After they type one command, they want to make sure that their display looks like yours. They consult your illustrations very carefully. And they read your explanations from beginning to end to make sure they haven't done anything wrong and that they understand this complicated process. These people read both sides slowly.

Here is an example of a tutorial in a two-column format:

INSERTING A RECORD

And now a quick lesson on how to insert a record into your file.

1. Look at the HELP screen again to find out the keys you need to insert a record and then go back to Review/Add/Change.

2. Put the cursor on an entry in Julie Aaron's record.

3. Hold down the OPEN APPLE key and type I.

Surprise!
Something new!

It's a blank record, in single-record layout. The record has the same headings as the other records you've seen in single-record layout.

The cursor is at the blank for Last Name.

PUT IN LOTS OF DISPLAYS

After people press a key, they want to know that they've done the right thing. Have they gotten the right display?

Particularly at the beginning of the tutorial, pause after every item that users type in to show them what the resulting display should look like. You'd be amazed how this reassures people that they're still following you and that nothing's gone wrong.

Like this:

```
5. Press Q, for Quit.               This lets you leave the
                                    Utilities Program.
                                    After a few seconds, you see
                                    the main menu of Apple
                                    Speller III.


   Apple Speller III    Copyright 1982, Sensible
                        Software, Inc,


   S_Speller Program
   U_Utilities Program
   Q_Quit


   Which would you like to do? [ ]
```

Also, if you're asking them to type something complex, and you have any doubts that they might get it wrong, show them what it should look like just before they press RETURN to enter it. (That way they can make corrections rather than plunging into limbo.)

DEFINE YOUR TERMS

Introduce each bit of jargon as a new word and define it. People don't mind some inside lingo if they feel they're learning it. What they hate is jargon that snubs and bewilders them—without any explanation.

For a tutorial that you've invited people to enter at almost any point, you might consider putting a list of key words at the start of each section, since you can't be sure that readers will have encountered them in an earlier section. That way, someone who's read the earlier sections can glance at the list and skip to the new material.

PUT IN PICTURES

Use pictures to orient the readers. Sometimes an illustration can help people locate a key, as in the picture from IBM's manual on BASIC shown in Figure 7.2.

Figure 7.2

Key(s)	Function
Del	Deletes the character at the current cursor position. All characters to the right of the deleted character move one position left to fill in the empty space. Line folding occurs; that is, if a logical line extends beyond one physical line, characters on subsequent lines move left one position to fill in the previous space, and the character in the first column of each subsequent line moves up to the end of the preceding line.

Copyright 1982 by IBM. Courtesy of IBM.

Pictures are particularly helpful for showing people how to perform delicate physical actions such as inserting disks. For instance, in my tutorial on the Apple Speller III, I worked with the designer Henry Korman to develop the diagrams shown in Figure 7.3 to demonstrate how to insert disks.

Figure 7.3

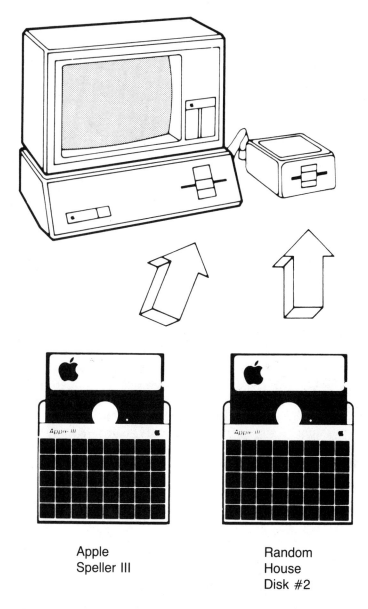

Apple
Speller III

Random
House
Disk #2

Use pictures to illustrate ideas. For instance, Figure 7.4 on page 88 is a drawing that helps readers figure out where they are when looking at a series of Mailing List labels. They can move back by pressing P (to go to the previous label), F (to go to the very first one), N (to go to the next one), or L (to go to the last one).

Figure 7.4

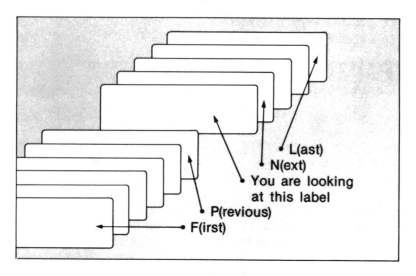

ANTICIPATE VARIATIONS

What if people have only one disk drive? What if they use a hard disk? If your program works with several hardware arrangements, each with its own pattern of commands, and if the differences show up in almost every step, then assign each arrangement its own section in the tutorial and just repeat the instructional material. Make sure you take a page at the beginning of the tutorial to tell people which section to use.

If the differences just occur occasionally, you might come up with a stylized representation, or *icon*, to indicate each type, and break away from the regular flow of text with a **boldface** phrase like "**If you're using a Profile . . . .**"

Then put in the icon and give the material that's specific to that machine. (You might isolate this from the regular text by surrounding it with a box.)

If there are two ways to do the same thing, say so right off, so readers don't think they're misremembering when you suddenly use RETURN instead of ENTER.

Sometimes one tutorial's got to be designed to run on three or four different machines. Here's how John Zussman handled that situation in his manual for ThinkTank, from Living Videotext:

STARTING UP THINKTANK

This section is divided into two parts. If you have a hard disk drive on your computer system, skip to the section on "Hard Disk Systems" later in this chapter.

Floppy Disk Systems

If you are operating ThinkTank on a floppy disk system, you will need at least two disk drives. Drive 1 is considered your main disk drive and is used to load and hold the THINKTANK PROGRAM DISK. Drive 2 and other drives contain ThinkTank data disks. Your drives and their controller should be installed in standard fashion (Slot 6, Drives 1 and 2 on the Apple II and IIe). Your dealer will normally take care of this for you.

Step 1: INSERT PROGRAM AND DATA DISKS

Depending on your computer, the ThinkTank package may contain two or three disks. One is labelled THINKTANK PROGRAM DISK and it contains the instructions your computer uses to run ThinkTank. The second is labelled THINK-TANK DATA DISK and it contains the sample outlines discussed in this manual. Once you learn how to use ThinkTank, you will create your own data disks to store your own outlines. If you have an Apple III, you have a third disk called the THINKTANK BOOT DISK; it contains the instructions your computer uses to start up ThinkTank.

(a) Apple II and IIe. Place the THINKTANK PROGRAM DISK in Drive 1 of your machine and your ThinkTank data disk in another drive. If this is your first time using ThinkTank, use the THINKTANK DATA DISK supplied with the program and insert it in Drive 2.

(b) Apple III. Place the THINKTANK BOOT DISK in the Apple III's built-in drive (Drive 1) and your ThinkTank data disk in another drive. If this is your first time using ThinkTank, use the THINKTANK DATA DISK supplied with the program and insert it in Drive 2.

SUMMARIZE

For people who are never going to read the reference material, but may want to turn back to what they have read, offer a brief summary of commands in the tutorial. (This should match what you put on your quick-reference card, by the way.)

The first time through the tutorial, readers may not remember everything you've taught them. Reviewing each subject after you've gone through it will give them a chance to reinforce it in their minds.

If your tutorial has a lot of sections, put a summary at the end of each one, so readers can review the material while they still remember part of it. Otherwise, collect all the summaries at the end of the tutorial. Figure 7.5 shows the summary VisiCorp provides at the end of its *QuickStart Course* on VisiLink:

Figure 7.5

Summary of
VisiLink Tasks

Task	To Get There, Press	To Leave Display	To Return To Main Menu
Back up your Utility diskette.	Forms Backup	(ESC)	Quit
Select Blank Forms			
Mark blank forms from the catalog.	Order Forms	(ESC)	Quit
Request blank forms from DRI. Enter your Personal ID and press (RETURN).	Order Communicate	(ESC)	Quit
Complete Blank Forms			
Select and create a completed form from a blank form. Type a filename and press (RETURN).	Define Create	(ESC)	Quit
Order DataKit Packages From Completed Forms			
Mark a completed form from a list of completed forms on the screen.	Order DataKits	(ESC)	Quit
Order a DataKit package by sending the completed form to DRI. Enter your Personal ID and press (RETURN).	Order Communicate	(ESC)	Quit
Leave Program			
Leave VisiLink program and go to VisiCalc program.	Quit Boot	---	---

GIVE PEOPLE A BREAK

It's hard work learning all this strange terminology, using this weird machine. Don't wear people out.

Make it easy for people to stop with a feeling of accomplishment. Suggest that they relax for a moment after every few sections. You don't want them driving themselves.

(You could even tell them how to turn the machine off if they're through for this session.)

ALLOW YOURSELF SOME ASIDES

You're talking to the readers. Every once and a while you can be enthusiastic. For instance, in explaining VisiCalc, one writer commented:

> How's that for speed?
>
> By the way, the coordinates of the cursor
> location are always displayed on the
> Entry Contents line in the upper left
> corner of your screen.

Warn people to follow you, not the suggestions on the screen. If they see an on-screen prompt like "Enter option:C," meaning that the programmer figured most people would choose option C, they may believe they're supposed to enter C, when you want them to enter L. Then they could innocently shoot off to some other part of the program and get so lost they'll never come back. Particularly at the beginning, beware of all the default responses indicated on screens you reproduce in your tutorial. People are very obedient if you tell them in advance.

ALLAY ANXIETY

If a frightening message is about to pop out at them, tell people not to worry. If the next few steps are going to be complicated, admit that they are—even for you. If you're using some awful term like *deferred execution*, show that you know it sounds terrible. "No, this section is not on last minute reprieves for condemned criminals."

Show sympathy, then. Whenever you see the program getting nasty, recognize that people will feel frightened. Crack a joke. It's OK. After all, this is just a tutorial.

RESTORE YOUR SAMPLE FILES

Sometimes you may set up some sample files for people to play with using the software you're teaching. That way, they don't have to spend a lot of time typing just to learn a few commands.

But you'll find that several people may want to use your tutorial. You want each of them to find the same file at the beginning. The key: don't *save* the revised file with its original name, so that users don't wipe out your original file.

If you must teach how to save a file, then have users save the revised file with a new name. And explain why. Later, you can show them how to delete files—that's when you can get the new one off the disk.

TEST IT. REVISE IT. TEST IT AGAIN.

When you think you're through, test your tutorial. Try it on some people who will tell you exactly what puzzles them; try experienced and inexperienced, middle management and entry-level employees. Stand there while they go through it. Watch where they slow down. Listen for the laughs.

You'll find lots of places where people misunderstand, enter weird data, get stuck, turn corners, or can't go back the way they came. You'll see that some problems stem from the program, and a few from your manual. You'll begin to see what you assumed users wanted—and what they really want. After watching real people use your tutorial, you'll want to do another revision.

When you've revised the tutorial for what you're sure is absolutely the last time, go through it one more time, very slowly:

- Have you really described what appears on the screen if readers do—or don't do—what you say?

- Have you really explained *default* in a way that makes sense to novices?

- Has the program changed since you wrote the first draft? Do you have debris from earlier drafts? (If what readers see on the screen no longer corresponds to what you wrote, you may make them feel frustrated, to say the least.)

If you've organized your tutorial carefully enough, you won't have to do massive rewriting—just a lot of tinkering.

TELL PEOPLE WHERE TO GO NEXT

Often people finish a tutorial and wonder whether they're ready to explore the real software. If they are, tell them so. If you think some readers may want a little more practice, and you've set up some exercises, mention the exercises and say whether they're required or optional.

Keep in mind how confusing the whole process is for beginners: a program, a tutorial, another manual, codes, keystrokes, maybe a separate reference card, and half a dozen disks. You may feel a little like a disciplinarian, but give firm guidance on what people should do next.

Figure 7.6 on page 94 shows how VisiCorp sketched out the various paths that users might take after completing the tutorial called *QuickStart Course*. The brave could just take out the pocket reference and start the program. The slightly less brave could turn to the user's guide and then start the program. The downright nervous could try out some of the sample applications described in the user's guide—a hand-holding tour of some already-written letters.

Figure 7.6

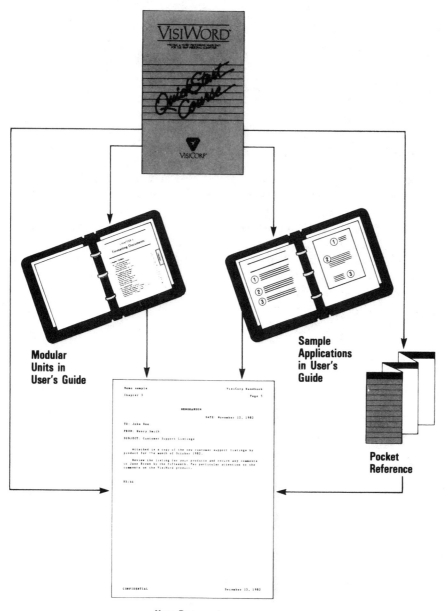

**Modular
Units in
User's Guide**

**Sample
Applications
in User's
Guide**

**Pocket
Reference**

Your Documents

A QUICK REVIEW

A well-designed tutorial can make readers feel the program will work for them and, better yet, may help them do their own job faster, better, easier. And happy readers recommend you to their friends. So, when you write a tutorial:

- [ ] Anticipate every move—every possible move.

- [ ] Be alert to whatever might puzzle beginners.

- [ ] Tell people how to use which parts.

- [ ] Carve the material into digestible sections.

- [ ] Introduce each section.

- [ ] Divide each section into a series of short steps.

- [ ] Show people how to get out.

- [ ] Separate what readers should do from what it means.

- [ ] Put in lots of displays and pictures.

- [ ] Define any unfamiliar terms the first time you use them.

- [ ] Anticipate the main variations of equipment.

- [ ] Summarize.

- [ ] Don't rush. And give everyone some breaks along the way.

- [ ] Allay anxiety.

- [ ] Restore your sample files, so the next person can start fresh.

- [ ] Allow yourself some asides.

- [ ] Test, revise, test, revise, test.

- [ ] Tell people what to do after the tutorial.

8

Creating
Computer-Assisted
Instruction

The Main Benefits
The Disadvantages
A New Way of Writing
Focus on Basics
Flash a Menu
Explain What You're Going to Do
Make Every Segment Short
Keep It Light
Play Foreground Off Against Background
Keep a Rhythm Going
Encourage Guessing
Catch Those Errors
Do the Boring Stuff
Give People Some Free Play
Sum It Up
Tell People Where to Go Next
A Quick Review

Creating
Computer-Assisted
Instruction

This is the way you might like to imagine two users musing over your latest manual. Unfortunately, since the nineteenth century, few people look for long and leisurely reads. In fact, some people today don't appreciate paper.

Even if Voltaire had written the manual and Maxwell Perkins had edited it, these people would probably find it dull, confusing, hard to get through. They'd say it reminded them of school. Focus groups of new customers report that they want to get going on the machine. Reading's not what they have in mind.

And think of what people go through using a written tutorial with an unfamiliar keyboard and video screen. Jon Butah, who has created computer-assisted instruction for Apple Writer, AppleFile, and Logo, says:

> We were watching people at the keyboard with the conventional paper tutorials, and the problem there was that people would look at the book, and look at the keyboard to type, and at the screen, so that they had three things to handle. Unless they are crackerjack touch-typists, which most people aren't, they have to glance at the keyboard to get oriented, especially the novice who may not be familiar with the Control key.
>
> They'll look at the keyboard, look at the book, look at the screen—bouncing around between those three things. We thought, "We've got to get it onscreen, so they don't have to struggle with the books." That was the initial impetus.

So writers began to put some user education on disks. That way people look at what's on the screen, then type, then look back at the screen. They are interacting with the computer.

THE MAIN BENEFITS

Paperless tutorials, often called computer-assisted instruction, offer several benefits:

- People get going fast. There's no book to slow them down. No reading to do first.

- Learning this way can be more fun and more exciting than learning from a book.

- Many people like using a computer to learn to use a computer. They feel cheated when they have to depend on printed materials.

- It's fast. In some cases, tests show that kids learn 40% more with computer-assisted instruction than with conventional techniques. Of course, the learning's not the same: they don't memorize as much, but they feel more at ease with the material.

- People find it friendlier. At least, it *can* be friendlier. That's up to you.

THE DISADVANTAGES

Yes, there are drawbacks. One is that any computer-assisted instruction is itself a program, even though it is not a very sophisticated one. Suddenly, you have to write within some rather strange limits:

- You may need to learn another program known as an *authoring language*. Authoring languages were originally developed so that teachers could create mini-lectures, followed by quizzes, all on the computer. Many limit you to rote drill. Most have trouble imitating whatever software you're teaching. (Their creators expected you to be teaching the names of the presidents or the capitals of the states.)

- If you don't find an authoring language you enjoy— and I'd say this is likely—you'll need to collaborate with a programmer. That will give you a lot more flexibility, but you'll still find areas where you have to bend to the requirements of programming.

- You may not be able to say very much. There is often a limit on how much you can write on each screen and on the total number of characters in your text. You may feel you are writing telegrams.

- You must anticipate most of the potential misunderstandings that users of the program may stumble into. Then your programmer (or authoring language) must catch the users making those goofs, and allow you to send helpful messages that show what to do to correct the mistake.

- Computer-assisted instruction involves you in a long and complicated process, much of which requires you to think like a programmer. (You're not really programming, thank goodness!)

A NEW WAY OF WRITING

In the past, most tutorials dealt with three media—the page, the keyboard, and the screen—but the page dominated. Now the screen dominates, and you get rid of the paper. And that means the way you write must change, too. Elizabeth Weal, a writer who has just completed her first computer-assisted instruction, called *Apple at Work*, says, "An interactive disk must be a lot more than an on-line book."

At first, writers tried using the text from books, but because the program responds to people, computer-assisted instruction begins to seem more like conversation. Jon Butah argues, "It's a dramatic dialogue between you and the program, so there's a natural tendency for people to anthropomorphize the program or the computer. They're going back and forth with it."

You need to think of the material as a kind of dialogue. Butah says, "The whole structure of the material becomes: we're inside the computer, and you're outside pressing the keys."

FOCUS ON BASICS

In this low-key drama you are creating, you have even less chance to expatiate on interesting sidelights than you do in a paper tutorial. Don't plan to teach a lot of advanced functions. You're going to be able to introduce people to the main features of the program—period.

You won't be able to teach users any variations, exceptions, or rules. In fact, what they gain here is more emotional than intellectual—a new confidence, a feel for the material, and a sense of the organization of the software.

Restrict yourself to fewer than half a dozen sections. No one section should take more than ten minutes. If the whole disk takes more than an hour, you're going to wear a lot of people out.

FLASH A MENU

At the beginning, offer an interesting title screen. (On a Logo interactive disk, users watch a complex pattern form while the titles appear.) Follow this with an outline of your material, presented in one display divided into three levels—title, menu, and comments.

Your readers should be able to select any section from the menu. (Don't force them to go 1, 2, 3 if you can help it—that feels pretty restrictive.) You might point to the section you suggest they try next. But don't insist on it.

Also, when they've done a few sections, they may forget which they've done. Help them out by signaling the ones they've done in this session. You should have your programmer put an asterisk next to these.

EXPLAIN WHAT YOU'RE GOING TO DO

Tell people up front some of the most common conventions you'll be using. For instance, you could explain the way the display will look:

```
In this program, we'll tell you something about Apple
Writer or ask you to perform a specific step by putting a
frame on the screen--just like the one you're reading
now. And behind the frame, you'll see an exact simu-
lation of the Apple Writer program.
```

Tell people how to go on. "Press RETURN to move forward." Rehearse that. Congratulate them when they manage it. This can be particularly important if you're putting simulation screens behind your text, since the simulation may include other advice, such as "Press SPACE BAR." Tell them how to back up when they want to (if your programmer can add this capability).

Reassure people that you'll keep them from fouling up. Explain how you'll handle mistakes:

```
And don't be concerned about making mistakes. We've de-
signed this disk so that we can catch you if you do some-
thing we aren't expecting.
    We'll beep the first two times you press a key we didn't
ask for. The third time we'll put a clarifying (we hope!)
message on the screen.
```

Be aware of the way you define mistakes. You might describe these as "doing something I don't expect," or "pressing a key I didn't ask for"—neutral actions, more like typos than serious errors. Remember that almost any error users make is your fault.

Don't cram too many explanations up front, though. Let people get going. If you can postpone describing some conventions, do so. People won't be able to remember very many, and if you describe four or five at once, users may begin to think they've got to memorize them.

MAKE EVERY SEGMENT SHORT

People have trouble reading a lot of text on the screen. Jon Butah says, "If there's a block of text of more than three or four lines, we find that people begin to feel uncomfortable. If you give them short paragraphs, they feel comfortable.''

KEEP IT LIGHT

Basically, this is a funny situation—all you little fellas running around inside the computer and the user outside pounding on the keyboard—so too much dignity will seem out of place. A light touch helps. For instance, when urging people to try typing something, recognize that they may type something obscene or revealing and that, because you've been talking together, they might feel embarassed. So you could say, "Type whatever you like. We promise not to look." Encourage them to take breaks: "And since we can't go anywhere, we'll be right here when you come back."

Not exactly a stand-up comedy routine. But asides like these play off the situation you're both imagining. As Elizabeth Weal says, "People like to laugh, especially when they're under the stress of learning something new." When explaining the idea of menus in *Apple Presents the Apple IIe*, Bruce Tognazzini and J. D. Eisenberg offer a real menu which includes some strange items. If you pick Bubble and Squeak, for instance, the computer responds like an unctuous waiter: "An excellent selection— British cuisine is so tasty."

When introducing word processing and data bases, Weal provides the reader with some tests:

```
A computer program that lets you use your computer to
type and edit documents is called a:

        a) random word generator
        b) word processor
        c) name dropper

A computer program that helps you keep track of nu-
merous related pieces of information or data is
called a

        a) data management program
        b) bit twiddler
        c) hodgepodge multiplexer
```

PLAY FOREGROUND OFF
AGAINST BACKGROUND

If you can, put displays from the real software behind your text, so users can see what you're talking about. For instance, in describing Apple

Writer, Jon Butah reproduced the data line, then described it in a box, like this:

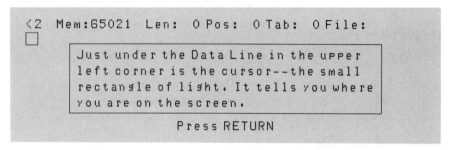

If you don't include displays from the software, include some graphics. A picture of files when you're discussing a data base or filer. A disk going into a drive. A keyboard with the key they should press lit up. You probably won't have room on the disk for really complicated graphics, but even stick figures will help.

Add sound, if you can. For instance, in the middle of a discussion of Logo users hear some beeps. It's a new character intruding. His name is Leo Logolover, and he's carried away with enthusiasm for Logo. That's why he keeps honking to get the user's attention. With that sound, the two-way conversation expands; people get the feeling of a crowd. It's more theatrical.

KEEP A RHYTHM GOING

Alternate between little lectures and exercises. Let users do something, then read, then do. As Jon Butah says:

> Keep a rhythm between the user reading something and the user doing something, so you don't have long stretches where the reader is pressing RETURN and reading text, pressing RETURN, RETURN, RETURN. That's deadly.
>
> We say, "This is how you delete a letter. You hold down the Control key and press the Left-Arrow key. Now you do it." And immediately people do it. And they're successful with it, and they think, "Hey, I can do this program. I'm not a dummy. I can use Apple Writer. I can use a word processor."

When the reader has played around for a while, tie the exercise to your main point. For instance, in learning Logo, users have to figure out how many degrees are in a right angle. They can guess 45 and be shown that's not right, then guess 130 and be shown that's not right. Finally they get it right, and Jon Butah tells them:

```
You had to experiment a little to find the right num-
ber. You've learned an important fact of geometry by
trial and error, not rote memorization.
```

ENCOURAGE GUESSING

Once you've explained how to do one function, see if readers can guess how to do the next one. If they get it, their confidence grows and their understanding of the program is confirmed. If they don't catch on, your response can direct them to the right path.

Elizabeth Weal uses this technique to suggest that data bases aren't that difficult, since they're based on ideas borrowed from ordinary filing systems. Before defining the term, she challenges the reader:

```
Each individual piece of information in a record
(that is, each flashing item) is called a
        a) tidbit
        b) entry
        c) smidgeon
```

Her wrong answers are just funny enough to warn people off, and if users happen to pick one, they get the response, "Not quite. Try again." That goes on until everyone's got it right.

CATCH THOSE ERRORS

Most of the time, catch any mistakes and disarm them, so the program doesn't go haywire. But don't react like a mainframe computer with messages like "ABEND, System Abort in progress." As Elizabeth Weal says, you should "make provisions for every conceivable error users can make and give people constructive suggestions when their responses indicate they're not understanding what's being explained."

If they guess wrong, encourage another try. If they make the same mistake two or three times, give them the answer: "Sorry, that's still not correct. A computer program that lets you use your computer to type and edit documents is called a word processor."

Don't be too clever, though. If you—and your programmer—can't figure out what users typed, or why, admit it. Say something like, "I didn't catch that," and then give a list of correct choices, or a hint, such as "Please type Y for Yes, N for No, or M for Maybe; then press RETURN."

DO THE BORING STUFF

If you want people to see what it looks like when they fill out a spread-sheet, have them type a few entries, then say, "OK, we'll do the rest for you."

If you run into difficult functions, such as positioning two types and three sizes of titles on a bar chart, talk about how this works, then show the titles floating into position. That way readers get the idea, without suffering the pain.

GIVE PEOPLE SOME FREE PLAY

Suggest breaks. After the third or fourth lesson, you could call for a seventh inning stretch.

Let people skip, too. If they get bored with a lesson, they should be able to return to the main menu, without having to page through every display in the lesson.

If possible, create sections in which people can exercise a little more freedom. You might let them get into a little trouble—nothing serious—then extricate themselves. They could type a few paragraphs and see if they can recall how to make corrections.

Jon Butah says:

> The ideal would be to present the material under very close control, and then to put them into a much freer situation and give them a general goal to go for, and say, "You've learned to move around and delete letters and paragraphs. Now here are a couple of letters. Move the first paragraph to the end." And we leave it totally open to them to try it. But unlike the actual software, we block them from getting into trouble.

SUM IT UP

Yes, summaries help people remember where they've been, remind them that they've learned something, and help them test their recall. At the end of each section, offer readers a condensed version of what you've just taken them through.

Better than a simple list of ideas: a quiz or an exercise in which people have to actually do something. As Elizabeth Weal says, "Some people like to test themselves. Others don't. That's why quizzes should be optional."

TELL PEOPLE WHERE TO GO NEXT

At the end of the disk, tell people what to do next. Don't leave them hanging, wondering whether to plug in the program, to open the manual, or to go out for a drink. What do you think they should turn to next? As Jon Butah says:

> People will either leave the disk and go to the tutorial for more work. Or, if they're more confident and more experienced, they might leave the disk and go directly to the program. For instance, with Apple Writer, they can leave the disk and go directly to the program. They wouldn't have to do the tutorial. But with Apple File, because of the overwhelming complexity of that program, nobody felt that way. They think, "Oh boy, this is good, but I don't remember all that stuff." So we make our directions very clear on the disk. We say, "You're finished now with the disk. Go now to the tutorial." It's very important to set people's expectations: What do I do next?

An interactive disk starts people off. It's not a reference manual. So you might explain what the reference manual offers them and when they might use it. In a way, you're advertising the rest of the documentation.

A QUICK REVIEW

When writing computer-assisted instruction:

☐ Focus on the basics.

☐ Show a menu up front and let people go back there anytime.

☐ Explain what you're going to do on the tutorial.

☐ Make every segment short.

☐ Keep the tone light.

☐ Play foreground information off against a background that shows what the program actually looks like.

☐ Keep a rhythm going between lecture and activity.

☐ Encourage guessing.

☐ Catch users' errors without making them feel bad.

☐ Do the boring stuff.

☐ Give people some elbowroom.

☐ Sum it up.

☐ Point out the next step.

9

Setting Up Reference Sections

What to Include
Adopt a Familiar Order
A Typical Function
Show How to Do Some Sample Tasks
Don't Forget to Summarize
When in Doubt, Make a Table
Provide Some Forms, Too
Report the Reports
Translate the Messages
Define New Terms
And, for Further Reading
Make a Handy Reference Card
A Quick Review

Setting Up Reference Sections

After a first reading—or glance—most people just use a manual for reference. That means they're looking up something. And that means they're already feeling a little nervous, maybe angry, certainly a bit frustrated.

They don't want to have to read pages and pages of commentary to find one code. They don't want to debate whether you mean A or B when you say C. They want to get back to work.

What information do they really need, then? And what can they live without? These questions will probably bedevil you as you write reference material.

WHAT TO INCLUDE

Where your tutorial introduces a smattering of key features, your reference must document everything a user could ever want to do with the software. Here are some important things to cover:

- The main tasks that people might want to use the program for and exactly how to accomplish them. Remember, a task is a piece of work in the user's office—not some obscure function deep inside the program. Writing a letter is a task. Deleting is just a function.

- Definitions of every term used in the program and your description of the program.

- What every function and every option on every menu does. Essentially, you're covering every choice a user can make.

- How different paths to a function affect what it will do. (Some routes may narrow the options or introduce odd behavior.)

- Explanations of every message, report, and signal that emerges from the program.

- Indications of what to do about various exceptional situations, including mistakes.

- Adjustments a user can make, so that the program behaves differently, offering more or fewer options.

- All the details a user needs to get the program started, or to keep it running, in various circumstances.

- Where to go for more information, if it's not all here.

For each program you write about, you'll decide whether users need more or less of each of these subjects. In general, tilt toward more, rather than less in reference sections. (No one reads it all.)

ADOPT A FAMILIAR ORDER

When you first put reference sections together, many look like long lists. You may cast around for a way to impose order on the various topics. Here are some rules of thumb:

- Put the common before the unusual. Then you can refer back to it each time it comes up. Some activities will crop up again and again; highlight those at the beginning.

- Organize around the things people might want to do—actions, jobs, procedures, tasks. Put these in an order most people would recognize as natural.

- Establish the context before revealing the details or the exceptions. Even a table needs an introduction and an appendix needs an outline at the start.

A TYPICAL FUNCTION

One way or another, you'll have to cover every function. Research on the way people actually use manuals suggests that for each function, readers want to find:

1. *A definition.* (What is it?)

2. *A little explanation.* (How does it work?)

3. *An example.* (Not too complicated, please.)

4. *A step-by-step procedure.* (If people could find it hard to apply or get to)

5. *Warnings about possible dangers and exceptions.*

The definition should come early, so readers can be sure they've reached the right section. The procedure, often known as a cookbook, because it resembles a recipe, should be separated from the other material, so people who just want to refresh their memory on some step can get to it quickly, without getting tangled up in an example.

If you've got the room, use white space to isolate each element in your explanation, like this:

————————————

CLS

Statement: CLS

Definition: Clear the screen.

Explanation: In direct mode, typing CLS and pressing RETURN will clear the screen immediately, and return the cursor to the home position.

You can also use CLS as a statement within a program. It has the same effect.

Exception: If you include CLS in a graphics program, the cursor will return to the center of the screen.

Example:
```
10 CLS
20 LET A = 50
30 PRINT A
40 END
```

This program clears the screen and prints 50 in the top left corner.

————————————

Once you figure out a way to describe each function, be consistent, so that readers who've figured out your method can apply it the next time to get information quickly, without having to figure out a new method.

Even when you have worked out a consistent way of exploring each function, you'll wonder how to present groups of functions. Look for an order that readers find familiar.

SHOW HOW TO DO SOME SAMPLE TASKS

Sometimes a simple list of functions leaves readers confused. How can they put all these little bits and pieces together to perform a task. Creating a pie chart and putting it in a report is a task. Calculating the interest on a loan and adding it to a memo that has to go out today is a task.

Be sure you include a few examples showing how a user could apply several of these functions to some of the elementary tasks they got the program for in the first place. If you don't think you've done this in the tutorial, you might add a few short chapters with examples of sample tasks.

Unlike a tutorial, these examples should be general. They resemble recipes in a cookbook, in that you ask readers to cut up some apples, but you don't specify whether to use Gravenstein, Red Delicious, or Granny Smith apples. In these recipes, you don't know what users will call their report, for instance. Here's an example of a recipe for a common task—incorporating data received from a remote data base into a letter:

Taking a Quote and Putting It in Your Report

1. Put your Communications Package Disk in the Main Drive and turn the power on.

2. Type R to Record what will be transmitted.

3. Type S for Services.

4. On the Services Menu, type Q for our Stock Quote Services.

5. When connected, type the code for the stock or stock category you are interested in. Immediately you see the current quotations. They also flow into your recording file, known as RECORD.FILE.

6. Press ESC to terminate the connection. Press it again to return to the Main Communications Menu.

7. Type Q to Quit the Communications Package.

8. Remove the Communications Package Disk.

9. Insert your Word Processor Disk, and press CONTROL-RESET.

10. Type C to Copy.

11. Type F to copy from a file, then type RECORD.FILE, and press RETURN.

12. The quotations now appear in your word-processing document. You are ready to write your recommendations in a report.

DON'T FORGET TO SUMMARIZE

However you organize your reference material, you'll find that good summaries help in two ways. First, when people read through the manual for the first time, they're likely to be dazed by all the new information; a summary helps them review and even memorize what they've learned. Second, after the initial reading, people like to flip open a summary page to find a quick command, a digest of a function, or a thumbnail sketch. At this point, they no longer require long explanations; in fact, they want to skip them.

The key to a helpful summary is its use. Ask yourself why someone would want a summary of this for a clue to what to put in it. Then keep explanations tight. (Make sure the index tells people where to look for longer ones.)

Leave plenty of white space. The eye should be able to zoom in on the crucial categories in a table, drawing, or checklist. Leave room between columns and between rows. You are not reprinting the phone book.

Think visually. A drawing may convey much more than text could. For instance, a sketch could show the steps involved in defining a record format. In writing, the first two steps pose a problem of repetition. A picture would let you avoid saying something like this:

> When you choose the Mail List Manager Standard Format you can then enter or modify the Mailing Record Format. After you've done that, you can enter the Mailing Record Storage Drive Number and Mailing List Name and return to the Main Menu.
>
> When you choose the New Record Format you can then enter or modify the Mailing Record Format. After you've done that, you can enter the Mailing Record Storage Drive Number and Mailing List Name and return to the Main Menu.
>
> When you choose a Previous Record Format you can then enter or modify the Mailing Record Format. After you've done that, you can enter the Mailing Record Storage Drive Number and Mailing List Name and return to the Main Menu.

All this information could be condensed in a picture, as in Figure 9.1 on page 116. Figure 9.2 is a picture that summarizes a whole program.

Figure 9.1

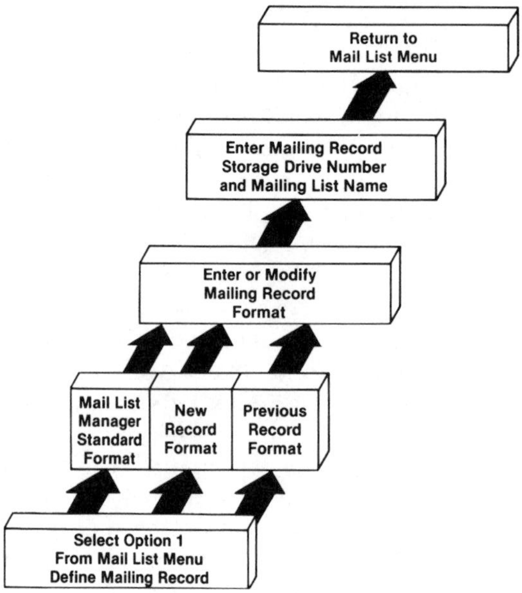

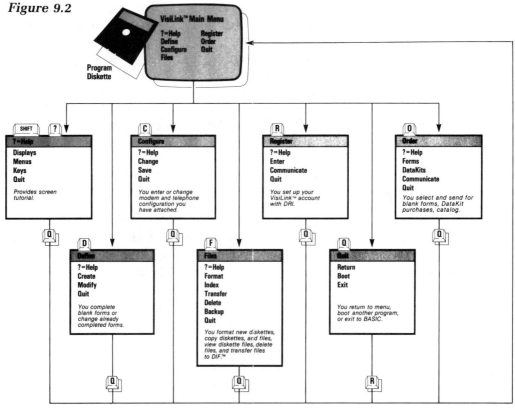

Figure 9.2

A summary often acts as a checklist. For instance, here's a summary from the end of a section:

> *SUMMING UP*
>
> Here is a summary of things you should know before you define your record format.
>
> - The names of your label fields, if any.
> - The names of your comment fields, if any.
> - Primary and secondary sort field names.
> - The number of lines in your label.
> - The maximum number of characters per line in your record.

Chapter summaries often provide you with the basic material for various appendixes and the quick reference card. Remember, then, to use the same format everywhere, so readers who figure out your conventions in one place can move easily to another place. If you set up two columns in the chapters, stick to that arrangement later.

WHEN IN DOUBT, MAKE A TABLE

Yes, more tables. But clear ones: pertinent, carefully thought out, and consistent in format from one to another. Creating a series of useful tables may take more work than writing a chapter.

Introduce your table, even if you only use a sentence or two, to give people a context. And don't be afraid to add an example or two afterward—or some notes. (Just don't clutter up the table itself.) Figure 9.3, for instance, shows how IBM presents a table of tempos available with the SOUND statement in BASIC.

Figure 9.3

The next table shows typical tempos in terms of clock ticks:

	Tempo	Beats/ Minute	Ticks/ Beat
very slow	Larghissimo		
	Largo	40-60	27.3-18.2
	Larghetto	60-66	18.2-16.55
	Grave		
	Lento		
	Adagio	66-76	16.55-14.37
slow	Adagietto		
	Andante	76-108	14.37-10.11
medium	Andantino		
	Moderato	108-120	10.11-9.1
fast	Allegretto		
	Allegro	120-168	9.1-6.5
	Vivace		
	Veloce		
	Presto	168-208	6.5-5.25
very fast	Prestissimo		

Here's another writing challenge: Which tables belong together? Figure out some of the reasons a person might turn to your tables. Then ask yourself: Which ones will they have to compare? Put those tables on facing pages. Here, for instance, are two tables, one on logical operators and one on operator precedence, from *Apple Business BASIC*. They follow a table on arithmetic operators. For a user, all three belong together.

LOGICAL EXPRESSIONS

Logical expressions are also called relational expressions and Boolean expressions. They are similar to arithmetic expressions, but use different operators. Where an example of an arithmetic expression might be $2+2$, $2=2$ is an example of a logical expression. The value of the first expression is 4, while the value of the second expression is "true," because 2 does equal 2. Likewise, the value of the logical expression $2=3$ is "false," because 2 does not equal 3. Arithmetic expressions evaluate to numeric values, whereas logical expressions evaluate to truth values.

Since BASIC doesn't understand the meaning of truth as such, but only the value of numbers, true and false have been assigned the numeric values 1 and 0, respectively. Thus $2=2$ has a truth value of 1, $2=3$ has a truth value of 0.

There are nine logical operators:

Symbol	Meaning	Example	Truth Value
=	Equal to	$3=3$	True
<	Less than	$3<1$	False
>	Greater than	$7>4$	True
<= or =<	Less than or equal to	$5<=4$	False
>= or =>	Greater than or equal *to*	$8>=5$	True
<> or ><	Not equal to	$4<>4$	False
AND	Conjunction	5 AND 0	True
OR	Inclusive disjunction	8 OR 3	True
NOT	Negation	NOT 4	False

OPERATOR PRECEDENCE

A precedence list for operators of logical and arithmetic expressions is given below, listed in order of execution from highest to lowest priority. Successive operators of the same priority are executed from left to right.

```
()
 + – NOT
* / MOD DIV
< > = >= =< <>
AND
OR
```

Such tables assume the reader already knows what priority means, and why precedence matters. These are, after all, only summaries.

Notice that the operators are in the left column in both tables. There's a reason for that. The writer established the left column as the column for operators in the first table, and even though there was plenty of room in the next table, the writer stuck to the convention so that someone could easily glance back and forth. In general, don't make tables about the same type of information look wildly different, even if there are some variations. Let someone be able to tell at a glance which columns deal with similar information.

If people have to read from left to right across ten columns of numbers, do something visually so they don't get lost on the way. Not too many lines. Perhaps some shading, every five lines. Perhaps a blank line after every tenth line.

Distinguish areas by color, when that's possible. For instance, when Allen Watson was showing memory maps in one manual, he faced this problem:

> There are several different kinds of soft switches that you use to bank-switch different parts of memory, and the way those switches work is not terribly consistent—very idiosyncratic. So I used color to show where the action was. I used the same map about five times, and then superimposed different colored areas on it, depending on which switch I was describing. For the part of memory that was inactive at the time, I used a ten percent gray background. For the part that was affected by the switch, I used a ten percent color.

And don't forget writing. Too many writers figure that a table is just an exercise in tabs and columns. Descriptive phrases can make a table meaningful—or a mess. The introductory paragraph, headings, labels, and footnotes can help the reader distinguish between all the possible explanations of these rows of letters, numbers, and codes. The writing's short, but vital.

PROVIDE SOME FORMS, TOO

Sometimes the system's so complicated a user has to do a lot of paperwork before turning on the power. For this, you might provide a copy of the actual display to be filled in or a form that reproduces the same fields in the same positions. Think through what a user really needs to know to fill out the form. For instance, if the program will accept no more than 30 numbers and letters in the "Street Field," then say so.

If the form is very complicated, you might number each field from top to bottom. Then attach your explanation to the same number on a facing page. That way readers can go back and forth. Some fields they know already; others they may want to look up.

Fill in the form, too. What you enter after the "QTY" label will indicate that this means "Quantity," not "Quality."

Structure your explanations so they will help someone who's trying to fill in the form. Offer useful information such as:

1. *Codes.* All the codes that the program will accept in this field.

2. *Format.* The correct format with an example. (For instance, "Enter the date month-day-year, like this: 9/23/84.")

3. *Cross-Checking Information.* Announce what the program will cross-check when the users fill in this field. For instance, what should they have entered first? And if they haven't entered that first, what error messages might they get?

4. *Definition.* If users might confuse this item with another, give a brief definition, so they know which one you're talking about.

5. *Warnings.* Warn people about possible surprises. If the program will automatically chop off the last five letters of any name longer than ten letters, let people know.

This process often turns up inconsistencies and odd sequences in the program. For instance, as you go through these steps, you may find that you have to enter the information in step 23 and add that to step 24 in order to put the result into the field numbered step 15. If you've been following the fields down the display, then the programmers got something out of order. Try to persuade them to rearrange the display.

If they won't, maybe you can change your numbering system. If that just adds to the confusion (Why is step 15 way down there on the display?), tell users in step 15 that they will have to wait to complete this one until after they have done steps 23 and 24. In other words, when the program's a nuisance, admit it.

REPORT THE REPORTS

If your program churns out many types of reports, show the reader at least one example of each. Use real reports, or at least some plausible dummy data. A blank report's too dull. Number the fields and use the facing page to explain what each field contains.

On long reports, you don't have to include all the data—just enough so people can see what each section looks like. Give examples of each major section.

As with input forms, you may find that the reports generated by the program have lots of ambiguous labels and a disorderly organization. Try to persuade the programmers to correct these. If you fail at this, just tell the users what's really meant, and how to overcome the confusion.

Where the system includes a variety of messages (say, any or all of the 15 error messages), explain all of them or refer users to the chapter that will.

When the program provides totals (such as number of transactions handled, number accepted, number rejected), explain how these calculations are made. And if someone can use these totals in troubleshooting, explain how.

Also, if the program generates some administrative data on every report (such as run number, run time, date of last update), do more than explain what these items mean; indicate which data the user can usually ignore. Not all data's equally valuable to your readers. You can help them zip through the report by telling them what they can skip.

Here's an example from a manual documenting an inventory program:

Your printer now kicks out a report on the product you want studied.

```
IMMEDIATE RESPONSE INVENTORY REPORT
DATE: 5/16/84    TM:00:15:01
PR: OJ      PR#:12-34A      SZ:1QT      VDR:TRCNA
PASZ:5 CPA: 12      CSS:14      TRIG:N
```

Here's how to interpret this report, field by field.

DATE   Date of the report.

TM   Time the report was printed. (This is military time. Midnight is 00:00:00. 1 p.m. is 13:00:00.)

PR   Product. OJ is the code for the product; in this case, orange juice.

PR#   Product Number.

SZ   Size. Here, one quart. (See Appendix B for list of all available sizes.)

Continued

VDR	Vendor. In this case, Tropicana. (See Appendix C for list of valid vendor codes.)
PASZ	Pallet Size. 5 means large. (Appendix D explains all pallet sizes.)
CPA	Current Pallets. The number of pallets of this product now on hand. 12. You've got a lot of orange juice out there.
CSS	Current Shelf Status. You have 14 quarts out on the shelf.
TRIG	Trigger. Is automatic reordering triggered by this inventory level? No. (That's the answer to your question.)

TRANSLATE THE MESSAGES

Suddenly the program stops. The screen goes blank and then a cryptic message appears saying, "Sys #341." The user wonders what's going on.

The programmer calls that an error message. But the term itself is insulting, implying that the user has fouled up again. Perhaps, when you start explaining these odd messages to the user, you can think of a more neutral phrase, such as *display message*.

List all error messages in alphabetical or numerical order. When people get error messages, they don't always know where these frightening interruptions come from. So don't sort them out by source or type—at least not here.

And don't leave out messages because you think they're so obvious. People wouldn't get that message if it was so obvious what they're supposed to do. When you leave out a message that they are looking at on the screen, people tend to think one or more of the following:

- I'm dumber than I thought.

- This manual's not about this program.

- What do I do now?

- I hate this manual.

Of course, some manuals just list the messages, and leave it to the user to figure out what to do about them. Here's how you could be a little more helpful:

- If the message reads "Abort, Retry, Ignore," explain why the user might have gotten such an awful set of options, and what each one will do.

- If the program spits out messages like "Error #33," make sure you've included every number, with a full explanation. (This seems obvious, but...) If one message got cancelled in the final version of the program, include the number and admit there's no message. That way people don't think you're hiding something.

- Say what can be done to correct the problem. Don't generalize. Take people through each step. If there's no solution, say so. But say what to do next. ("Return to your dealer and purchase a new computer.")

- Don't say things like "You entered too many digits here," without adding the relevant rule: "Please just put in six numbers here—no more."

- If users have to read some other section before correcting their "mistake," at least tell them where that section is.

- If even after the user has corrected the mistake, the display still says "System Error $1#2," remember to tell the user how to get moving again.

When one message covers half a dozen problems, indicate what they are, and how to solve them all. For instance, when a word-processing program announces that it has an input/output error, you could suggest that people fiddle with their disk drive doors, adjust the disk, and see if the printer has any paper in it. Or ask a series of questions that imply the solution, as in this example:

```
LABEL NOT FOUND—> XXXXX
```

A Go statement contained the label argument XXXXX, but no such label exists in the program.

- Have you spelled the label correctly in the Go statement? If not, type the Go statement again.

- Did you type letter I for number 1? letter O for number 0? If so, retype.

- Is the use of uppercase and lowercase identical in the label and the label argument? If not, retype the Go statement.

DEFINE NEW TERMS

When you mention a new term for the first time, you can help beginners by defining it—perhaps in the margin, or in a footnote, so that experts don't trip over it. But what about the person who dips into your book somewhere past that first reference, and wonders what the word means? A glossary defines the words that might be unfamiliar to some readers—bits of jargon, acronyms, commands, and phrases that apply only to this subject. The more inexperienced your readers, the larger your glossary should be.

The entries in your glossary might be thought of as a subset of your index. In the index, you have to include words you don't use in the text. For instance, if you call a certain feature Start, then you may need an entry that reads "Begin—See Start." But in the glossary you only have to define terms that you use in the text.

It's hard to determine all the words a novice might find puzzling. I recommend that you test your manual. Ask someone who doesn't know the program to read through the manual and underline any words or phrases that seem obscure. Have you defined all those?

If someone needs help badly enough to look up the word, they want more than a tight-lipped minimum. So add an example, as in this entry:

---

device name The name used in SOS pathnames to refer to a particular device, without regard to what files are associated with the device. Device names begin with a period and a letter, followed by up to 13 alphanumeric characters. For example, the device name of the disk drive built into the Apple III is .D1 regardless of what disk is in the drive.

And feel free to add a sentence or two of advice, as in this entry:

---

floppy disk A 5-1/4-inch flexible disk, or smaller. Remember not to touch the magnetic surface of a disk; handle it only by its plastic cover.

You might distinguish the term from others it's often confused with. Or spell out its parts, so readers understand that this is a general term, encompassing all those smaller ones. Or, if there's a perfectly good synonym, say so. Don't be shy about referring people to other entries, but give the gist of those entries here so the casual reader doesn't feel compelled to flip back and forth.

The first phrase—not exactly a sentence—just defines the term. (You can assume the verb *is* or *are* is between the term and your phrase.) That phrase may have to be a bit dry to be precise. But after that, you can loosen up and get a little more conversational.

By giving a little extra in most definitions, you can make your glossary a lot more helpful than a dictionary—and a lot more specific to your subject.

AND, FOR FURTHER READING

Sometimes you'll want to send your readers to other manuals, books, and magazines for further information. Good idea.

You'll usually want to add some details:

- Explain who the book or periodical is for and what they can expect to get out of it.

- Warn readers about hard texts and simple-mindedness. Some want primers, others prefer puzzles.

- Give the price, along with the publisher's name, address, and phone number—so your readers can actually get ahold of the book.

For instance:

Personal Computer Age

A fairly friendly magazine aimed at people who've already used their computer for a few months and like to tinker. Lots of reviews of new hardware and software. Columns about graphics, law, education, games, and music. A few program listings.

Price: $24.00 for 12 monthly issues

Publisher: Personal Computer Age
10057 Commerce Avenue
Tujunga, CA 91042

(213) 352-7811

MAKE A HANDY REFERENCE CARD

A handy reference card comes out of your manual and sits next to the keyboard. Basically, people want a quick way to recall the necessary keystrokes, syntax, and codes. Something they can add their own notes to. Just the essentials, then. No elaborate explanations. Only a few footnotes and references.

Arrange the material by function. Too many reference cards just list the commands in alphabetical order, and some don't even give them in order. This slows access.

Remember that readers turn to the card to recall how to do something. So arrange the commands according to that something.

Not like this:

A	ARRANGE
D	DELETE
F	FIND
I	INSERT
K	MAKE A DUPLICATE
L	CHANGE A LAYOUT
R	CHANGE RECORD SELECTION RULES
Z	ZOOM IN OR OUT TO REVIEW 15 RECORDS AT A TIME

Why not? Because if readers wonder how to make a duplicate, they might not think to look at "K" right off. Sure, they can find the command here. But not as fast as they could this way:

TO ACCOMPLISH THIS:	DO THIS:
Add Characters	Move cursor to spot, enter letters.
Insert Characters	Position cursor to right of where you want to begin inserting.
	Press CONTROL-I.
	Insert text.
	When through, press any of these keys: UP- or DOWN-ARROW, CONTROL-I, RETURN, CONTROL-TAB, or TAB.
Replace Characters	Position cursor on top of the character you want to replace.
	Type the new character over the old one.

What information do people have to look up, over and over, using the program? Put that on your card, too. For instance, in the Mail List Manager, users have to know a lot of maximums:

```
MAXIMUM NUMBER OF CHARACTERS PER:
        DISKETTE NAME              31
        FIELD NAME                 11
        LABEL CODES FIELD           6
        LINE OF FIELD NAMES
        (INCLUDING DELIMITERS)     33
        MAILING LIST NAME          31
        MAILING RECORDS FILE
        NAME (IN DRIVE 5)          10
        MAIL LIST MANAGER LOCAL
        FILE NAME                  10
        MAIL LIST MANAGER
        PATHNAME                   62
        PHONE FIELD                20
        RECORD                    105
```

Here are some ideas of what you might put on the card. (Don't put them all—remember, the card must be handy.)

- ASCII character set and codes

- Conventions

- Definitions of key terms

- Examples

- Illustrations showing the way different levels of the program interconnect

- Instruction sets

- Restrictions, limitations

- Rules, in a nutshell

- Sequences of commands necessary for housekeeping, such as system configuration

- Specifications

- Summaries of all commands

- Syntax of every statement, command, and expression

- Tables showing valid moves and permissible sequences

- Translations and conversions (from hexadecimal to binary to decimal, for instance)

Basically, if you can't put it some information in a table, exclude it. A few footnotes will help, but don't litter the baseline with them. Perhaps a hint of other manuals to turn to.

If you have more than a few folds in your card, you might consider devising some method to help people find their way around. I recommend a little table of contents at the start and page numbers on each fold, so people can tell if they are moving forward or just looking over the pages they looked at before. Also, if you use both sides of the card, you might color the back, so users know immediately which side they're looking at.

If you arrange things neatly, you may be able to fit all the commands of one type on a particular fold. Then users can just find that fold, bend everything else out of the way, and plunk the card on the keyboard.

A QUICK REVIEW

In general, useful reference material:

☐ Puts the common before the unusual.

☐ Is organized around what people want to do.

☐ Establishes a context before giving the details.

☐ Avoids repetition, and avoids "go to's."

☐ Gets people going fast, without a lot of reading.

☐ Provides some sections focussed on the tasks that users want to do as part of their job—not just the functions of the program.

For each function, be sure to provide:

☐ A definition.

☐ An explanation.

☐ An example.

☐ A step-by-step procedure, if needed.

☐ Exceptions and warnings.

Helpful summaries:

☐ Concentrate on the main point (what users most want to know about the subject).

☐ Give bare-bones instructions with minimal explanations.

☐ Do not start with exceptions.

☐ Stand off from the regular text, in plenty of white space.

☐ Rely on drawings when possible or helpful.

☐ Appear in the same format throughout.

Readable tables:

☐ Present similar material in the same way.

☐ Use visual cues to distinguish rows and columns in complex or crowded tables.

☐ Have clear introductions, headings, labels, and footnotes, explaining what the numbers mean.

Sample forms for input:

☐ Correspond clearly to the fields on the screen.

☐ Say what each field name means, distinguishing it from similar ones.

☐ Define what the program will or will not accept, showing all permissible codes in the correct format.

☐ Key all explanations to the fields on the form.

☐ Show how the program may respond.

☐ Warn readers about possible surprises and confusions.

☐ Show a filled-in version.

Sample reports:

☐ Show part of each section.

☐ Key explanations to each field.

☐ Include all possible codes, error messages, and administrative data.

Program messages:

☐ Aren't called error messages.

☐ Include all messages in one list. (How would a beginner know which type this one is?)

☐ Translate any jargon.

☐ Tell people what to do about it. If there's an applicable rule, say what it is.

☐ Tell readers where to go for further information.

Glossary entries:

☐ Appear for every term introduced in the manual.

☐ Do not have lockjaw.

☐ Do not simply repeat stock phrases.

☐ Give examples when they might help.

☐ Refer to other entries, but give the gist of those entries, so people don't have to keep flipping back and forth.

☐ Include some advice.

For Further Reading:

☐ List only the most helpful books and magazines.

☐ Explain who the book's for, and what the reader can expect to get out of it.

☐ Warn the reader about level of difficulty.

☐ Provide a way to get the material—a publisher, address, price, and perhaps even a phone number.

Quick-reference cards:

☐ Arrange material by functions.

☐ Include material someone would need, but might not easily recall.

☐ Stick to tables and lists.

☐ Have related material on the same fold.

10

Drawing Up Your Index

Making Up Entries
Multiple References
Detail
Subdivisions
The Same Idea
See Also
Synonyms
Singular or Plural
Including References
Punctuating
Sorting
Revising
A Quick Review

Drawing Up Your Index

An index offers readers hundreds of ways into your text. Like a table of contents, your index helps people skip to the material they really want to read.

Of course, you can't draw up a final index until you've got final pages. As you write an alpha draft, you should start figuring out what words and phrases you want to include, so you don't have to do all that thinking at the last minute.

It's a picky business, making up an index. And as you do it, you may ask yourself, "Why bother?" Here are some reasons. A good index can do all this:

- Help readers find a particular topic, even if it's not a chapter or section heading.

- Make up for the fact that a manual is not an electronic data base with fast and random access.

- Reveal what's connected with what.

- Show what has been left out.

- Give browsers a general idea of the subject matter of the manual.

- Indicate which terms you consider standard, or nonstandard.

With those purposes in mind, your index should be:

- Complete

- Accurate

- Easy to search through

- Helpful to both novices and experts

Of course, each of those ideals must be compromised somewhat:

- No index is truly complete—readers wouldn't want it to be. What people want is intelligent selection, a psychic anticipation of every word they might ever look up, and an equally intuitive exclusion of hundreds of words they don't care about.

- Similarly, accuracy is relative: In a manual for a word processing program do people really want to know every page that refers to the word *word*?

- The more references, the more frighteningly long the index looks. Is that easy or hard? For whom?

- And who can predict all the phrases a novice might look up? (Experts are more predictable.)

That's why I say indexing takes thought. It's not just a matter of mechanically piling up some file cards and alphabetizing them. For instance, how do you decide what to put in and what to leave out?

MAKING UP ENTRIES

You might review what readers will be looking for—starting with the main subject of the manual and its subdivisions. Look, for instance, at your glossary—that's a mini-index in itself. Don't forget your own headings. If a topic's important enough to have a heading, it belongs in the index.

In this way you can come up with a rough list of key words—words you're going to index. This list will help when you read through the final manuscript. You'll have the key words in mind as you go, and they'll tend to jump off the page at you.

As you read through, you might underline every key word whenever it comes up. Then write it on a slip of paper and add the page number of each reference. In this way, you can check later if you're not sure you caught each place it is mentioned. Along the way, you may think of several questions.

Multiple References
What if there are three or four ways to refer to the same topic? Make the one most readers would think of the main entry. Don't leave the other ways out, since they might help someone else find the subject. Just add "See Disk Drives," or whatever the main entry is. This way you indicate what you consider to be the standard term and you don't condemn readers for not knowing that.

Detail
How specific should an index be? Get down to the level of the text. If the text mentions external disk drives, and you feel that's significant in the

context, index *external disk drives*. (Otherwise you would just index *disk drives*.)

Subdivisions

When should a topic be subdivided? When you get more than about a dozen references, you might start thinking about subentries—or, possibly, separate listings. (Clumsiness, not length, is the real sign that you need to subdivide.)

For instance, after going through thirty-odd pages, you may have a dozen references to reports. Going back through the manual, you might find those could be divided up into separate entries for: *Report*, *Report Catalog*, *Report Format*, *Report Menu*, *Report Name*, and *Report Title*.

And when the *Report Format* entry gets too heavy, you might start subdividing that into *Labels*, *Options*, *Screen*, and *Tables*. If you've already created an entry for *Margins*, then you might add another subentry under *Report*:

Report

       Margins   *See* Margins, report format

The Same Idea

What if different people might look up the same phrase or idea in several ways? Invert the phrase. If your main entry is *Disk Drives*, don't forget to include *Drives, Disk*. This way readers find a reference on the first pass, rather than thinking that disk drives are not mentioned in the index or the manual.

Decide which is your main entry, and tell the readers to look there: *See* Disk Drives. Don't be afraid of prepositions if using them can make these entries clearer. A preposition can show the connection between a subentry and its main entry:

Margins   6, 8, 10
            Setting up   8
            Looking at   10

See Also

When should an index use *See* and *See also*? Not very often. But if you must . . .

Use *See* when you are referring readers to the main entry from the entry of a nonstandard term. Use *See also* to refer readers to related subjects that they might not have thought to look at.

Synonyms

How can you make sure you've included every synonym readers might use? You can't be sure. But once you're sure you've included every synonym you use, look at specialized dictionaries in the field and manuals from your competition. These will suggest a few more ways of describing the same thing. Include them, and say, "See . . . ." Focus on key ideas rather than little details.

Singular or Plural

Should most entries be singular or plural? Singular, as a rule. When in doubt, follow the common expression. For instance, under *Disk*, you might have subentries like this:

Disk

Backup	(because it's a single process)
Blocks	(because no one's likely to care about one particular block)
File types	(because there are several)
Volume	(because it's a collective noun)

This is often a matter of tone, not rule. You'll have to listen for the odd note. For instance, if the text tells the readers not to plug the computer into a series of extension cords, you might use *Plug*, but *Plug* sounds odd. So use *Plugs*.

INCLUDING REFERENCES

Don't include every page that mentions a topic. Only refer to significant text—sentences that might really help readers who look up this topic.

Use page numbers, not section numbers, not chapter numbers. Do not distinguish between the parts of a page, such as notes, figures, or marginal glosses.

If the text discusses assembly language for four pages, use an en dash:

Assembly language   25–28

But if the text is really about something else and just happens to mention assembly language on each of those pages, list them separately:

Assembly language   25, 26, 27, 28

Again, if you find too many page numbers piling up after a given entry, start subdividing into main and subentries. Or ask yourself: Are these all meaningful references? Perhaps you could drop a few.

PUNCTUATING

Capitalize the first letter of each entry. Don't put a comma between an entry and the page numbers. Leave two spaces before the page numbers. But if you've got some modification of that entry, use a comma in the middle, like this:

Menus, Quick File   23

Don't put a period at the end. When you have subentries, just indent them:

Disk
    Boot   6
    Program   7
    Sample files   5

If you have to include a numeric entry, spell it out, so you can fit it into the alphabetical list.

SORTING

Sort entries in alphabetical order. Don't stop alphabetizing a phrase when you come to the end of the first word. Ignore the blank, any accent marks, punctuation, and any capitals and look at the next letter. This is known as alphabetizing verbatim, and it produces lists like this:

Record   12-18, 24
Record, Adding   14
Record, Definition of a   18, 24
Record layout   3
Record selection rules   16
Records, Length of   12

File nothing before something.

In general, include all entries in one index. Occasionally, though, you'll find that this produces an ugly mix of hexadecimals, acronyms, memory map locations, plus words. If you're sure—and I mean sure—that readers will know beforehand that these are hex codes, then provide a separate index for them. This looks better, but you still risk having some readers think you haven't indexed any of these other items, because they're not in the main index. Be sure to include the little index as an entry in the larger one so readers can find it.

REVISING

When you've updated the text, revising an index can be harder than making up a brand-new one. Even professional indexers grow pale at the thought. But if you don't revise the index, you can leave readers with something that looks like an index but isn't.

If you haven't changed much of your text, and you know exactly which pages got changed, you might just scan through your original index looking for those page numbers. Make up slips of paper with the page numbers for each reference. Then sort the slips by page number. That way you can go through, page by page, seeing how much of your original index still matches the text. It'll take another pass to add any new terms that have cropped up.

If you've made extensive revisions in the text, forcing complete re-pagination, then you may find it's easier to begin your index anew. Don't just look for the key words you used before: keep an eye out for words and phrases you never mentioned in the first draft.

One other thought: If you have a computer alphabetize your index, make sure some human checks it. I've found that many sort programs can't handle subentries and odd punctuation.

A QUICK REVIEW

A quick review of what the average reader wants your index to do:

☐ Include every topic treated in a major or minor heading.

☐ Include every special term, abbreviation, code, and acronym in the manual.

☐ Include synonyms for words readers might think of before remembering your term for the subject.

☐ Use indentations to show subordinate topics.

☐ Give the information here, rather than telling people to "*See also* . . . ."

☐ Include only the key page numbers for the useful pages.

☐ Appear in alphabetical order.

Refining Your Style

Noun Clump
Before the Before
Runt
Whazzat
Passive Nobody
Its Its
The Dead Hand
Long Words
Cliches
Trailing Off
Parallels That Aren't
Half a Contrast
Mechanicalness
Miss Krinkow's Rules
Dumb Rule #1: Never Start a Sentence with *Because*
Dumb Rule #2: Never Say *I*
Dumb Rule #3: Watch Out for *May and Might*
Dumb Rule #4: Never Use *About*
Dumb Rule #5: Don't Use *Then* So Often
False Good Cheer
Bloodless Writing
A Quick Review

Refining Your Style

Some writers work hard to present themselves in this way: complex, occasionally brilliant, well armored, overplumed, and ready to fight anyone who laughs. But you probably want the style of your manuals to be friendly. That takes even more work.

After you've done a draft, prowl through the manuscript looking for stylistic tangles—constructions that could trap, mesmerize, confuse, or even terrify your readers. Some of these snafus look so odd that anyone can see the danger; others are so familiar that you pass right by them, ignoring what they might do to readers who follow you.

You have to train yourself to recognize these ornate messes. The more you get used to spotting them and transforming them into simple prose, the easier it becomes to sidestep them when you are writing new material. What you learn from revising gradually seeps into your fingers, so that you no longer create Double No-No's and One Bite Intro's.

Here's an anthology of stylistic pitfalls with suggestions on how you might turn them into plain talk.

NOUN CLUMP

A string of nouns. A clumsy way of avoiding two or three phrases or clauses. Confusing because readers lose track of the point and wonder when it will ever end. Here are some examples from real manuals:

- *The Office Design Management Worksheets User's Manual*

- *The Microcomputer System Development Monitor Control Program*

- *The Run Time System options menu prompts . . .*

Is the first one a manual for people who manage office designers? In the second one, who's controlling the monitor? Where do the hyphens go in the last one?

If you find you've spawned a noun clump, take a deep breath and give it some air. For instance, you might revise the last one this way:

———————

The messages that prompt you to choose one of the options on the Run Time System . . .

———————

BEFORE THE BEFORE

Creates a dizzying feeling that time has dissolved. Backs into the present, crying "Before that, but before that, but before that." Results from not organizing the material in time sequence. For instance, notice how the time sequence is reversed here:

———————

Before you go on to the detailed explanation concerning the function you are about to study, you should first load the SET UP file. If you have not already created that, see APPENDIX A for the procedure. Remember that as a preview to the SET UP file, you must insert the SYSTEM disk and reboot. Before you do that, though, be sure to save your material on the disk.

———————

Best solution: Sort out what you want people to do first, second, and third. Keep moving forward in time.

RUNT

Shockingly short—a one-bite intro. Tells readers as little as it can. So compressed it's cryptic. For example, here's the entire preface to a 200-page manual:

> **PREFACE**
>
> This manual is a general reference for the standard data transmission techniques used with our modem. It does not discuss user interfaces, but it does mention the effect of user options.

What techniques? Which modem? Is this the right manual? And where can a person find out about user interfaces? This tells more about what the book does not do than about what it does. It's not much of a preface.

To revise, take more space. Prefaces and overviews set the tone for the whole manual. Make it easy for the reader to figure out what's to come. This is no place to skimp. You might devote at least one sentence to each chapter, so the reader can get a sense of the overall design of the manual. That also makes it easier to skip ahead.

WHAZZAT

An unfamiliar term. Leaps out at the reader. Often appears in introductory material. Never mentioned before, it makes readers question their memory or their competence. Here are some examples from the first few pages of manuals:

> • Then boot your system again.
>
> • Re-initialize.
>
> • Your word processing package will allow you to perform functions such as block moves, zero slashing, right justification, fractional spacing, strikeover, and mask-making by using one of the 13 programmable function keys.

What's *boot*? Did readers do that before? When? And what about *re-initializing*? Do readers realize they have already initialized? And what are all those functions? Should readers already know them? If they don't know what zero slashing is, are they such klutzes that they should stop right now before damaging such a sophisticated system? Or did the writer describe all these before, and they just forgot? Maybe they'd better turn back a few pages.

To wipe out Whazzats, go through the manuscript just looking for terms you may not have defined earlier. Don't assume readers know them. Find the first mention and add an explanation. And if you mentioned something 20 pages ago, but not since then, remind readers that they've already heard the term before and tell them, gently, what it means. Even people who know what a block move is will appreciate it if you say what you mean by the phrase.

PASSIVE NOBODY

Implies that events take place without anyone doing anything. Moves files, desks, and ideas without any assistance from a human being. Makes readers wonder whether they should be doing something—or just sitting there waiting for the system to perform. It turns actions into states of being. It's somewhat mystical, but tends to put readers to sleep. Here are some examples:

- The filenames *can be removed* when the RFIL command *has been entered* and *accepted*.

- Potential sources of trouble *may be discovered* during the system's startup phase.

- An option *is preselected* for your approval; if approval *is granted*, that option *is initiated*.

By whom? Does the system do this? Do I do this? Who's responsible around here?

All forms of the verb *to be* turn other verbs passive: *is, are, was, were, has been, have been, had been, will be, won't be, shouldn't be,* and *haven't ever been*.

To get more active, say who does what. Assign responsibility to the system or to the program or, if necessary, to the reader. If you have to tell readers to do something, don't pussyfoot around—tell them. (Are you slipping into the passive because you don't dare to order readers around?)

Avoid thinking of the system in a state of rest: This is . . . , That is . . . . Or even a series of states: This will be . . . , That was . . . . Concentrate on actions. Who changes what how and when?

ITS ITS

A crowd of neuters—nonpersons who investigate, judge, and find guilty without ever appearing. Frightening because they are ghostly; puzzling because they might refer to the reader, to the writer, or to some system. Here are some examples:

- It has been determined . . . .

- It will be clear that . . . .

- It is often thought that . . . .

Who determined that? Who thinks it's clear? Who ever thought that?

When the air grows thick with these *its*, get out your wand and turn them into people. Don't talk as if the program thinks.

THE DEAD HAND

Makes a perfectly human action into an idea or object. Mummifies whatever you do: turns *I decided* into *It was decisionized*. Some examples:

- The insertion of new channels by means of digitization and modulation or a combination of the two can mean an increase in cost-effectiveness and a utilization of previously idle time frames.

- Transmission via satellite requires frequent resynchronization, due to the satellite's attraction to the sun and the moon.

By turning these clunky nouns back into verbs, you can reveal who does what and make your point clearer. For instance, you might rewrite the two examples this way:

- You can digitize or modulate signals so as to insert new channels. This saves money, because we can use more of the carrier more of the time.

- The sun and the moon draw the satellite out of its circular orbit, so you have to keep changing your aim when you transmit.

You'll note that it takes real rewriting to resuscitate these verbs. They were well buried in their noun forms. To revive them, you actually have to rethink what you meant.

LONG WORDS

Sometimes you can't avoid a long word—it may be the only precise way to describe something. But a long word can act as a big club, threatening the reader. Think how you'd feel if you were warned:

Finalization of these requirements is a condition of commencement of utilization of the system.

Here's a translation:

You have to do this before you can start using the system.

Often you can find a short word that will do just as well as the long one. Even a series of short words will be easier to understand. We all used to get extra points in English class for calling lying *tergiversation*, but this is not English class.

CLICHES

Old and tired and flat, a cliche sounds like it means something, but just what isn't clear—it has been used to mean so many things that readers may nod, recognizing the cliche, without being sure what you intend by it. And if you go on using cliches, the nodding may continue, until the readers are asleep.

Here are some particularly boring examples:

- This is a user-friendly program.

- Back to square one.

- What's the bottom line?

- When you're interfacing with a client . . . .

- This is a turnkey system.

How do cliches get into your prose? You may be puzzling about what to say and a prefab phrase rises in your mind. With relief, you figure that phrase more or less covers what you want to say. And you know your readers will recognize it, so that establishes some kind of bond, right? Sort of. But is the phrase accurate or merely convenient?

Beware of that feeling of relief when you seize on a cliche and fit it into your paragraph. That's a sign that you've taken the shortcut to less meaning.

TRAILING OFF

A sentence that starts off crammed with ideas but ends up in a ditch. Usually an accident. Caused by impatience, when the writer hurries the main point of a sentence into the first few words, then wonders how to end it all. Here are some examples:

- Report generation to specified requirements can also be accessed.

- A function known as CATALOG, that displays the volume number and list of all files on a given diskette, also exists.

- The requirement for at least one completed form cannot be gotten around.

Here's how you could rewrite these sentences:

- You can also specify the way you want reports generated.
- To display the volume number and a list of all the files on a given diskette, use the function known as CATALOG.
- You must have at least one completed form.

A cure for sentences that trail off: Build up to a climax. Put the most significant or the most interesting information, the very reason for the sentence, at the end.

PARALLELS THAT AREN'T

Jolt readers in the middle of a list. The items may be similar, but the way you present them isn't. For instance:

You'll need the following equipment:

- A RS 232C interface.
- An Apple III computer.
- You have to have a printer, too.
- Don't reconfigure your system yet, though.

The list began as a series of noun phrases, each a piece of equipment. Then the writer thought of a printer, but forgot the list. So instead of a noun phrase, readers find a new sentence. And once that happened, all parallelism dissolved. The last item doesn't even mention equipment—it's really the beginning of a new paragraph.

In general, shifting the way you present items in a list (switching from a series of nouns to a verb, for instance), startles readers, makes them go back to reread, and raises questions about how to understand you. So whenever you have a list, keep all the parts of it in the same grammatical form.

HALF A CONTRAST

Implies a contrast, but deprives readers of the other half. Heavily emphasized *only* and *not* suggest some other possibilities—never spelled out. Here are some examples:

- Only RAM may be used for this operation.

- This chapter will not cover questions of bad disks.

- On the one hand, such errors may lead to system failure, incorrect data, or in some cases, disk erasure. Next we will discuss pathnames. Pathnames are . . . .

What could the reader use besides RAM, anyway? What will the chapter discuss if it doesn't cover bad disks—and where can curious readers find out about those? And why bring it up anyway? Did the writer think of including them, then rule them out? On the one hand, this; on the other hand, what?

When you're thinking of a contrast, envision a seesaw. You can get one side up in the air—but what about the kid on the other side?

Or maybe you don't really have a contrast in mind. If that's the case, wipe out the signals that tell a reader a contrast is coming. For instance, you might rewrite the examples this way:

- For this operation, you must use RAM.

- This chapter discusses ways to make sure your disks work the way they're supposed to. If you think you have a bad disk, turn to Appendix A for help.

- On the one hand, such errors may lead to system failure, incorrect data, or disk erasure. On the other hand, these errors may not cause you any problems at all, if you have used the right pathname.

  Pathnames are . . . .

MECHANICALNESS

Prose that clanks. Phrases and whole paragraphs that you've read five times before in the same manual. A rigid and repetitive way to describe similar phenomena. For instance, one manual introduces two different functions this way:

- FITR is a command. This command dictates parameters for the R files. The parameters involved are described below. This command should be invoked only by a systems analyst, or supervisor.

- RAXR is a command. This command dictates parameters for the XR files. The parameters involved are described below. This command should be invoked only by a systems analyst, or supervisor.

Now that may be accurate. But it's lazy, and readers begin to feel that a machine is doing the writing. To avoid mechanical prose, combine whatever can be combined so you only say it once. For instance, here the writer could have started off saying that the following commands should only be invoked by a systems analyst or supervisor, then provided a table:

Command	Dictates Parameters For:
FITR	R FILES
RAXR	XR FILES

Don't slip into elegant variations to escape mechanicalness. You may make readers think the two commands are very different when they're not.

MISS KRINKOW'S RULES

Back in high school, Miss Krinkow gave us all a bunch of rules that didn't make a lot of sense. They did to her. They were designed to keep us from making horrendous blunders. We learned to follow the letter of the rule, not the spirit. So we still misapply them.

And in following Miss Krinkow's rules, we often make our prose ten times more complicated than it needs to be. Here are some of her dumb rules, with my reasons for breaking them.

Dumb Rule #1: Never Start a Sentence with *Because*.

She said this because so many of us wrote things like, "I like jam. Because it is sweet." But that's no reason to change *because* to *due to*, or *as*, or *since*, when those just add ambiguity. For instance, substitute *because* as you read these examples:

- Due to the fact that the file is now empty, you can delete its name from your directory without harm.

- As the disk is formatted, you may proceed to enter the following text.

- Since you have inserted the Utilities disk, in the built-in drive, you can hear a whirring noise.

Because makes a good beginning.

Dumb Rule #2: Never Say *I*.

She thought you should only tell objective truth. She did not believe in subjective truth—or at least, that wasn't what you put on paper. This is the result:

- One can easily see . . . .
- The writer's own experience can testify . . . .
- It is obvious that . . . .

When you're writing a manual, you usually don't need to talk about yourself. But if you do, admit it's you.

Dumb Rule #3: Watch Out for *May* and *Might*.

Miss Krinkow scared us all with her red pencil marks circling *may* and *might*. So we just gave up using them, even when they might apply. We knew it took more words, but at least she wouldn't yell at us. Try these sentences with *may* and *might*, and listen to the difference:

- There is a possibility that you have only one disk drive.
- How could this have happened? There is the possibility that when you opened the first box you damaged the disk.

On the other hand, don't use *may* to give permission to readers, as in "You may enter alphanumeric characters here." *Can* is less pompous.

Dumb Rule #4: Never Use *About*.

Miss Krinkow objected to all inaccurate guesses. She hated it when we wrote that the baseball game lasted "about two hours." So we learned to leave that dangerous word out, substituting much longer but safer phrases like these:

- In the approximate vicinity of
- Relating to the subject of

- In reference to

- With respect to

You may now discard all those. Write about things, and if you have to indicate that your statement is fuzzy, say something like "It takes about two hours." We know what you mean. If you still feel uncomfortable about being imprecise, say why you cannot be more precise.

Dumb Rule # 5: Don't Use *Then* So Often.
Miss Krinkow hated paragraphs that went like this:

We ate lunch. Then we played ball. Then we had a snack.
Then we went out in the woods. Then we saw a snapping turtle.

We didn't know why she disliked *then* so much, but we learned to use lots of longer phrases instead. (We also got rid of *now*, for the same reason.) For *then* we wrote phrases like these:

- At that point in time

- During that previously mentioned period

- Within that time frame

Wonderful, eh?
 So use *now* and *then*. They're short, but they do the job. And if you're using them too often in a paragraph, don't blame them—it's just you getting repetitious.

FALSE GOOD CHEER

Pasty smiles. Routine congratulations. Trained welcomes. Rehearsed enthusiasm. "Isn't calculating fuel burn patterns for jets over Germany fun?"
 That's engineered, not friendly. Watch out for excessive jolliness—where you're really forcing yourself to be cheerful.
 This is tricky. You want to sound encouraging, open, human. But you shouldn't have to try too hard.

BLOODLESS WRITING

Some writers give you the impression they have no senses. Touch is unknown to them, and taste and smell are taboo. Evidently, they never hear or see anything that's not already in the program or the equipment.

As a result, readers get none of those helpful asides that tell them that the disk drive will make noises, but those whirrings are OK. Readers may begin to think that the writer has no feelings. And, as people with six senses operating, they intuit that behind the manual there is no one alive.

So describe. Admit what you go through. Confess to hunches and physical reactions. Stop every once in a while to say what you notice about the display, the monitor, the keyboard, the drives. That will help readers imagine what you're doing—and who you are.

A QUICK REVIEW

A friendly style:

☐ Breaks up all those noun clumps.

☐ Organizes material in time sequence.

☐ Allows your introductions to grow so they aren't runts.

☐ Defines unfamiliar terms.

☐ Replaces passive sentences with a name and an action.

☐ Replaces anonymous *it* with a person—and an active verb.

☐ Omits long words when you don't need them.

☐ Cuts cliches.

☐ Revises sentences so they don't trail off.

☐ Keeps each item in a series parallel.

☐ Completes any contrast with its second half.

☐ Doesn't get too mechanical, rigid, and repetitive.

☐ Doesn't fake good cheer.

☐ Shows all your senses are alive—in the writing.

Indulging in Humor

Understand the Reversal
Allow Yourself Some Admissions
Make Your Wordplay Accessible
Keep It Informal
Show Your Sympathy
A Quick Review

Indulging in Humor

Humor brightens up the landscape. A good joke lightens readers' labor, helping them to understand the material from a new angle. It may bring to the surface feelings that have been buried, such as fear, anger, or awe, depriving these emotions of their ability to paralyze comprehension. In general, good humor helps you show readers that you sympathize with them in their efforts to learn.

That's no reason to force yourself to be funny. You'll just end up straining yourself. But if you feel like it, indulge. Here are some suggestions for the indulgers.

UNDERSTAND THE REVERSAL

Most humor depends on a quick change. For instance, some time in the thirties, Dorothy Parker, who had just come from the *New Yorker's* offices, was going to a party. At the door she collided with a stunning show girl, who drew back to let her by, saying, "Age before beauty." Miss Parker marched quickly through the door, smiling, "No, dear—pearls before swine."

Miss Parker had recognized one cliche, thought of another that could apply, and tossed it over her shoulder—all in a few steps through the door. Part of the joy in her throwaway line lies in the quickness with which she reversed a snub.

Most good jokes end by reversing our point of view—suddenly. In an instant we see losers become winners; falsehood revealed; wit win. We may begin to smile as we recognize that this new perspective makes more sense than the ideas we had before. If we had time to talk, we might say it sounds more like the truth. But the very suddenness of the reversal provokes the laugh.

Thus, if you're thinking of a joke, keep the switcheroo in mind—and save it for the very end. Here's an example:

Very, very small numbers (between about .0000000000000000000000
0000000000000003 and —.00000000000000000000000000000000003)
will be converted to zero by the computer. (We hope that was the right
number of zeros.)

Not much of a joke. But all those zeros set up a feeling of extreme per-
snickety precision, a kind of computer mystique that could frighten the
innocent, maybe even make them question whether their math is up to all
this fraction-splitting. You may need to include the exact figure, but be
aware that it could turn some readers off. The parenthetical comment
deflates any awe readers might feel, allowing them to go on.

Here's another example:

Those who like formal terminology will recognize that this is merely a
system of rectangular Cartesian coordinates. Those who don't like fancy
talk can just think in terms of columns of bricks.

Again, the writer feels required to point out the Cartesian reference, but
warns readers first that the text is about to get formal. Having done the
formal bit, the writer returns readers to "normal" with an excuse—that
was just fancy talk. True. But by describing all these rectangles as a bunch
of bricks, the writer defuses any feeling readers may have that they are
missing something important, and at the same time offers a clear physical
image that explains the idea.

ALLOW YOURSELF
SOME ADMISSIONS

At times, you have to explain some junky piece of jargon, a pointless
feature, or an annoying drawback. Traditionally, technical writers were
supposed to pretend that all of these were wonderful, or at least the best
users could expect. But that approach just gives readers indigestion.

When you find yourself having a hard time describing something
honestly, or when you look at what you've written and think that monkeys
have been at the keyboard again, add some asides in which you admit that
you too find these terms a bit odd:

Creating an Empty Dictionary

This sounds like a crazy idea, but the Utilities program lets you create an
empty dictionary in order to create a brand-new dictionary from scratch.

Or:

Keys You Must Use Precisely

The computer is not smart enough to accept substitutes, unless the programmer specifically instructs the computer to do so.

Each of these passages allows readers to see that the writer, too, shares
some feelings of contempt for the computer or the program. By admitting
that you share these feelings, you align yourself with your readers.

MAKE YOUR WORDPLAY ACCESSIBLE

Don't be professorial. Avoid puns that depend on readers knowing something academic, even if it's in a field outside of computers. Wordplay pulls
a fairly cheap reversal of perspective: what sounds like one thing turns out
to mean something else.

Jon Thompson, manager of the Apple II editorial group, asks this question of writers: "What do you call the floor of a French kitchen after you
drop a bomb on it?" Give up? The answer: "Linoleum blown apart."
Groans all around. Thompson sighs, and continues:

> Ah me. Anyway, here's the thing. If you had somehow never heard of
> Napoleon Bonaparte, or if maybe you'd just never heard his last name,
> you wouldn't get the joke. At a party, that's no big deal, because you
> can usually fake it. But in reading a manual, you not only miss the joke,
> you might wonder if you've missed something important, too. And
> you'll feel left out.

In these circumstances, readers may also lose their concentration. They
have to pause and shift gears. They may lose the connections between
those fragile bits of information they've been trying to store away.

Of course, for those who get the joke, humor may give a deeper appre-
ciation of the subject. So if 99% of the audience will get the joke, it's
probably OK to sacrifice the understanding of the remaining 1%. But how
do you calculate percentages like that? Often, you can't.

If your work gets translated and sent abroad, you can figure that most of
your puns, turns of phrase, and double entendres will get lost. Or worse,
they might turn into a puzzling mess.

So make sure that any wordplay works against the professorial. Often,
it's the computer term that's so obscure it freezes out two-thirds of the
audience. A touch of humor can at once explain it, and invite people back
in. For instance, here are some explanations:

Computerniks call this list of numbered descriptions a menu. It works like a menu at a roadside cafe. If you want scrambled eggs with hash brown potatoes, toast, jelly and coffee, you can just say, "I'll have a number 5."

Virtual means existing only conceptually, as a collection of parameters inside the computer. A *virtual pen*, for example, need never run out of ink the way an actual pen does.

CONTROL-G is called BELL for historical reasons: The present keyboard design is based on that of the teletype. On that venerable machine, CONTROL-G rings a real bell.

I'm not talking about Johnny Carson openers. Just a hint of disrespect for the poor old teletype and the venerable menu.

KEEP IT INFORMAL

In general, humor seems to work best where your style's already informal— in introductions, examples, and tutorials. The tone there prepares people for asides, jokes, even a few puns. No one's working when they look in these sections. They're learning—edging into the subject— and humor gives them a break.

In a reference section, however, a joke is an annoying interruption when users are just looking for a fact. They are not looking for sympathy, or even an admission that something's difficult. They just want to know what's what.

SHOW YOUR SYMPATHY

Attitude's more important than punch lines. A real sympathy for readers, a recognition of what you've had in common with their suffering. As James Thurber, a master of deadpan, says, "That humor is the best that lies closest to the familiar—which, for me, is usually humiliating, distressing, even tragic."

So admit to yourself, before writing, what makes you feel confused, upset, embarassed, or unhappy. As you write, give readers some details in little reminiscences that help them recognize that you have felt as confused as they do. That way, even though they may just have been feeling very lonely, faced with this know-it-all expert, now they realize that the expert's just a person, like them, who has gone through the same irritation, anxiety, frustration they're going through. As E. B. White says, "Humorists make trouble pay."

Here's how Allen Watson, an experienced writer, showed that he knows people have some anxiety when they unpack their computer: "This manual is designed to answer the question: 'What's inside the box?'"

And here's how one tutorial admitted what happens if someone goes astray: "All you get for your pains is an error message."

Your attitude toward readers and the subject shows up throughout the manual. That's why jokes aren't as important as sympathy and good humor.

A QUICK REVIEW

When you feel like including a little humor in your manual, make sure that the humor:

☐ Makes clear the reversal of perspective.

☐ Allows some admissions on your part.

☐ Keeps all wordplay accessible.

☐ Appears only in the more informal and optional sections.

☐ Shows your sympathy for the readers.

13

Designing Your Images

Creating a Look
Laying Out the Elements
Dreaming Up Images
What Might Make an Image?
Where Is It?
What Is It?
How Does It Work?
Why?
What's on That Level?
And Below That?
But What's the Big Picture?
What Are the Steps Involved?
And If You Don't Feel Comfortable Sketching
Think of What the Artists Need
A Quick Review

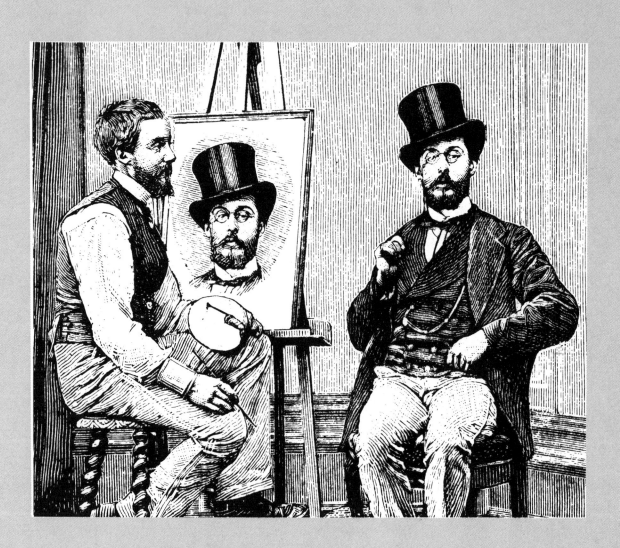

Designing Your Images

Most manuals look unpleasant. Crowded and complicated, their layout makes them hard to read. Text, text, text, that's all you see—there are very few pictures, and those few are dark smudges, murky and irrelevant.

In this chapter, I'll give you a few tips on creating a strong layout and including interesting pictures. As you design the images for your manual, you might reflect on the idea that some people think visually, others physically. As a writer, you probably learn most from words. But not everyone does. A clean, meaningful design can help everyone learn your subject matter faster; one brilliant image can suggest relationships that words would take pages to convey.

CREATING A LOOK

If you have a chance to create or revise a layout, rejoice. You've got a rare opportunity. Start by thinking about the general look you want. Your manuals reflect your management's attitude—and budget:

- If the budget is stingy, management may want to save paper and printing charges by jamming text to the margins and photocopying the whole manual. You'll get a grubby look.

- If management wants to look well heeled, they may authorize you to print your manual and use a lot of white space. Your manual will look expensive, perhaps even generous.

You must make some key decisions at this stage:

- How are you going to reproduce the manual? Will you be printing it on a dot-matrix printer, then photocopying it? Copying the output of a letter-quality printer? Offset printing? Laser printing a series of originals each time you need one? Typesetting, then printing? This one decision affects almost every other decision that follows. (If you're photocopying, for instance, you're probably stuck with $8\frac{1}{2}$-by-11-inch pages.)

- What kind of paper are you going to use? Glossy? Pulp? Near cardboard? Standard photocopying paper?

- What size and shape will your pages be? Large squares with plenty of room for pictures? Or tall and narrow with room for only one column of text?

- What typeface will you use? Sleek modern typefaces without any wiggles or twists at the end of the letters? Older typefaces, reminding readers of the *New York Times*, books of the thirties, the nineteenth century, or the Renaissance?

- In general, how much white space will you allow? A lot or a little? Will you have wide margins or tiny bands of white around the edges? Will you allow much room between paragraphs?

- How colorful will your pages be? Will you print in two colors—black and one other? In four colors—enough for full-color photographs? Or will you stick to black and white?

- What kind of cover, binder, or box will enclose the manual? The package will make a strong first impression on users before they read a word.

LAYING OUT THE ELEMENTS

Once you've made some decisions about the general look of your manual, you need to design the elements. For instance, a footnote is an element. If you're going to have such an element, what position, typesize, and style of type will you assign it? (Essentially, you're laying out every possible element in terms a typesetter will understand.)

Here's a list of common elements you may have to design:

1. *Asides.* Do you want a special format for information that is not essential?

2. *Figures.* Illustrations, diagrams, maps.

3. *Headings.* Of several levels: large, medium, small, perhaps even tiny.

4. *Icons.* Small drawings indicating disk drives, for instance, or elements in the computer that you refer to regularly.

5. *Key terms.* Will you use boldface type for these?

6. *Lists.* How will you handle bulleted lists, numbered lists?

7. *Marginal glosses.* Definitions of key terms in the margin.

8. *Prefatory material.* Will you have a special format for disclaimers and copyright and trademark information?

9. *Running heads.* Chapter titles and section titles.

10. *Running text.* The main body of your manual.

11. *Sample screens.* Will you photograph these? Set them in a different typeface? Put gray behind them?

12. *Special keys.* For instance, will you use a special symbol for the RETURN key? For ARROW keys?

13. *Subscripts and superscripts.* Text above and below the line. Do you have a lot of mathematical formulas, for instance? How will you set them off from the regular text?

14. *Summaries and quick-reference material.* Do you want these set in smaller type?

15. *Tables of contents.* How will you show the difference between various levels of headings? Will there be chapter tables of contents?

16. *Tables.* How many different kinds will you use?

17. *Text that the readers must type.* Perhaps you want to show this in a special typeface that makes each letter look like the key they're going to type.

18. *Titles.* Manual title, chapter titles.

19. *Tutorial text.* Will you arrange this in two columns? Will you number the steps?

20. *Warnings.* Are you going to set them in red type to alert people?

Complicated, huh? It can take you more than a year to resolve these design questions, and even when you get a basic design you like, you'll probably go on tinkering with it from one manual to the next.

A few cautions. Don't create too many distinctive elements. You can jazz up a page to the point where the reader gets dazzled, but can't read. For instance, you may at first be attracted to the idea of setting different elements in different typefaces and sizes. But that makes an incredibly jumpy page. Use restraint, then.

Remember, too, that the main point of the manual lies in the running text. Every other element must help readers get through this material—not draw attention away from it.

So discard any element that does not actively support the meaning. For instance, you may think about some decorative symbols on certain pages. If these are just for decoration, eliminate them. A reader has only so much attention; don't waste it.

DREAMING UP IMAGES

You may not get very many chances to design the look and layout of a manual. But every time you begin writing a new book, you can—and should—start imagining the illustrations.

Nancy Hecht, who helps writers create illustrations for their manuals, says that writers need to remember that verbal and visual languages work differently. She offers this comparison:

Verbal Language	Visual Language
Presents things in temporal order.	Presents things in space.
Moves forward one item at a time.	Presents different things simultaneously—all at once.
Uses names to point to things.	Represents the thing itself.
Constructs meaning out of discreet units and categories.	Constructs meaning out of continuous lines and textures.

Images can do more than show where a certain key is or how to put a disk in a disk drive. "An image represents what the words talk about," says Hecht. "An image shows the whole, so that words can point out its attributes. The image acts as the thing that your words point or refer to."

Images can also function as advance organizers, telling readers where the discussion is headed, offering a context for ideas that will be presented. Hecht says:

> The readers can adopt a well-designed illustration as a mental image. They can hang plenty of verbal explanation on that basic framework. If an image is correct, unambiguous, and efficient, and if it shows appropriate relationships among parts, then it will support increasingly complex explanation as the readers learn more and more about the core concept.

Traditionally, writers write, revise, revise—and only at the last minute think of pictures. Unfortunately, that tends to make all pictures decorative or pasted on.

To grow pictures along with your text, go through your table of contents and mark the sections that seem most likely to benefit from illustrations. This way, you can plan your writing with pictures in mind. You can assign some instruction to text, some to illustrations.

Look for opportunities for pictures; don't just wait until you can't avoid one.

WHAT MIGHT MAKE AN IMAGE?

Keep in mind the questions that occur to you as you delve into the program. The answers to these questions may suggest images for your manual.

Where Is It?
If the readers aren't familiar with the keyboard, you can use an illustration to help them locate obscure keys. For instance, Figure 13.1 shows how John Zussman tells Wordvision users to find the Print key.

Figure 13.1

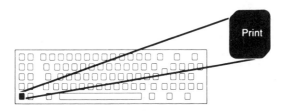

Copyright 1983 by Bruce and James Program Publishers, Inc.

What Is It?
Sometimes you have to refer to a physical object that you're afraid some readers may not know. Again, an illustration can help. Figure 13.2 shows how Zussman defines continuous-form paper.

Figure 13.2

Copyright 1983 by Bruce and James Program Publishers, Inc.

How Does It Work?

When you want people to perform some activity that they may never have heard of before, think of an illustration. One way you'll know you need some pictures is when you realize that the programmers are relying on metaphors—such as *scrolling*. The word *scroll* used to be a noun, referring to a long piece of papyrus rolled up on a stick. But in a text editor, you must actively *scroll* through the long text, viewing it through a small *window* which is, of course, the screen. The metaphors get tangled. Unscramble them with a picture, as in Figure 13.3.

Figure 13.3

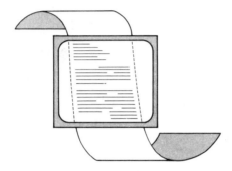

Why?

Sometimes a verbal explanation is just not enough to show why a term makes sense. For instance, Figure 13.4 shows a chart IBM uses to demonstrate how ASCII characters are made up of dots in a 5 x 7 matrix—creating a dot-matrix image.

What's on That Level?

As they dig deeper into a program, readers may begin to sense that they are going up and down tunnels, never quite sure how far they are from the surface. Diagrams help readers get their orientation. For instance, when users reach the command level of Apple III Pascal, they have a number of commands available, as shown in Figure 13.5 on page 174.

And Below That?

Programs offer options hidden behind options. To help readers see what they could get into, use diagrams such as the one in Figure 13.6 on page 174. Keep the diagrams consistent with what they have seen earlier.

Figure 13.4

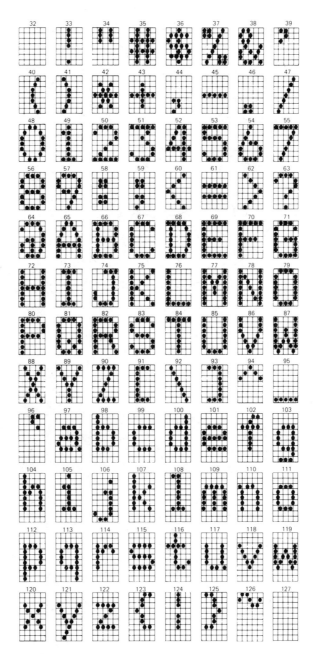

Copyright 1983 by IBM. Courtesy of IBM.

Figure 13.5

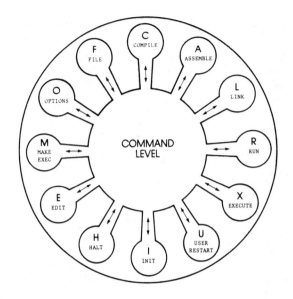

Figure 13.6

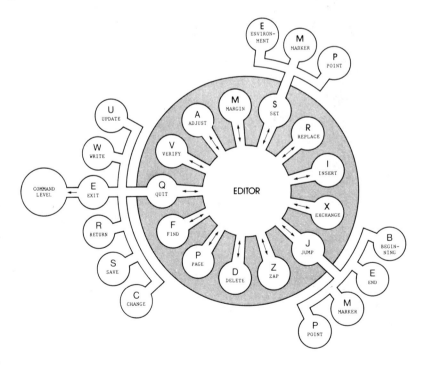

But What's the Big Picture?

From one menu, your readers may dip into half a dozen submenus, where each option may lead to yet another submenu or several prompts requesting more information. People have trouble understanding what their choices are on the main menu, in part, because they can't see what the next choices will be. So show them. Figure 13.7 shows how VisiCorp lets readers look ahead of the main menu in VisiLink™:

Figure 13.7

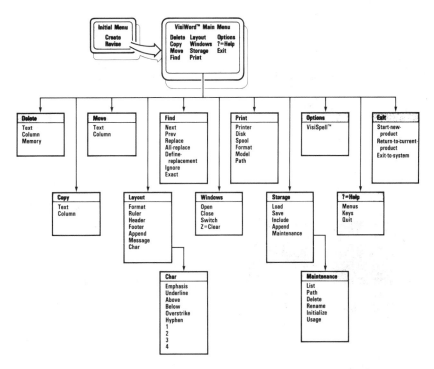

Copyright 1983 by VisiCorp.

What Are the Steps Involved?

More important than menus are actions. Images help illustrate the sequence of key actions people can take when using the program. Think of these images as a series of snapshots. You're not showing every keystroke now—just the gist of the activity. For instance, Figure 13.8 shows the

images conceived by Henry Korman, a design consultant, to introduce readers to the key steps they would be taking while using Apple
Speller III:

Figure 13.8

You Do This	The Speller Does This
1. Start your word processor. 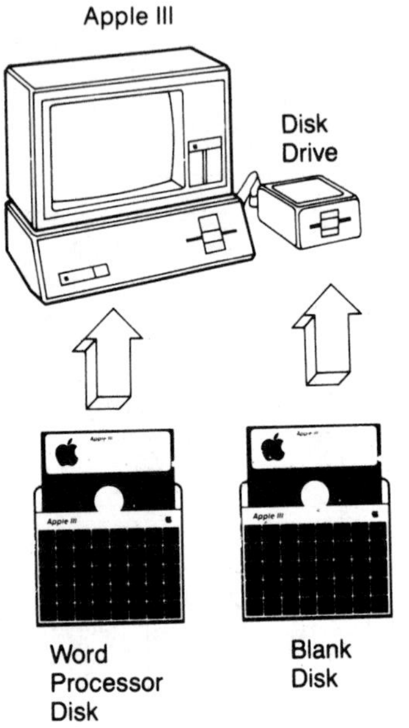 Put your word processing program disk in the built-in drive and a blank disk in the external drive.	

You Do This	The Speller Does This
2. Send text to disk. Word Processor Disk Letter Disk Write a letter and send it to the disk in the external drive. Remove your word processing program.	

You Do This	The Speller Does This
3. Start Apple Speller III. Apple Letter Speller III Disk Disk Put Apple Speller III into your built-in drive. Leave the disk containing your letter in the external drive.	

You Do This	The Speller Does This
4. Select document.	

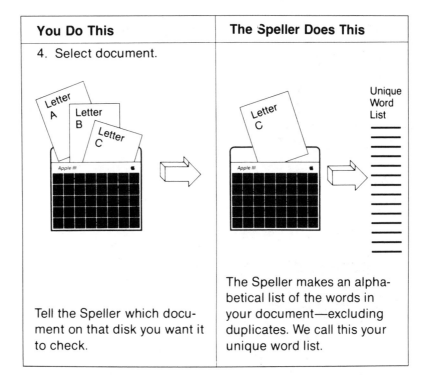

	The Speller makes an alphabetical list of the words in your document—excluding duplicates. We call this your unique word list.
Tell the Speller which document on that disk you want it to check.	

You Do This	The Speller Does This
5. Put in dictionary disk.	

Dictionary
Disk

Remove Apple Speller III program disk and put in a Random House dictionary disk.

You Do This	The Speller Does This
6. Select a dictionary.	

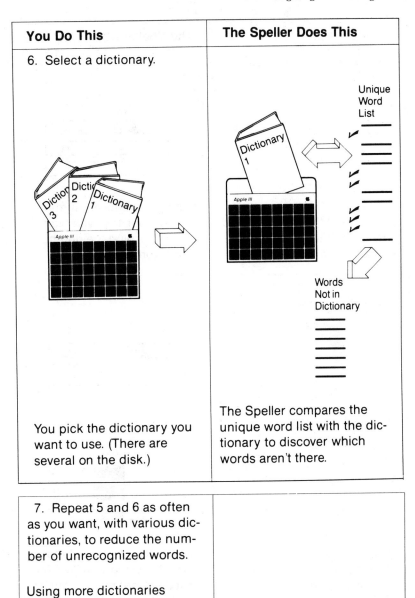

You Do This	The Speller Does This
You pick the dictionary you want to use. (There are several on the disk.)	The Speller compares the unique word list with the dictionary to discover which words aren't there.

7. Repeat 5 and 6 as often as you want, with various dictionaries, to reduce the number of unrecognized words. Using more dictionaries means more words will be recognized as correct. (That way you'll have fewer words to look at when correcting.)	

You Do This	The Speller Does This
8. Examine highlighted words. You look at the unrecognized word in context and decide what to do about it.	Word The Speller shows you three lines of your text with high-lighting around the unrecognized word.
9. Have Speller guess word. If you're not sure of the spelling, you can now have the Speller guess which word you meant—or list out similar words from the dictionary.	Word Guesses Your Word The Speller guesses at the correct spelling of your word. (But it will not guess right if you mistyped more than one or two letters.)

You Do This	The Speller Does This
9. (alternate) List words from a dictionary.	Dictionary ⬇ Possible Words with PPL APPLE APPLICA———— APPL—— —PPL———— —PPL—— —PPL———
[?] [P] [P] [L] [=]	
If the Speller can't guess what you meant, you can have it look up all the words that come close. Spell out the pattern you want matched; the question mark stands for a single letter you are not sure of, the equal sign for any number of letters.	The Speller shows you every dictionary word that matches the pattern. You spot the word you're after.

You Do This	The Speller Does This
10. Replace misspelling with correct spelling. 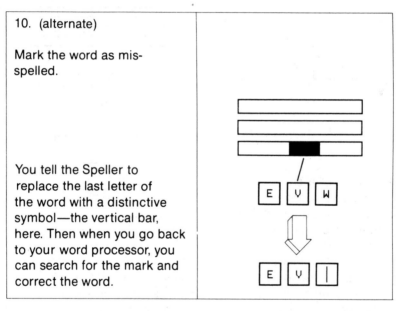 You can now do something about the spelling of the word. In this case, you type in the correct version.	The Speller replaces the misspelling with the correct spelling.
10. (alternate) Mark the word as misspelled. You tell the Speller to replace the last letter of the word with a distinctive symbol—the vertical bar, here. Then when you go back to your word processor, you can search for the mark and correct the word.	

You Do This	The Speller Does This
10. (alternate) Ignore the word. If you decide the word's spelled right, even if it's not in the dictionary, you can leave it as it is. It's OK.	

10. (alternate)
 	
Add the word to a dictionary because it's correct and will be used in the future.
 	
   a. Decide what dictionary to add word to.
 	
   b. Tell the Speller the new dictionary's name.
 	
You can tell the Speller that this word is all right and should be added to the dictionary.
	Old Dictionary New Dictionary

11. Repeat 8, 9, and 10 until all words have been looked at.	

You Do This	The Speller Does This
12. Remove cleaned-up text. You can remove your corrected document now. And if you marked some words, you can now go back to your word processing program, search for the marks, and correct those words, too.	 Letter Disk

AND IF YOU DON'T FEEL COMFORTABLE SKETCHING

You don't have to draw, to create images. You have to write. You face a writing challenge when you describe a picture you envision so that an artist can give you a real drawing.

Think of What the Artists Need

The artists are your audience, at least while you're writing little descriptions of the illustrations you'd like. Artists need to know about these things:

1. *Relationships.* What goes above what? What's on either side? How are they connected?

2. *Alignment.* What lines up with what?

3. *Scale.* What's bigger, what's smaller?

4. *Detail.* Which details matter? Can you provide a good photo? Which details do you want left out?

5. *Purpose.* What's the point? What message are you trying to get across?

6. *Text.* Which words do you want the artist to put in the picture? (A complete and accurate text!) Be sure to distinguish this text from your own description.

7. *Equipment Needed.* What gear should the artists include? And where can they find it?

8. *Perspective.* If odd, say how and why.

9. *Color.* What colors should be used, and what do they mean? Be consistent.

In general, avoid lyricism. Don't leave everything up to the imagination of the artists so they draw a blank—or worse. Be unambiguous. As the art coordinator, Nancy Hecht, says, "Please try to anticipate any and all possible points of confusion—it is better to overexplain than to leave some points dangling."

A QUICK REVIEW

This chapter has given you a whirlwind tour of art in manuals. Here's a slow review.

In designing a look for your manual, you need to pay most attention to:

☐ Reproduction Method

☐ Paper

☐ Page Size and Shape

☐ Typeface

☐ White Space

☐ Color

☐ Covers

You should decide on the position, typesize and style of type for each element:

☐ Asides

☐ Figures

- [ ] Headings
- [ ] Icons
- [ ] Key terms
- [ ] Lists
- [ ] Marginal glosses
- [ ] Prefatory material
- [ ] Running heads
- [ ] Running text
- [ ] Sample screens
- [ ] Special keys
- [ ] Subscripts and superscripts
- [ ] Summaries and quick-reference materials
- [ ] Tables of contents
- [ ] Tables
- [ ] Text that the readers must type
- [ ] Titles
- [ ] Tutorial text
- [ ] Warnings

Use images to answer key questions, such as:

- [ ] Where is it?
- [ ] What is it?
- [ ] How does it work?
- [ ] Why?

☐ What's on that level?

☐ And below that?

☐ But what's the big picture?

☐ What are the steps involved?

In describing an illustration you want in the manual, be sure to tell the artists what you want in terms of:

☐ Relationships

☐ Alignment

☐ Scale

☐ Detail

☐ Purpose

☐ Text

☐ Equipment Needed

☐ Perspective

☐ Color

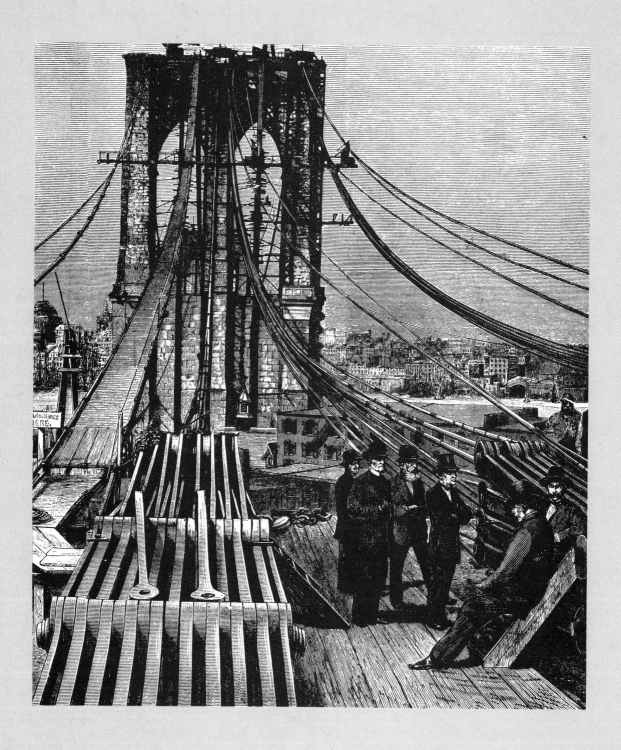

PART FOUR

Revising

Chapter 14: Rewriting
Chapter 15: Testing Your Manual

14

Rewriting

Ask for Comments from the Team
Listen Hard
Call a Meeting
Take the Long View First
Check Back—But Not Too Often
Plan for Updates and Revisions
Deciding When to Update or Revise
Call an Update an Update
Read What the Readers Say
Talk to Anyone Who Can Help
Recognize When Rewriting Means Writing It All New
A Quick Review

Rewriting

Like housework, revising's never done. You polish one patch, scrub another, wash away smudges, patch the rough surfaces, and find at nightfall that you've got to do it all again. In fact, revising's what you'll do the most of as a technical writer. Your own manuals, in three or four drafts. Somebody else's. From quick fixes to wholesale rewrites, you're constantly cleaning.

If you had time enough, you might wait a few months before picking up the manual to revise it. That way you'd be cold. You could look at it as a stranger might. After a vacation like that, you would no longer remember all those half-conscious choices you made as you concocted a particular sentence. You would no longer treasure a paragraph because it was hard to write. You might not even remember the product that well, so you could see where beginners might get confused. But, alas, you usually won't get that much time. You have to start revising while you're still hot.

So you need help from the rest of the team. You depend on their comments, meetings, and decisions. As a writer, you know that your manual will someday be revised, probably by some other writer. So you can make that writer's job easier, by asking for help from your readers and technicians, laying the groundwork for future revisions. Here's how to work together on revisions.

ASK FOR COMMENTS
FROM THE TEAM

Seems simple. But comments don't come easily from most people. Help team members out by using a cover letter to suggest what to look for, what to say, and when.

Ask them what's missing, what's undecided, what's wrong. If you have specific questions about a chapter, put those in. Point out what you've assumed—particularly if you're not sure that everyone agrees.

Include your current schedule. Emphasize the dates when you need their photographs, illustrations, prototype hardware or software, specifications—whatever. Emphasize how much the schedule for the manual will slip if you do not get those on time. And, yes, when you send out a draft, set a definite deadline for return with comments.

When you get to a beta draft, warn them that unless they object to something violently, you're not planning to change much. (Don't encourage them to waste their time.) At final draft, explain that it's too late to change anything except what one writer calls deadly technical errors.

LISTEN HARD

After all the comments come back, Rani Cochran, who wrote the owner's manual for the Apple III+, takes all the marked-up manuals and lays them out on a large table:

> I copy the comments from page 1 of all 15 manuals, and then I turn a new leaf on my nice new copy and do page 2. I put down everything. When I just made a clear error or some dumb typo, I only have to write down one thing. But when the question is one of style or approach or organization, I often get four or five conflicting comments. I make a note of all of them and attribute each one, because it's my duty to sort them out. Often I'll have to negotiate on matters of content and audience.

You may want to start with the most helpful reviewers. Connie Mantis, who has written manuals on word processing and telecommunications packages, says:

> Some people actually think up solutions. I decided to pinpoint my best reviewers, the ones that really seemed to know what they were doing. For instance, there's one guy who not only catches the technical stuff, he notices a lot of the grammatical stuff that nobody else caught. So I said, "He's my prime guy." Plus he offers solutions. So I said, "I'll always do his first, then I'll go in descending order, because then I already have a lot of questions answered." I knew that by the time I got to somebody else's comments, who had just written "Huh?", it was already rewritten, or I knew how to fix it.

CALL A MEETING

When five different reviewers disagree, invite them to a review meeting. You might sum up the questions that you view as unresolved, so everybody can think about them before coming.

If possible, get your supervisor to monitor the meeting. You're too close to the material—intellectually and emotionally. Connie Mantis says:

It's not good to be your own monitor. There are two reasons. One, you just feel like killing everybody. Even if they liked it in general, they're making all these little snipes. It seems like everybody is saying how stupid everything is, how stupid the words are, and they're battling each other. But the other reason you don't want to be your own moderator is you're writing notes like crazy.

Usually, a review meeting starts with general comments. People say, "I hated all the humor," or "You should cut all the examples," or "You repeat yourself too much." Listen, but nudge people into a page-by-page discussion of the manual. That way you can tell what they really mean by these broad pronunciamentos.

For a while it will go like this, says Connie Mantis:

OK, nothing on page 3, nothing on page 4, and then page 5, and everyone will chime in and say, "Well I think blah blah," and then they'll start to line up and you'll have completely opposite views. They can begin to fight out these issues.

You can short-circuit some of these debates if you've reasoned out the whole argument before. But some arguments are necessary. Someone else has to make a decision or win a point—and you'll just write it down. Without the meeting, these confrontations might never take place. As Mantis says:

This page-by-page stuff brings it to a head. You get to the point where everybody must say something. Everybody's being beaten out of the bushes. They've got to own up that they are really thinking this or that. No more hiding. No more running into the corner. Finally, everyone must agree—somehow.

Of course, these debates can drag. "People get off on wacky tangents," Mantis says. "They go on for hours and get all purple in the face. They get frothy." That's when the moderator must step in and say, "OK, you two, go off and make a decision, and tell the writer by Tuesday." Or, "This is too trivial to talk about anymore. Here's what we're going to do."

Between comments and the meetings, you should be able to resolve outstanding issues. This will help your style. When you're writing to accomodate three or four interpretations, you must get ambiguous. Once the team decides what they want to do, you can weed out several of these sentences and say it straight.

TAKE THE LONG VIEW FIRST

When you've collected all these reactions, you may feel snowed under. Resist the temptation to start clearing away details. Look first at the lay of the land. Consider structure before style. One organizational change may solve a lot of tangled syntax in sentences that you wrote to excuse the disorder.

Think of form as a series of promises to the readers. Do you fulfil each one? If so, your form probably makes sense. But if you keep jumping back and forth, think how you might sort out the sections. Look at any transitions that have caught several reviewers' eyes: sometimes that means that you've got topics out of order and couldn't quite justify the mess.

Also, to avoid that anxious feeling that you have 400 hours of work to do in a week, get an idea of the main types of changes you'll be making before you get overwhelmed at the sheer number. You'll see they fall into certain categories. Once you've decided what to do about each category, your job will be a lot less complicated.

If you've gotten a smattering of comments about your style, ask yourself which traits people noticed. Often people hit on one mannerism, marking that throughout. But they may well be bothered by a general tone, of which that trick is just a symptom. Don't rush to revise your style, though. Ask yourself these questions:

- How many people want me to change my style? If it's a majority of your reviewers, listen. If it's a weird minority, listen, but don't be too quick to act on their advice. Figure out your own solutions.

- What's their background? Are they really speaking up for users? If not, thank them and forget it.

- Is this just one irritating habit? If so, just fix it.

- Are reviewers reacting to a whole style? If so, you'll have to go back and figure out your audience again, and get agreement on the team about the new tone. This will mean detailed rewriting, so warn people that it will take longer than an average revision.

CHECK BACK—BUT NOT TOO OFTEN

To encourage reviewers, show that their comments have made a difference. Return their marked-up copy, with your revision. That way, they can compare, line by line, to see how you acted on their advice. And write a memo to each reviewer, summing up the ways you have followed their ideas, or disagreed—and why. Here's an example:

MEMO

To: Maude
From: Mel

Here's how I used your suggestions for revision.

Page	Subject of Comment	Action Taken
1	TITLE	Yes, I agree. "A Grand Tour" is a little grand. I've replaced that with "Introduction."
1	Keycaps	I agree. This material belongs later in the chapter.
2	"Equipment"	No. *Configuration* is a crummy word. I see no reason for using—or teaching—this particular hunk of jargon.

Don't go through too many revision cycles, though. People read most attentively the first time through. From then on, they tend to look only at areas they're anxious about. And after several drafts, many people skim so fast that they miss the fact that pages 20–30 appear in back of page 79. You can wear reviewers out, particularly when they are not deeply involved in the project, so try not to circulate more than three drafts.

PLAN FOR UPDATES AND REVISIONS

As soon as you finish your manual, it becomes a candidate for someone else to revise. You can help another writer with those updates by the way you handle some parts of the manual—and by writing notes directly to that writer.

As you write your manual, keep asking the team which parts of the product are most likely to change. See if you can keep the changeable features in an appendix, isolated from the main text. That way the next writer can update that small section and make a few changes in the table of contents and index, without bothering any other parts of the manual.

In the back of your manual, ask the readers to help by sending you detailed comments. I don't like the standard reader-response cards that ask for general praise. ("Do you like the style of writing in this manual? What do you like most about this manual?") The answers to these kinds of questions are no help to a writer.

Instead, make up a reader-response card that will elicit real answers. Show readers you're interested by asking real questions. Most pollsters find that people take a long questionnaire as evidence that you will actually use their responses, rather than throwing them into some statistical pot. This encourages them to write in. So go through each chapter, like this:

READER RESPONSE CARD . . . . PAGE 2

In Chapter 4, on Utilities:

    Have you changed the character sets?
        Did you have any trouble? What kind?
        How should we change the manual to help?
    Have you had any trouble creating a dictionary?
        What kind?
        What should we add to the manual to help?
    Did any dictionary maintenance functions misfire?
        Which ones did the manual help you on?
        What did you want more help on?
        Where did we steer you wrong?
    Did we use any terms we forgot to define in the glossary?

That way, if anyone writes in, you'll get the kind of data you or the next writer can really use in a revision. Not just "Yes," or "It was very nice."

I know that when you complete your manual, you may not feel like thinking about it a minute longer. But take a few days to help out the next writer—the one who will have to revise it later. You can provide the next writer with these things:

- Old memos—the ones that explain the reasoning behind the design and approach you took.

- A letter from you, one writer to another, saying what you would like to have done, what you suggest doing if there's time, what to watch out for.

- A copy of the printed manual, with notes on everything you'd change if you could—from typos, illustrations, and errors to whole sections you would add or subtract.

- A copy of your last electronic version, plus a paper copy, with all last-minute changes marked on it. That way the new writer won't have to proofread a hundred pages to locate 18 words' worth of corrections.

DECIDING WHEN TO UPDATE
OR REVISE

You don't make this decision alone. As the program itself gets fixed or improved, your original manual becomes outdated. When someone finds a gigantic problem deep inside in the program, the programmers may begin to suggest that putting out another edition of the manual will take care of it. As readers write in, you begin to find out that certain passages just don't make sense.

If there's a danger to users' health or data, you'd better let them know fast. You don't have time, at first, to revise the whole manual, but you do have time for a quick fix or an errata sheet (an admission of error). Sometimes you have a few days to make a few changes—nothing more. Rani Cochran says, "With quick fixes we are correcting typos and adjusting little tiny things with the next reprinting of the manuals, Version A, Version B, Version C."

If you've got a lot of corrections, and they've got to be fixed before the next version of the manual, you may have to turn out an errata sheet. But please don't call it an errata sheet. Try using a title like *We Goofed!* And don't limit yourself to mistakes in accuracy. Now that you've got the chance, go in and tidy up typos, ambiguities, and brief omissions.

If you send out change pages (users are supposed to substitute those for the unfortunate originals), recognize that most people will stuff them in a binder somewhere and lose them. Very few change pages reach their destinations.

When you've sent out half a dozen errata sheets or change pages, you will probably be convinced that it's time for some real rewriting. But you won't get the go-ahead until your supervisor and the whole team agrees.

At this point, you and your supervisor should probably campaign for enough time for a real revision, or at least an update brochure, rather than a series of patches. Patches look like they'll save time, but each patch makes the original a little messier. You end up taking more time, and doing a worse job in pieces. So resist the pressure to do a series of quick fixes when what's really needed is a complete rewrite or a booklet explaining the ways the team has upgraded the program.

CALL AN UPDATE AN UPDATE

Sometimes the team makes some changes in a product, but you don't have the time to redo a whole manual or a series of manuals. If you're lucky, you can change a few pages and slap the new versions into the next printing. If you're not so lucky, the changes will affect a hundred different references in the original. In that case, you may need an updated brochure.

Dick Leeman, a writer who worked on an update of a language designed to accomodate new hardware and to expand some of the features, figured that readers would have already read the original manual. But he had to review some of the material in that manual to show where changes affected the language so that readers could see how things worked and why—before and after the changes.

He set up a series of tables summarizing how the system worked in each version, like this:

Version 1.0	Version 1.1
Allows 2 libraries per program	Allows up to 6 libraries per program
PROGRAM LIBRARY FILE:	PROGRAM LIBRARY FILE:
Limit: one per program	Limit: one per program
Same directory as program	Same directory as program
Takes name of program	Takes name of program
Cannot be shared	Cannot be shared
	OR REPLACE THE PROGRAM LIBRARY FILE WITH . . .
	LIBRARY FILE NAME:
	Lists pathnames of up to 5 library files
	Limit: one per program
	Same directory as program
	Takes name of program
	Facilitates library file sharing
	LIBRARY FILES
	Up to 5 can be used in one program
	Takes any name except that of the program, .LIB or .CODE extension
	Can be shared between programs
SYSTEM.LIBRARY	SYSTEM.LIBRARY
Must be on system disk	Must be on system disk

To show how these features affected every stage of a programmer's work, Leeman added a chapter of running commentary. He says:

> This takes the user, a professional program developer—perhaps someone who hasn't been doing it that long—through the complete program design, development, coding, compiling, and executing of one application, so that you can see in particular how the new features work. It's deliberately conversational, as if I were looking over their shoulder.

READ WHAT THE READERS SAY

If you've been assigned to do a thorough revision of a current manual, your best source of information is the audience. They know what worked for them, what didn't, and where they went wrong.

So look through letters, reader-response forms, and any other feedback. For many products, there'll be what I call user input reports. These ask users for comments about the product, but many of those comments apply to the manual. You might put a digest of the comments on a large data base, coded to indicate how severe the problem was (Critical, Medium, Can Wait).

Here are some typical reader comments, about various manuals:

- Not clear how window works to keep cursor from falling off screen.
- Should say that kernel must be in first sector to get a self-booting disk.
- Tutorial needed with lots of examples.
- This manual is very poorly written.
- Would like to know how to write driver files.
- Page 101 does not work; regardless of setting, left margin remains the same.
- You mention double-strike, but don't tell me how to do it.
- Page 55, change line 160, not 180 as indicated.

Rani Cochran, one writer who has relied on reader responses, says:

> Each one of these comments has to be treated with respect. Some individual, maybe in a state of high dudgeon, took the time to write in. But the reports themselves have to be treated with a great deal of caution. I was checking one report and discovered that I was making the same mistake in reading that the user had made. And I discovered this after plowing through five related manuals trying to find what the incorrect reference in the original manual could have been. I had slipped a comma, just as the original reader had. That meant rewriting one sentence, not five manuals.

Reader comments are a great help in making quick fixes. You can go to the engineers, get an answer, and fix it so it will appear in the next printing. Don't forget to take the comments off the data base or the next writer will think these things still need to be fixed.

TALK TO ANYONE WHO CAN HELP

As you start a complete revision, talk to the last writer on the project, the people who've had to repair or maintain the product, and the people who are about to change it.

Remember that the last writer on the project may not be too happy to have you rewrite all that wonderful prose. Rani Cochran says:

> I think that anyone who is going to revise a manual needs to get a good shot of diplomacy vitamin before going in to talk with the original writer. It can be very touchy. This is where a supervisor can be a great help to smooth the way, because the original writer is a great source of information, and must therefore be comfortable. The supervisor can tell the revising writer what approaches to take with the original writer, and pave the way by going to the original writer.

She adds:

> Another great source of information for revisions is communications from the technical folks in-house to the folks in the field. These may contain that very information, in great detail. Now the revising writer looks at those, with the attitude, "Here are folks out in the field, thrashing through, sharing their efforts with each other, and with us." Here the question is not "Is this true?" but "Can I use this sample program in my manual, or is it proprietary?" or "Does it really apply?"

RECOGNIZE WHEN REWRITING
MEANS WRITING IT ALL NEW

Sometimes what starts out as a revision turns into a brand-new manual. You may begin trying to preserve the original, then realize you can't.

That's an important decision. Rani Cochran, whose revision of the Apple III owner's manual turned into a whole new manual, says:

> I wasted a lot of time when I first began revising, trying to retain the structure of the old manual, trying to respect the original writer's style, trying to fit in. Finally I got my courage and just did it my way.

If the software or hardware has changed a lot, you face that kind of decision. Remember that your manual is often just part of a series. So you must decide whether all of these manuals need to be rewritten. At first, the team will resist such an idea since it takes time and money. But in some cases, it may make more sense.

   If so, you're back at the beginning, sketching out a new document design. That's why I say revising never stops.

A QUICK REVIEW

Here's a review of revising:

☐ Ask for comments—and listen.

☐ Call a review meeting to get outstanding issues resolved.

☐ Take the long view first: work on structure before you tinker with details.

☐ Check back with reviewers.

☐ Plan for future updates and revisions.

☐ Read what all the real users say.

☐ Make quick fixes—this week.

☐ Send out errata sheets or change pages as you go.

☐ Call an update an update.

☐ Recognize when rewriting means writing it all new.

☐ Talk to anyone who can help.

Testing Your Manual

Get Started Early
Decide What You Want to Test
Estimate Your Time
Recruit Real Users
Figure Out How Many
Relax
Start with a Lecture
Set a Problem—for Reference Manuals
Watch Carefully
Ask, But Don't Argue
Make Notes as You Go
Discuss It Afterward
Congratulate Yourself
And Repeat
A Quick Review

Testing Your Manual

Professional testers make sure that the program does what it is supposed to and that the manual accurately reflects the program. But as a writer, you need to perform a very different form of testing.

Meg Beeler, who has organized a lot of testing for manuals like her own *Applesoft Tutorial*, says that just watching people as they read—or stop reading—can give you ideas. "It's an enormously valuable insight into how people use your book: what they read, what they gloss over, what frightens and excites them, what confuses them."

When you test your manual on people who resemble your actual audience, you may be surprised at what you discover—steps you left out, tricky or ambiguous passages, descriptions that no longer match the words on the display, phrases that make some readers guffaw, perhaps even a few outright mistakes. And you'll get to chat. Beeler says, "One of the reasons testing is fun is that you get feedback from the people who are really going to be using the manual." They'll tell you what they liked, offer suggestions for sorting out the hard parts, plead for more pictures.

In the process, you may find out how to improve your manual so much that the next time you have somebody test it you can prove:

- The training really helps people to use the program effectively.

- The language is clear throughout the manual and the organization encourages efficient use.

- You don't move people along too fast, and you didn't leave out any steps.

- Most people can zip through your writing without getting bogged down, upset, or lost.

When you test a manual, go beyond verifying its accuracy. You're making sure that it works—that it teaches readers to use the program.

That's why you will probably want to concentrate on tutorials. You can watch people go through each step, seeing where they succeed and where they go wrong. You will also want to test reference volumes, but these demand more planning and more time, so you probably won't test them as often.

Here's how to test your manual.

GET STARTED EARLY

Beeler warns, "Planning the testing, finding the testers, and arranging for all the equipment does take time. And if you're rushing around and you feel chaotic when you begin, it doesn't help. So leave yourself plenty of time to prepare."

In the weeks before you have other people test your manual you should be testing it yourself. Make sure that every step of the tutorial matches the way the software really behaves.

Then try it out on resident experts, people who know the program or people who know how to put a manual through its paces. The purpose is to fix every bug you can before you put the manual in front of people who represent the users. (Otherwise you're wasting their time and your own.)

You should clear all the irritating mistakes out of the manual before bringing in people to test it. If a tester gets started and your tutorial crashes the program, you can be sure you haven't done your homework. Also, you should feel confident of the organization of your manual by the time you test it. You hope that testing will validate what you've done. (That's why you've already done so much revision, right?)

DECIDE WHAT YOU WANT TO TEST

Are you going to test the whole tutorial? Or just a few sections? Do you want to pick six functions, hand testers the entire manual, and see how long it takes them to succeed at all six? (That's a good way to test your reference sections, index, table of contents, summaries, and overviews—how fast can people find something, and how much sense does it make when they get there?)

You may have certain rough spots in mind, too—particular choices you're not sure of, transitions you fear may be weak, questions of order. Make up a checklist of questions you want answered, but be prepared to face a hundred more from the people who actually try out your manual.

ESTIMATE YOUR TIME

Figure out how long you think it will take a slow beginner to go through all the material. (The slowest I've encountered: ten pages an hour on a tutorial.) This depends on how heavy your pages are—with text and thought. To get an idea, you might try the material on one person who has no experience with the program and use his or her time as an average.

If you have a lot of material, consider dividing the testing into morning and afternoon sessions. Build in some breaks. Leave time for lunch. And keep your schedule fairly flexible. Remember that you can probably count on some disasters: a machine will overheat at the last minute or a disk drive will refuse to talk to the computer.

RECRUIT REAL USERS

Recruit some people who resemble your target audience. Ask friends; call friends of friends; pester your coworkers for suggestions. You don't want professional testers, you want people who might actually be using the program. If you can afford it, pay them. (A lot of people will test your manual once for fun, but on your next project they want cab fare.)

Remember that your audience probably includes several types of users. For instance, when the writers decided to test the manuals for one accounting package, they wanted some bookkeepers and some accountants who had never touched a computer and some of both who had—four distinct types of users. To test a spelling checker, I recruited secretaries, writers, and managers. I made sure some of each group could spell ten-gallon words, and some couldn't; some knew computers well, others had just met the machine.

When you talk to someone before they come in to test your manual, Beeler says:

> It's crucial to tell them that the purpose is to find your mistakes. You should discuss this the first time you talk to them, and repeat it when they're about to begin testing. Say, "We don't want you to know anything; it's fine; we're not looking for what you know, we're trying to find our problems."

Reassure them that this is not a high school quiz. You are not a teacher, trying to flunk them. You are a writer asking for their help.

FIGURE OUT HOW MANY

Figure out how many people you want to watch at once. I emphasize watching them personally, because you'll find out much more that way than if you send them home and ask for comments. (The usual comment: "Oh, it was nice.") Beeler suggests that you can only give close attention to two or three people at once.

You could ask someone else to join you, perhaps a programmer on the project or an editor who knows the manual. Then you might be able to have half a dozen people in a room at once.

Or you can work with just one person at a time. That way you can really explore each problem as it comes up, and find out—in detail—what brings on confusion. (Sometimes you're forced to test people one at a time; for instance, you may have the only prototype of a new machine.)

Now you can calculate how many machines you need at once, how many copies of the software, how many disk drives, printers, outlets, and desks—oh, and copies of your manual. (If you're writing for more than one type of machine, you'll probably want to test them all.)

Conduct the testing wherever you have room for all these people and machines: your office, a meeting room, the training center. I've even done it at home.

RELAX

On the big day, calm down. To get the most out of this kind of testing, you have to be receptive. Beeler says:

> Remind yourself that the purpose of this exercise is to get information and to make the manual better. You won't facilitate the process at all if you're defensive or attached to your manual. If you have trouble with that, you might pretend that the manual is someone else's. If people sense that you don't want to hear what they have to say, then they're not going to tell you.

Before you go into the testing room, remind yourself that your purpose is to diagnose what's wrong and to figure out roughly what to do.

START WITH A LECTURE

Don't just launch people into your manual. Take some time to explain what you want them to do. Thank them for coming, and point out again that you're looking for your own mistakes—not theirs. Beeler says:

> Emphasize that you are looking for problems in manuals; if they don't understand something, or get stuck, or get confused, it is probably the fault of the book. Tell them that you want them to speak up, whenever possible, if something seems wrong, or if they have suggestions.

Most people have been trained in school never to mark in their books, never to object to some confusing passage, always to blame themselves if something goes haywire. You've got to overcome years of indoctrination to persuade them to tell you when something's inaccurate or obscure.

Remember, too, that for the last 30 years or so, the people who programmed mainframes made ordinary folks feel foolish. So many people come to the computer with a legacy of fear: "I'll never understand computers. And if I can't follow the directions, there's something wrong with me." That's why you need to stress that you're trying to uncover your own errors, not their incompetence.

You may want to explain how to turn on the machine, handle disks, and run the printer—unless that's in the tutorial you're testing. Give them an idea how long it will take them to do the testing. Assure them that you'll be there all along, and that you want to hear what they have to say as they work.

Then have them open their manuals and—on the count of three—go.

SET A PROBLEM—
FOR REFERENCE MANUALS

A good way to test reference manuals is to pose half a dozen problems for people to solve. If you select the problems carefully, you can find out whether beginners can locate basics, obscure facts, and advanced features. You need some proof at the end that your testers have actually succeeded. And, if possible, you need to study the way in which they go about solving the problems—or get lost.

In this way, you will find out how people actually use reference manuals. For instance, new users tend to do a lot of trial-and-error searching through the table of contents. If the headings there reflect an ordinary person's view of the functions, readers succeed; if the headings have too much jargon, readers get lost.

Mary Dieli, a student of documentation, recently watched a great many people using a series of reference manuals built around recipes, step-by-step directions on how to use a feature. She found that readers tended to follow this process of solving problems:

1. They define the task they want to accomplish.

2. They look in the table of contents for a key term representing a feature they think may help them solve the problem.

3. They find that term in the table of contents, turn to the right page, and look for a definition or a brief explanation of the feature's function or purpose. They look for an explanation to confirm that they have found the appropriate solution.

4. They find and follow the procedure, the step-by-step instructions for using the feature.

Novice users, Dieli concluded, look for a definition first, an explanation second, and the procedure third. As a result of this testing, she suggested that writers distinguish these elements visually and verbally.

She also discovered that some illustrations contained so much information that novices got confused. She recommended pointing out the important features for the reader.

WATCH CAREFULLY

Watch what each of the testers does. Don't count on them raising their hands to ask you what's going on. Beeler says:

> Especially when they first start, they're very reticent. They'll just sit there reading an obscure page over and over again.
>
> See if people get lost. In the process of watching them, you'll see the nonverbal stuff they do when they hunch over or start fidgeting or sit there for a long time staring at the main menu. You get a lot of clues you would never get from just talking to them afterward.

Think of odd behavior as a symptom. To find out what's really bothering them, though, you'll have to ask.

ASK, BUT DON'T ARGUE

So ask. Ask what's bothering them. You have to be alert to recognize that people are in trouble, but when you spot it, ask them what's confusing. Make a note in that part of your copy of the manual. Beeler says:

> When you see someone stopping, you need to ask them why. They may not know why they have stopped, but what they say will give you some clues. I've also found that right there on the spot they can give you good ideas for fixing the problem. Otherwise, you'd have to go home and sit down and think about it for three hours before you knew what to do.

Talking with people takes away some of the authority they invest in you. After all, you're an expert. But when you laugh and joke about the problems you've had making the manual clear, they begin to see that they can really help you, and that you're the one who's made the boo-boos.

You may well feel like defending yourself. Don't. It doesn't matter what you meant; if the readers don't understand, it's your fault. So shut up and take notes.

People you don't need to take too seriously: the Helpful Harry's who spend their time looking for trouble, being picky, not really trying to do the work you've outlined, spending more time rewriting than performing. These people are too conscientious to make a good test case. (Ordinary users don't spend their time figuring out how to rephrase your first paragraph.)

MAKE NOTES AS YOU GO

You'll probably think you can remember everything. But use a pencil to help. Sometimes, with the help of the testers, you'll be able to reorganize a section or some steps on the spot. Other times, you won't have time to do anything besides mark the spot where someone got stuck or make a few cryptic notes to yourself.

When you're listening to someone who's gone astray, mentally check what they say against a set of questions you've come up with before testing. Go over the same ground after you've collected all the manuals and collated all your notes. For instance, ask yourself these questions:

- Do the explanations make sense? Are they in the right spot?

- Do people know why they should do each step? Do they see where they're headed?

- Do some readers tend to skip a particular instruction? Is it called out clearly enough? Can they see that it's an instruction?

- Which passages are murky—and why? Is it poor organization? Clumsy wording? Have you mentioned a term without defining it?

- Are you talking above their head or beneath their contempt?

- Do you carry on too long about some things?

- Where have you included outdated or incorrect information?

- Does everything you've said hold true on all possible systems with all possible hardware hooked up?

- Do people laugh at your jokes?

- Can people find things using the index, table of contents, and quick-reference chart?

- What spots need rewriting, for whatever reason?

- After reading the manual, can people actually use the program to do some work?

- Do people come away feeling cheerful, encouraged, even confident?

DISCUSS IT AFTERWARD

Hold a general discussion at the end. When people have finished going through particular steps, they can tell you how they reacted to the program and the manual in general. You might start with a broad-based questionnaire to get them thinking about broader issues, then lead a freewheeling discussion.

You'll get an idea of the level of difficulty you've posed for different readers. Is one section too hard for beginners, too slow and simpleminded for the more proficient? You'll be able to talk with the testers about ways to navigate between those rocks.

Listening to each other, your testers may come up with good suggestions. They can also comfort you. As Meg Beeler says, "If they've just found a huge number of problems and your ego is feeling a little weak, you may also discover they still liked your manual a lot." So . . .

CONGRATULATE YOURSELF

Testing keeps you alert every second, so you may feel drained afterward. But recognize what sections worked, what explanations made sense, what transitions went by without a hitch.

You've got pages of notes, but you've already done the hardest work—diagnosing what's wrong and figuring out roughly what to do. After that, the writing will go quickly. Also, you've caught a lot of errors now, so you can correct them before you go to typesetting—not on some errata sheet slipped into the box just before shipping.

AND REPEAT

Then do it all again. Once you've fixed your manual, test it on a fresh crew to make sure you've really improved it. In some places, you may just have introduced chaos where order reigned before.

And, if you can get the time, keep testing until you're sure the final version works smoothly and causes no problems.

A QUICK REVIEW

Here's a checklist for testing:

☐ Get started early.

☐ Decide exactly what you want to test.

☐ Set up a schedule.

☐ Recruit some people who are like your target audiences.

☐ Figure out how many people you'll watch at once.

☐ Calculate what equipment you need.

☐ Calm down.

☐ Begin by asking for their help in spotting your mistakes. Encourage them to speak up.

☐ Set up some problems to be solved using the reference sections.

☐ Watch what they do.

☐ Ask what's going on, what they think, why they pause.

☐ Make plenty of notes.

☐ Hold a general discussion at the end.

☐ Congratulate yourself.

☐ Repeat until your manual is perfect.

PART FIVE

Helping Other People Write

Chapter 16: Reviewing Someone Else's Manual
Chapter 17: Softening Up the Software

Reviewing Someone Else's Manual

Your Aims
What to Watch For
Preserve the Manual's Consistency
Maintain Your Innocence—and Sympathy
Communicate with the Writer
A Quick Review

Reviewing Someone Else's Manual

When you're asked to review someone else's manual, you may feel like a street cleaner. You're supposed to march through the manual, straightening syntax, drawing clarity out of chaos, filling in holes, cutting away tangle so people won't slip or get lost.

Part of what you're doing, then, is critical. You must think like an editor and act as a representative for the people who will really have to use the manual later.

And part of your task is creative. You may scribble in better phrases, snappier openings, simpler expressions. When you've completed your review, you must write up your general conclusions in a way that will be useful to the manual writer.

YOUR AIMS

When you review a manual, you should have these aims:

- To clear away stumbling blocks and unnecessary distinctions from the paths of readers.

- To spot the writer's messy habits so they can be cured before they irritate readers.

- To assure that the manual's organization makes sense, leads readers gradually through the instruction, and provides various paths through the reference material.

- To establish a reassuring record of consistency and accuracy.

Sure, the writer could do all this alone. The Roman poet Horace suggested that after you write a poem, you should put it away for nine years before editing it. That way you could look at it as a stranger might and cut ruthlessly. Manual writers don't have that much time. As a reviewer, then, you speed up the review process and make it more thorough.

Every writer needs a reviewer. Leslie Liedtka, who has edited dozens of manuals, argues that like an editor, a reviewer can provide another set of eyes:

> When you're looking at something you've written yourself, you don't always notice your problems; you don't notice you've made an error. You thought it was such a great idea, and you wrote it down, and you may not notice that you've got a split infinitive and a word misspelled and you're not following some standard.

WHAT TO WATCH FOR

Watch for murk—moments of darkness in the prose. These arise from problems of style, organization, and consistency.

You'll probably notice stylistic problems first. Passages of jargon. Haste or slowness. Changes in tone. Lack of variety in sentence structure. Passive verbs spreading like rot. Peculiar personal quirks, blindspots, and odd twists of phrase.

Try not to get lost in correcting these awkward stretches. You can become so involved in rewriting that you lose track of the way you are moving forward through the text. You have ceased being a stand-in for readers.

Readers care more about meaning than style. So make at least one pass through the whole manual to assure that all of these are true:

- The organization makes sense and can be understood without a lot of reading.

- The organization seems to accomodate the needs of average readers.

- It is clear why each section follows the one before.

- Readers don't have to jump forward and backward in the manual to figure out how some function works. What should come first comes first.

Laurel Rezeau, another editor, says,

> The main thing we're looking for is that it's easy to follow what the writer is trying to say. And that means an overall organization that is clear and makes it clear what the point of each individual part is and how the parts all relate to each other. When a writer is working on explaining individual things, sometimes that overall cohesiveness and the point of each section can get lost.

You're spotting omissions, too. Writers can be so immersed in the subject that when they first use a term they forget to include a definition. It's up to you to say, "Oh, you need a marginal definition here, or maybe you could define it in the text."

PRESERVE THE MANUAL'S CONSISTENCY

Here is where your critical facility becomes most important. Watching for absolute consistency of references, for instance, seems to require a different way of thinking than writing does. But consistency is important for the reader.

When the writer uses three different terms to refer to the same object, some readers will imagine three different objects. The head of Apple's editorial group, Jon Thompson, says, "When all the lists are punctuated differently, and *database* is spelled as two words in one place and as one word in another, and there are serial commas in one place and not in another, after a while there's a cumulative effect."

At first this inconsistency just confuses readers, who begin to think there's some significance to the variations and try to figure out what they mean. Then inconsistency begins to sap their confidence in the reliability of the manual. After a while, inconsistency can drive even the most dedicated readers crazy.

To help readers concentrate on the subject, not on the writer's infinite variety of terms, punctuation, organization, and style, you may have to make several passes through the manuscript, checking on the way a whole range of elements are handled. You're making the manual consistent in all these ways:

1. *With the product.* The manual's got to match the product. That's the minimum requirement. You should use the manual and see if it really describes the product accurately.

2. *With the standards in other manuals.* And with standard American English.

3. *With its own terminology.* As Leslie Liedtka says, "You can call a computer by ten different names, but we want to pick one name and use that over and over. We don't want to confuse people."

4. *With its own organizational principles.* If one section is organized with definition first, then example, then procedure, all similar sections should be too—or have a good reason not to.

5. *With its own design.* If the writer uses marginal glosses for definitions in five sections, then starts using marginal glosses as if they were subheadings, make a note. Readers' expectations have been set up—and frustrated.

6. *With its own style and tone.* Beware of extreme gyrations of tone—these often occur when writers write sections at different times under wildly different pressures.

7. *With its own cross references.* Often a writer changes a chapter title but forgets to update the table of contents. Or the guide to the manual still has titles that disappeared two drafts ago.

MAINTAIN YOUR INNOCENCE— AND SYMPATHY

Don't be too doctrinaire. You may have certain rules you always follow when you write. It's tempting to apply them everywhere, even when they don't really apply.

Instead of trying to make the other writer measure up to your ideas, stick to your role as stand-in for the users. Not a writer, a user. "Try to forget everything you know about the computer," says editor Leslie Liedtka. "Read the manual as if it's the first time you've ever read one, so you say, 'Now wait a minute. They're telling me I'm supposed to be using this file, but I didn't even make it yet.'"

That means more than applying a bunch of rules. You may encounter passages that puzzle you, but don't seem to violate any known standards. "You'll be reading along, and something just doesn't sound right," says Liedtka. "Maybe half the times there's something wrong. Don't be afraid of your instincts, though. Follow it through. Raise that red flag. Ask a lot of questions." You don't have to have a solution to raise a question.

COMMUNICATE WITH THE WRITER

As you write your comments, show your sympathy for the poor writer. Remember how you react to expressions like *Terrible!* scratched in the margin. Or, *This part stinks!* That hurts. And it's a rare writer who can overcome the consequent resentment to go on and fix the passage. So be polite in your comments.

Be helpful, too. Provide details that will help somebody to rewrite— exactly what bothered you, which phrase derailed you, what word sounded sour. Make specific suggestions, too, not vast criticisms. You are not grading a paper. You are helping a coworker.

Use your imagination, too. See if you can imagine why a writer is making the same goof over and over. Once you have an idea of the way the writer is operating, you can make suggestions for new ways of thinking. Here, for instance, is the way editor Jon Thompson makes suggestions:

You have a tendency to use the passive voice, and here's an example of it, and here's why I think you may be falling into the passive voice.

Possibly you're thinking more about the product than about the reader, so you tend to say "The disk can be booted by inserting it," as opposed to saying, "You can boot the disk." Once you get consciously thinking about the user, instead of the product, that will help.

Also, keep in mind that it's the writer's manual. Make sure that at least some of your comments show that you believe the writer should have the final word.

Of course, your first read-through will probably produce a lot of marginal comments, crossings-out, attempts at rewriting. Resist the temptation to take that version and hand it back to the writer. It looks too horrible.

Figure out the patterns you've spotted. Take the time to sum up what you like (first!), then your main complaints (linked directly to recommendations). That way, the writer won't feel that everything you say is an attack. The writer will be able to see that all those red marks are really six mistakes multiplied throughout the pages. That takes some of the sting out. And it reassures the writer that six decisions can solve a hundred problems.

So write a cover sheet digesting your work. Here's a tip on the approach you might want to use in that letter. Keep your focus on the manual, not the writer. Editor Roy Rasmussen, who never uses red ink ("I don't think green is quite as upsetting"), suggests:

> Instead of saying something like "You wrote this sentence awkwardly," a better approach would be to say something like, "I think we need to do something to improve this sentence" so that the focus is on the sentence. And if you use *we*, that includes the writer and the reviewer in the task of improving the sentence, rather than putting them against each other.

If you have a chance, talk with the writer in person before returning the marked-up manual. Make your points out loud. That way, they're more likely to be understood when read. Also, you can lessen the shock ("What are all those marks?"), by talking about what you like and showing you have confidence in the writer's ability to make improvements in the draft.

Your suggestions can help the writer improve the accessibility and reliability of the manual. When you see the next draft, you'll see right off that the writer has not taken all of your suggestions. But, if you've done your review with thoroughness and tact, you'll find the next version clearer, stronger, easier to understand. That's your reward.

Of course, then you may well be asked to review the next draft.

A QUICK REVIEW

Here is a reminder of what to do in your review. Make sure that the style is:

☐ Free of jargon.

☐ Not too fast or slow.

☐ Appropriate in tone, without sudden changes.

☐ Active, not passive.

☐ Alive with variety—not monotonous.

Make sure that the organization:

☐ Makes sense.

☐ Accomodates the needs of different users.

☐ Makes clear why one section follows another.

☐ Puts first things first.

☐ Leaves nothing out.

Assure consistency so that:

☐ The manual matches the program. It is accurate.

☐ The manual never violates company standards or the standards of English.

☐ The same term is used for the same object throughout.

☐ The design of each element looks the same throughout.

☐ Similar sections are organized the same way.

☐ Style and tone do not vary from one part to another.

☐ The table of contents matches the actual titles and headings.

And as you write comments for the writer:

☐ Note anything strange, even if you don't know what to do about it.

☐ Be specific.

☐ Show sympathy and respect for the writer.

☐ Sum up what you like and what you recommend.

Softening Up the Software

Keep Track of the Irritations

Do Less, Not More

Help Users Guess

Don't Lead Users Astray

Don't Make Users Feel Stupid

Block Any Jargon

Help Users as They Go

Make All the Menus Look the Same

Group Activities the Way Users Think of Them

Provide Some Examples

Give People a Way Out

Do Some Homework

A Quick Review

Softening Up the Software

Here's a new job of rewriting: softening up the software. A program contains a good deal of language. It has a style of its own and an organization. As a stand-in for users, you can—and should—help revise the program itself, particularly the part users actually see, known as the user interface.

Traditionally, writers took whatever program they were given and wrote about it. When the writing got tangled, they may have cursed the illogical and ugly program they were describing, but few dreamt of asking that the program be reshaped.

More and more, these days, writers are being asked to do just that. Essentially, if you find a program irritating, you should say so—and suggest how it could be made friendlier. Work alongside the programming team to improve the program's social behavior. At the least, teach the program to say "Please" and "Thank you."

As a writer, you're a representative of the people who are going to use the program. So react—then step in to help the programmer make modifications. You can save users a lot of trouble and make your own job of writing the manual a lot simpler.

Bruce Tognazzini, author of *User Interface Guidelines* for the Apple IIe, sums up the aim: "Make the product easy to learn and make it easy to use." But that's not easy to do. He says, "For most programs with a good human interface, the design of that interface consumes more design time, is more prone to bugs, and is harder to test than any other part." That's where your experience as a writer can help.

KEEP TRACK OF THE IRRITATIONS

As you try out early versions of the software, be aware of all the minor irritations. As you work your way through a new program, you might ask yourself questions like these:

- Is what I have to do at each point fairly simple?

- Do I perform the same kind of function in the same way throughout this program?

- Do all menus, commands, help screens, and prompts look alike? Or are there so many variations that I lose track of what they have in common?

- Can I remember the way the program works—or figure it out based on a little experience, without having to look it up in my notes?

- Does the program include enough help for me as a beginner? And if I know all that, does the program let me skip it?

- Does the program help me recall commands, rather than insisting I memorize them all?

- Does the program sometimes make me feel stupid?

- Does the program trick me?

Make notes as you go and talk them over with the programmers. In the rest of this chapter, I will suggest some general principles to consider as you work together to make the program a bit friendlier.

DO LESS, NOT MORE

As you make your way through the program, do you sometimes find you're getting lost in a maze? Are you branching so often you can't find your way back up the tree you came down? Have you forgotten that you are on the fifth level, with no way to jump back to the main menu?

See if there is a way the programmer could combine several screens to reduce the number of menus. Also, think about rewriting the actual options so they're clearer.

HELP USERS GUESS

When users make wrong guesses or typos, does the program slap their hands or crash? Does it tell them that they've just made an error, when in fact it just couldn't find the filename they inadvertently added one letter to?

Perhaps you could talk the programmer into adopting some form of what Tognazzini calls the Disambiguator, so the program "understands" what is meant before users have finished typing:

> On each keystroke, the list of possible words is scanned for a matchup of as many letters have been typed so far. As soon as only one match can be found, the word has been found and can be completed by the program.

That means users don't have to type a lot. (The more they type, the more mistakes they make.)

And if you're feeling very generous, you could persuade the programmers to revamp the program so it makes guesses when people mistype a filename or command. You might create a new error message, too:

```
I'm sorry, I don't recognize that filename, Do you
mean ""LETTERS.TEXT?''
```

DON'T LEAD USERS ASTRAY

If users type in a mistake—letters for numbers, for instance—does the program accept that for the moment, let them go on processing for a few hours, then announce that it can't come to any conclusions, because there's an "Input Error"—leaving it up to the users to discover what it was? Protest to the programmer and write an error message to be included in the program at the moment the mistake is made.

Here are a few errors that shouldn't be errors:

- Lowercase letters for uppercase, or vice versa. Plead with the programmer to accept either one.

- Significant spaces. As Tognazzini tells programmers, "Users look upon a space as a lack of a character, not as a character." Try to persuade the programmer to accept "ABC. TEXT" as if it were "ABC.TEXT."

- Options that aren't available yet. Lobby to leave them off the menu until those functions are actually installed in the program.

If you notice the program makes it easy to destroy a lot of work, plead for a warning message before the program goes ahead. Create a warning, like this: "YOU ARE ABOUT TO DESTROY WORK. If you really want to do this, type 'Yes, I do.'"

DON'T MAKE USERS FEEL STUPID

If users are in the middle of making a mistake, the program should say so—and not in obscure terms like "SOS Error #64" when the manual only lists 16 errors. Volunteer to write a message explaining what has happened and how to correct the problem.

Instead of phrases such as *illegal delimiter*, designed to frighten and shame users, try politeness:

- Apologize for misunderstanding.

- Ask users what they mean.

- Suggest what users can do to correct the problem.

You can write polite messages, like this:

```
I'm sorry, I didn't understand that. What file
do you want to look at?

(Type it in now. For help, press OPEN APPLE-?)
```

BLOCK ANY JARGON

A lot of computerese frightens ordinary folks, but programmers are quite attached to it. So you may have a difficult time explaining to programmers why users do not understand acronyms such as ASCII, CRT, and I/O, even after these clunkers have been used over and over in menus and messages. When you talk to the programmers, suggest equivalents in plain English. Or at least offer to translate the jargon on a help screen.

HELP USERS AS THEY GO

Some programs promise to help the users, but when asked provide only a few skimpy phrases. Sometimes the help messages are not relevant to the task at hand. Sometimes there's too much text, so the real help gets buried.

Changing the help strategy is difficult, because so much of it depends on the willingness of the programmers. If you can, persuade them to slice up the help and make it available where users really need it. This kind of help should be crisp and abbreviated, somewhat like a quick-reference card. For instance, at a minimum, you could let users know all the commands they can use at this point and what those commands do. When they are entering a filename, they may want to know about the conventions required—but they probably don't care about formatting a text file.

Again, if you can talk the programmers into it, create two lines of help—one for beginners, and another (much thinner) for experts. Perhaps the programmers can figure out a way that experienced people can turn off all the help screens at the beginning to speed up processing.

If there's no room in the program for real help, make sure that the prompt lines don't seem to promise it. What little the program does offer should be labeled accurately.

MAKE ALL THE MENUS LOOK THE SAME

Think of all the menus as tables of contents. Variations in format make people wonder if there's some significance in the difference. So you might persuade the programmers to be consistent. Show them how to be consistent by typing all menus in a standard format, with the top part devoted to a title, the middle part for the options, and the bottom part for the prompts, instructions, or error messages:

```
ThoughtFull Program                     MAIN MENU
_____
What you can do:

        1. Open a Thought File to Work on
        2. Combine Two Thought Files
        3. Save a Thought File
        4. Discard a Thought File
        5. Quit the ThoughtFull Program
_____
Type number you want, and press RETURN

        Press ? for Help.
```

In general, number the options. As Tognazzini points out, more than half the people who use computers can't touch-type, so they don't know where the various letters are. Numbers are easier to find and just as easy to recall. Also, numbers don't get confused with the mnemonics for commands. Is it Option E they want, or Option 5—Erasing?

Make sure that the way users select an option is the same on every menu. This is fairly easy for programmers to fix.

When all the menus follow this general design, users will get the idea. Then they won't keep having to learn a new layout each time. They can focus on their work.

GROUP ACTIVITIES THE WAY USERS THINK OF THEM

Think about the order and grouping of options. For instance, on the following menu, why is Deleting a File the first option when Creating a File is the third one? And why when users select Option 2 are they told that before they can use that they have to choose Option 4?

```
GEOGRAPHY FUN              FILE MENU
───────────────────────────────────────────

    1. Deleting a File
    2. Combining Files
    3. Creating a File
    4. Selecting Files to Combine
    5. Renaming a File
    6. Naming a File
    7. Saving a File
───────────────────────────────────────────

Type number of selection, and press RETURN:
```

If people have to do one thing before another, persuade the programmer not to present both on the same screen as if they were equal options.

Similarly, a programmer may consider two subroutines very similar and so group them together. But users don't think of them as similar at all. Tognazzini points out that in a music program:

> Saving created music and loading that music for later playing are highly similar programming tasks and can quite possibly be done using the same basic subroutines. But while it is structurally logical to share code between them, it is intuitively wrong to dump the two options adjacent to each other on a menu. Saving should be grouped with other music-creation options; loading with both creation (for editing) and playing.

In general, fight to keep the order of options similar to the order suggested by common sense.

PROVIDE SOME EXAMPLES

When users are asked to type in the date, do they type all of the following, and get rejected?

- August 6, 1984

- 8.6.84

- 6 AUGUST 84

- August 6 '84

- August the Sixth, Nineteen Eighty-Four

In cases like this, it should be fairly easy to persuade the programmer to let you offer an example—and a form to fill in:

```
Please type in today's date, in this order:
month, day, year. Example: 9/30/83.

__ /   __ /   __ /

Month   Day   Year
```

GIVE PEOPLE A WAY OUT

Have you ever wondered how to get out at the end of the program? The hidden command—the one you needed but couldn't see on the command line—was something like Q for Quit. But you were busy typing E for End or pressing ESCAPE.

ESCAPE should take users back to the previous menu and from minor menus to the main one. ESCAPE should only work within the program. And if pressing ESCAPE means that users are about to exit from one of the main modules (Accounts Receivable on a large general accounting package, for instance), then plead with the programmer to put in a message asking users if they really want to do that, yes or no? As Tognazzini says:

> This will keep the user, who was acting in haste to begin with, from having to wait an extended period of time while you reload the module. (Such a charitable act on your part can extend the life of the keyboard and other fragile items within arm's length of the user.)

But once they're back at the main menu, how do they get out of the program?

On the main menu, make sure the programmers provide some option—a variation on QUIT, or just Q— that lets users stop the whole program. As Tognazzini says, "Users feel positively trapped by programs with seemingly no end; they forget that the power switch solves all."

A QUICK REVIEW

I've just covered some of the most obvious places to look. You'll find that every program has its own problems in the user interface. Spotting these, figuring out how to fix them, and then selling your solutions to the programming team will challenge you. Remember that you're in a unique position to see all parts of the program from a user's point of view. You may be the first to notice inconsistencies, niggling annoyances, and downright goofs. As a member of the team, you can help make the program itself be a little more friendly. And later, when you actually write the manual, you'll find you have an easier time, because you don't have to explain away so many horrors.

Here's a checklist of the ideas I suggest for improving the user interface on the program you're working on. I'm sure you can add to it.

☐ Work with the programmer to make the program easy to learn and easy to use.

☐ Reduce the number of menus and levels.

☐ Help users guess.

☐ Don't lead users astray.

☐ Don't make users feel stupid.

☐ Eliminate jargon.

☐ Provide help along the way.

☐ Make all the menus look the same.

☐ Group activities the way users think of them.

☐ Provide examples.

☐ Help people escape.

Appendixes

A Sample Style Sheet
For Further Reading
Glossary

A Sample Style Sheet

To achieve a consistent style and terminology within a series of manuals, you and your fellow writers will probably develop a series of standards, codified in a style sheet. A style sheet says how to do it—whether you're wondering about capitalizing *operating system* or hyphenating *data base*.

Each time you run into an area of uncertainty (Should I capitalize every letter? Use boldface? Use italics?), talk with the other writers. Try to decide on a common approach.

That common approach should be recorded on your style sheet. In this way, the style sheet grows and gets refined.

You'll probably want to adopt some style manual as the authority, so you don't have to decide common issues of grammar, punctuation, and idiom. You might, for instance, rely on *The Chicago Manual of Style* or *Words Into Type*, plus your favorite dictionary. That leaves you special issues, particular to your company or products, to resolve on your style sheet.

Here is a sample style sheet. Each paragraph indicates a decision made by at least half a dozen writers and editors at Apple. Since these standards grow and change every week, this style sheet's already out of date. It's just an example. You'll grow your own.

accessory card   Use *peripheral card* for general references. See *peripheral card*, *controller card*, and *interface card*.

accessory slot   Use *expansion slot*.

acronym   Always say what it stands for when you first use it. When forming the plural of an acronym without periods, do not add an apostrophe before the *s*. See *ANSI, ASCII, BASIC, EBCDIC, IEEE, ISO*.

addresses   Abbreviate *avenue* (Ave.), *building* (Bldg.), *block* (Blk.), *boulevard* (Blvd.), *place* (Pl.), *square* (Sq.), and *street* (St.) in specific references. Use U.S. Postal Service abbreviations for states (no periods). Separate state and zip code with two spaces. For example:

The Book Co.
15720 Hawthorne Blvd.
Lawndale, CA 90260

address, memory   See *memory address.*

affect, effect   *Affect*, as a verb, means to influence. *Affect*, as a noun, is best avoided. (It is occasionally used to describe an emotion.) *Effect* as a verb is rarely used and means to cause. *Effect* as a noun is more common and means result.

afterward   Not *afterwards.*

allow   See *enable.*

all right   Not *alright.*

alphabetic   Not *alphabetical.*

ANSI   Acronym for *American National Standards Institute.* An industry standards organization.

any time   Not *anytime.*

appendixes   Not *appendices.*

application software   Not *applications software.* Applies the system's resources and capabilities to perform a particular task, such as text processing or data base management.

arrow keys   Do not capitalize *arrow* in general references.

articles   Do not use in references to keys when the manual uses keycaps ("press CONTROL," not "press the CONTROL key"). Always use articles when referring to disks: *the disk, a disk.*

ASCII   Acronym for *American Standard Code for Information Interchange.* Use acronym only after first reference.

as, like   *As* is a conjunction and should be used to introduce clauses. *Like* is a preposition and requires an object. It is also correct to use *like* as a conjunction if it is followed by a word that may be regarded as a simile.

assembly language (n.) *assembly-language* (adj.)   Not *assembler language.*

auto-repeat   Note hyphenation.

back panel   Not *backplane.*

backplane   Use *back panel.*

backspace (n., v., and adj.)

backspace key   Use DELETE.

backup (n., adj.) *back up* (v.)

backward   Not *backwards.*

ball-point pen   Note hyphenation. Hyphenate same as *felt-tip pen*.

BASIC   A computer language. Acronym for *Beginners All-purpose Symbolic Instruction Code*. (No apostrophe.)

baud   Not necessarily the same as *bits per second*.

because   Preferred to *since* when expressing a cause-and-effect relationship.

bitmap   Refers to correspondence between bits in memory and dots on the display. See *dot matrix, raster*.

black-and-white (adj.)   Note hyphenation.

blank, blank character   Use *space character*. Acceptable to use *space* for subsequent references.

blinking cursor   Preferred to *flashing cursor*. Acceptable to use *flashing* to describe the display after using the FLASH command.

board   A built-in part of the computer. See *card*.

boldface   Use for computer jargon, tags in boxes, glossary terms, figures and tables, sometimes for lead-in to paragraphs. See *italics*.

Boolean logic   Note capitalization. Capitalize same as *Boolean algebra*. Named after George Boole.

boot   Use *start up*.

braces   Not *curly brackets*. *Curly brackets* might be used to define *braces* when the term is first used.

built-in (adj.)   Note hyphenation. When used in a callout, caption, or title, do not capitalize *in*: Built-in.

built-in disk drive   Use instead of *internal disk drive*.

buttons on the hand control or *hand-control buttons*   Not *paddle buttons*.

callouts   Capitalize same as titles and captions. Use a period at the end of all callouts for a figure if any of the callouts are complete sentences or long phrases. See *capitalization*.

can, may   Use *can* to express ability, power, and so on. Use *may* to express permission or possibility.

cancel   Unconditional, permanent halt that carries connotation of undoing something. Can use *cancel* instead of *halt* to avoid awkwardness. See *halt, suspend, stop*.

canceling, canceled   Not *cancelling, cancelled*.

capitalization   Use the following rules to capitalize titles, captions, and callouts:

- Capitalize the first and last word.
- Usually capitalize the second word in hyphenated compounds: *High-Resolution Graphics*, not *High-resolution Graphics*. Exception: *Built-in Disk Drive*.
- Capitalize prepositions of. four letters or more: *About, With, From, Between*.
- Don't capitalize coordinating conjunctions: *and, but, or, for, nor, yet, so*; or articles: *a, an*, and *the*.
- Don't capitalize *to* in infinitives.

captions   Capitalize same as titles and callouts. Use a period at the end of a figure or table title when more information follows the title. See *capitalization*.

card   Removable accessory that plugs into an expansion slot. See *board, controller card, interface card*, and *peripheral card*.

card names   Capitalize name including *card*. Do not capitalize when used generically as in *80-column card*.

caret   Use to describe this character: ^. Not *circumflex*.

catalog   Preferred to *directory*, except in Pascal references.

central memory   Use *main memory*, as distinct from *peripheral memory*.

central processor   Meaningful only in contrast with *peripheral processor*. Never *the unit* or *CPU*.

chapter   Capitalize in specific references: Chapter 8, Chapters 4 and 5.

character   Use to refer to what the keys on the computer's keyboard stand for. There are 128 characters in the ASCII alphabet. See *symbol*.

chip   Don't use without first introducing *integrated circuit* and *silicon chip*.

circumflex   Don't use to describe this character: ^. Use *caret*.

code file   Two words.

cold start (n., v.) *cold-start* (adj.)   Never *coldstart*.

column   Not *character position*. (The Apple IIe text display consists of 24 rows and 40 (or 80) columns of characters.)

command   Something you type to make something happen immediately. See *instruction, statement*.

command names   Use initial caps for names of application program commands, but do not capitalize *command*: the Find command, the Execute command (not eXecute command), the Save command, the Verify command. See *key word.*

communications   Acceptable to use plural, especially when referring to a system.

company   Abbreviate or spell out according to company's preference. Same as for *corporation* and *incorporated.* Examples: Software Publishing Corporation, Peachtree Software Incorporated, Apple Computer, Inc.

computer   The physical thing (what's inside and part of the case, including keyboard). See *system.*

computer voice   A special monospaced font used only for: what is seen on the display, program listings, and what users type. Zeros in computer voice should have slashes. Use backslashes to indicate this in manuscript. See *keycaps.*

connector   Be more specific.

   plug: connector with prongs or pins

   socket: connector with holes

   slot: long, skinny holes on main board

   edge connector: corresponding connector on peripheral card

   jack: small, round one-pin socket

Never use *male* or *female* in reference to types of connectors.

console, CRT   Don't use when you mean *video monitor.*

constant   Sequence of characters that stands for a particular, unchangeable value.

CONTROL   The key. Not CTRL. (Applies to Apple IIe and Apple III.) Word *key* unnecessary in manuals that use keycaps. Can also use *control* in general sense: control characters.

control-character (adj.)   Note hyphenation. For example: control-character commands.

controller card   A type of peripheral card that drives or controls a peripheral device. More specific: *disk controller card, printer controller card.*

controlling   Not *controling.*

coprocessor   Not hyphenated.

copy-protected (adj.)   Note hyphenation. Do not hyphenate when used as a verb or predicate adjective: The disk is copy protected. See *write-protected.*

corporation Abbreviate or spell out according to company's preference. Same as for *company* and *incorporated.*

CP/M *Control Program for Microcomputers.* An operating system.

CPU Use *central processor.*

curly brackets Use *braces.*

cutout One word. A hole in the back panel of the computer. Also used to describe the oval hole in disks (but not the write-enable notch).

dark-on-light Note hyphenation.

dashes Use two hyphens to indicate dashes in manuscript—with no spaces around them.

data A plural noun, which must take a plural verb. Try to avoid in favor of *information.*

data base (n., adj.) Always two words.

data file Two words.

DB-9 connector Try to use *9-pin connector* (same for *DB-11* and *DB-25*), especially in tutorials and user manuals. *DB-9 connector* acceptable in more technical manuals. However, if you use *DB*, explain that the connector is shaped like a *D.*

dealer Preferred to *dealership.*

default Try to avoid the verb and noun. It is less objectionable when used as an adjective. Explain carefully with first use.

DEL character Not *DELETE character* or *rubout character.*

DELETE The key. Not *DEL key* or *backspace key.* Word *key* unnecessary in manuals that use keycaps.

desktop (adj.) Not *desk top.*

device name Two words. See *filename, volume name.*

different from Not *different than.*

differently than Not *different than* or *differently from.*

directory Avoid in favor of *catalog*, except in Pascal references.

disk Not *diskette.* Always use article: *the disk, a disk.* Never use as a short form for *disk drive. System disk* preferred to *program disk.*

disk drive Good generic term for referring to drives. Unless there is a particular reason for being specific, use *disk drive.* When mentioning particular device, do not capitalize *disk drive: disk drive 1.* See *built-in disk drive.*

diskette   Obsolete term. Use *disk.*

disk names   Usually follow what the label says and italicize. Do not use quotation marks or capitalize *disk.* Continue to use all caps for disks that do not have new labels, which are uppercase and lowercase.

Disk Operating System   Capitalized in specific references to *DOS.* Lowercase in generic references.

Disk II drive   Use for first reference when you mean that specific model. Otherwise use *disk drive.*

display   What appears on the screen.

display device   Device connected to the computer for displaying text or graphics. More specific: *video monitor* or *television set.*

display pages   Capitalize *page* to distinguish from memory pages: high-resolution graphics Page 1, text Page 2. See *page.*

display screen or *the screen*   Where text or graphics appear.

DOS-formatted (adj.)   Note hyphenation. For example: DOS-formatted disk.

dot matrix   An array of dots. Usually refers to a method of forming characters on a printer or display device. See *bitmap, raster.*

double check (n.), *double-check* (v.), *double-checking*   Note hyphenation.

DOWN-ARROW   Note capitalization and hyphenation. Replaced with an icon and keycapped when typeset. Word *key* unnecessary. When referring to more than one of the arrow keys, *arrow* is not capitalized. In manuals that do not use keycaps, use *Down-Arrow key.*

drive   Use *disk drive* except in passages where it becomes cumbersome.

due to, due to the fact that   Use *because of* and *because.*

EBCDIC   Acronym for *Extended Binary-Coded-Decimal Interchange Code.* Don't use acronym without explaining what it stands for.

effect, affect   *Affect,* as a verb, means to influence. *Affect,* as a noun, is best avoided. (It is occasionally used to describe an emotion.) *Effect* as a verb is rarely used and means to cause. *Effect* as a noun is more common and means result.

e.g.   Use *for example.*

electromagnetic interference   Note spelling. Also known as *EMI.* Don't use acronym without explaining what it stands for.

embed   Not *imbed.*

enable   Avoid in favor of *turn on* or *allow*. *Enable* is acceptable in references to circuitry. Hardware enables; programs allow.

ensure, insure   Use *ensure* to mean guarantee. Use *insure* for references to insurance.

enter   Don't use when you mean *type* or *press*. *Enter* is appropriate when referring to data. You enter data, type words and characters, and press keys. Also acceptable to say, "Now the computer wants you to enter some information." See *press, type*.

entitled   Use *titled*.

envelope   Not *sleeve*. The paper holder for the disk in its black jacket. See *jacket*.

equal sign   Not *equal's sign* or *equals sign*.

ESC @, ESC E, ESC F   No hyphen because you don't have to hold down the ESC key while pressing the second key. In manuals using keycaps and computer voice, ESC is keycapped and the following key is set in computer voice. See *keys*.

etc.   Use *and others* or *and so forth*.

expansion slot   Not *peripheral slot* or *accessory slot*. Can also use *slot* without qualifier. Lowercase even in specific references: slot 1, slot 6.

fanfold paper   Note spelling.

felt-tip pen   Note hyphenation. Hyphenate same as *ball-point pen*.

female connector   Use *socket*.

fewer, less   *Fewer* is used with individual items; *less* with quantity or bulk: Fewer hedgehogs require less food.

figures and tables   All figures and tables should have titles and be referred to in the text. See *captions*.

file   Use only to refer to a collection of information stored as a named unit on a disk or other storage device. In references to a file, think of it as a file folder that holds information. You save the contents of memory *in a file on a disk*. What is in memory is a program, picture, document, worksheet, or model.

filename   One word. In specific references, use all caps to agree with catalog and directory listings: Name the file PAPERDOC; Run the Utilities program UTIL.CODE by pressing X and typing UTIL. See *volume name*.

file types   Two words: text file, code file, data file, destination file, SOS file, source file, work file.

finish   People finish; *things* are done. For example: I will take a nap when I finish working. The machine is done collating the copies. It is incorrect to say "when you are *done* transferring files . . ."

firmware   Software that resides in read-only memory. See *software*.

flashing cursor   Use *blinking cursor*. Acceptable to use *flashing* to describe the display after using the FLASH command.

flexible disk   Use to introduce *floppy disk*. Never use *floppy* as a noun. Acceptable to mention popular term *floppy* when introducing *flexible disk*: a flexible, or floppy, disk is used to store information. See *rigid disk*.

floppy, floppy disk   See *flexible disk*.

following (adj., n., v.)   Not a preposition—use *after*.

   Correct: The meaning of the record variable reference is determined once, before the statement *after* DO is executed.

   Incorrect: The meaning of the record variable reference is determined once, before the statement *following* DO is executed.

game controller   Use *hand control*.

GAME I/O connector   The connector on the main board. Note capitalization. See *hand-control connector*.

game paddle   Use *hand control*.

graphic (adj.)   Preferred to *graphical*, although there may be times when a distinction can be made.

gray   The color. Not *grey*, except in *greyhound*.

green-phosphor screen   Note hyphenation.

grey   Use *gray*.

grounded outlet   Not *grounding-type outlet*.

halt   To stop a process unconditionally without the possibility of later resumption. Can use *cancel* instead of *halt* to avoid awkwardness. See *cancel, halt, suspend*.

hand control   Not *hand controller, game controller,* or *game paddle*.

hand-control buttons or *buttons on the hand control*   Not *paddle buttons*.

hand-control connector   Not *game connector*.   The connector on the back panel. See *GAME I/O connector* (the one on the inside).

hand controller   Use *hand control*.

hard disk   Use *rigid disk*.

hex   Use *hexadecimal* for first reference. *Hex* acceptable for subsequent references.

hexadecimal   Use short form *hex* only after first reference.

hexagonal-head screw   Preferred to *hex-head screw*. Note hyphenation (same as *Phillips-head screw*).

hex-head screw   Use *hexagonal-head screw*. Note hyphenation (same as *Phillips-head screw*).

high bit   *high-bit* (adj.) not *hi-bit*.

highlighted, inverted   *Highlighted* is acceptable in this sense: The default value is highlighted. Use *displayed in inverse* instead of *inverted*.

high resolution (n.), *high-resolution* (adj.)   Not *hi-res* or *high-res*. Note hyphenation.

hyphenation   The general rule for hyphenation is that when two words modify a noun as a unit and not as two individual modifiers, a hyphen joins those two words. We follow this rule when:
- Confusion might result if the hyphen were omitted (read-only memory, machine-language program, rigid-disk drive).
- One of the words is a past or present participle (free-moving graphics, DOS-formatted disk).
- The two modifiers are a number or single letter and a noun (80-column text card, D-shaped connector).

Notable exceptions: *word processing* and *data base* are never hyphenated.

Also, do not hyphenate two words when one is *very* or an adverb that ends in *ly*: newly completed bridge, very good time. See specific compound in style sheet.

ICs   See *plurals*.

identifier   Sequence of character that can be used as the name of something and is constructed according to definite rules. An identifier that refers to a variable is the *name* of the variable. One that refers to a statement in a program is a *label*.

i.e.   Use *that is*.

IEEE   Acronym for *Institute of Electrical and Electronics Engineers*. An industry standards organization.

imbed   The preferred spelling is *embed*.

incorporated   Abbreviate or spell out according to company's preference. Same as for *company* and *corporation*.

indexes   Not *indices*.

information   Better than *data*. See *text*.

in order to   Rarely necessary. Better just to use *to*.

input (n., adj.)   Never use as a verb. Use *enter* or *type*.

instruction   Part of a machine-language or assembly-language program that is executed directly by the processor. See *command, statement*.

insure, ensure   Use *ensure* to mean guarantee. Use *insure* for references to insurance.

interface card   A type of peripheral card that implements a generalized interface to other devices. More specific: *serial interface card, parallel interface card*.

internal disk drive   Use *built-in disk drive*.

interrupt   A running program can be interrupted only at the hardware level.

inverse, displayed in   Not inverted. Can also use *light-on-dark* or *dark-on-light*, which are always hyphenated.

invoke   Use *call* or *load*.

ISO   Acronym for *International Standards Organization*. An industry standards group.

italics   Use for explicit references to other manuals; words as words, letters as letters, phrases as phrases; and emphasis. Italics also should be used after *stands for* and *labeled* to avoid problems with punctuation and quotation marks. For example: INIT, which stands for *initialize*, is used . . .; See the column in the directory labeled *EOF* . . . . See *quotation marks*.

jacket   The black cover that holds a flexible disk. See *envelope*.

keycaps   Used for function keys (ESC, ESCAPE, DELETE, CONTROL, SHIFT, RETURN, RESET, ALPHA LOCK, CAPS LOCK, ENTER, SPACE) and for single keys in combination keystrokes (when joined by hyphen). See *keys, computer voice*.

keypress   One word.

keys   Use all uppercase letters for labels. Use keycaps for function keys (ESCAPE, DELETE, CONTROL, SHIFT, RETURN, RESET, ALPHA LOCK, CAPS LOCK, ENTER, SPACE) when typeset. In combination keystrokes, hyphens signify that the keys should be pressed simultaneously:

   CONTROL-SHIFT-N   (all three keys pressed simultaneously)

   ESC N   (not simultaneous)

Continued

Use *type* for those keys representing printable characters. Use *press* for nonprinting keys as well as buttons on hand controls and combination keystrokes.

Use keycaps for each key in simultaneous keystrokes—even single characters. Word *key* unnecessary in manuals using keycaps.

keystroke   One word.

key word   A word that identifies a particular type of statement or command, such as IF or CATALOG. Follow capitalization of programming language.

kilobyte   1024 bytes, or two to the tenth power. Use K only after introducing kilobyte.

label   See *identifier*.

labeled   Not *labelled*.

lay, lie   The transitive verb is *lay*. It takes a direct object. *Lie* means to recline. It does not take a direct object. The difference between *lay* and *lie* is the same as the difference between *set* and *sit*.

Present	Past	Present Participle	Past Participle
lay	laid	laying	laid
lie	lay	lying	lain

When *lie* means to make an untrue statement, the verb forms are *lie, lied, lying, lied*.

LEFT-ARROW   The key. Replaced with an icon and keycapped when typeset. Word *key* unnecessary. When referring to more than one of the arrow keys, *arrow* is not capitalized. In manuals that do not use keycaps, use *Left-Arrow key*.

less, fewer   *Fewer* is used with individual items; *less* with quantity or bulk: Fewer hedgehogs require less food.

letters as letters   Letters are italicized when they are particularly referred to: the *i*'s and *o*'s, the *n*th power. See *italics, plurals*.

light bulb   Two words.

like, as   *As* is a conjunction and should be used to introduce clauses. *Like* is a preposition and requires an object. It is also correct to use *like* as a conjunction if it is followed by a word that may be regarded as a simile.

light-on-dark   Note hyphenation.

line   Not necessarily the same as *statement*. One line may contain several statements or one statement may extend across several lines. See *statement*.

line feed   Two words.

line numbers   Don't capitalize *line* or use comma in numbers of five digits or more: line 50 and line 43567.

lists   Use numbered lists for sequential steps or when you want to show a hierarchical relationship. Numbered lists should be introduced with a main clause followed by a colon. The first word of each item should be capitalized, and each item should have ending punctuation. Bulleted lists generally fall into three categories. The following examples show the most common lists and how to punctuate and capitalize each one:

Unbroken Syntax—No Colon; Final Punctuation Ends List
(Normal sentence broken into a list to emphasize the parts of a series.)

The parts of a computer system are

- a computer
- a display device
- one or more disk drives.

Typical List—Main Clause Followed by Colon; No Item Punctuation

You can do any of the following word processing tasks quickly and easily:

- editing
- printing
- writing

Complex List 1—Main Clause Followed by Colon; Item Punctuation
(If any one of the items is a complete sentence, then the first word of each item should be capitalized and the item should end with a period.)

Here are just a few of the things macros do for you:

- They save you the trouble of changing your margin settings every time you want to type a list or other indented material.
- They provide you with automatic headings, which display the chapter number and title, the current main heading, and the page number.
- They eliminate the need to count the blank lines between one element and another—not to mention the need to remember how many blank lines there were supposed to be.
- They act as visible markers in your document, so you can jump to the next head or marginal gloss directly, even if you don't remember what it contains.

Complex List 2—No Colon; Item Punctuation
(Complex sentence broken into a list. If any of the items is a clause—that is, a group of words that contains a subject and a verb—then the first word of each item should be capitalized and each should end with a semicolon, except the final item, which should end with a period.)

Continued

For each of the macro commands described here you'll see

- What the command looks like and an example of how it should appear in your text file;
- What the command tells the system to do;
- What the sample passage will look like when you use the command to print it out;
- What the same passage will look like when set in type.

lock   See *protect.*

Logo   Not *LOGO.*

low bit   *low-bit* (adj.) not *lo bit.*

lowercase (n., adj.)   Not *lower-case* or *lower case. Uppercase and lowercase characters* preferred to *upper- and lowercase characters.*

low resolution (n.), *low-resolution* (adj.)   Not *lo-res* or *low-res.* Note hyphenation.

machine language (n.), *machine-language* (adj.)   Note hyphenation.

main logic board   Not *motherboard* or *main circuit board.* Can also use *main board.*

main memory   As distinct from *peripheral memory.* Don't use *central memory* or *CPU.*

male connector   Use *plug.*

mass storage device   Acceptable to use in reference to rigid-disk drive. Do not use to refer to 5¼-inch flexible-disk drive.

may, can   Use *may* to express permission or possibility. Use *can* to express ability, power, and so on.

memory address, memory location   For clarity. Can use just *address* and *location* for brevity. Never *memory cell, cell.* Main memory is a collection of locations. Each location can hold one byte and is identified by address. The location contains the information. Zeros in addresses do not have slashes unless set in computer voice.

memory pages   Do not capitalize *page* and spell out numeral to distinguish from display pages: zero page, page one. See *page.*

mode   A state of the system that determines the system's response to users' actions. Avoid when not absolutely necessary. *High-resolution graphics* preferred to *high-resolution graphics mode.* You enter or leave a mode, not turn on or turn off a mode.

modem eliminator   A type of cable or connector used to correct incompatibilities between devices.

monitor   Acceptable to use for *video monitor* only after first reference.

monitor cable   Use *video cable.*

Monitor program   Note capitalization to distiguish from *video monitor.*

motherboard   Use *main logic board.*

name   See *identifier.*

name plate   Not *nameplate.*

9-pin connector, 11-pin connector, 25-pin connector   Preferred to *DB-9, DB-11,* or *DB-25.* Good idea to mention connector's distinguishing characteristics: 20-pin, D-shaped connector (note hyphenation). See *connector, DB-9.*

non- (prefix)   Usually not hyphenated: noncomputer, nongraphic, and nonprinting; but non-alphabetic, non-null, and non-editing, because they look terrible without hyphens. For *non-write-protected* it is better to say *not write-protected.* And *non-certified* is what we get from Legal.

null character   ($00). Not *zero character.*

number sign   Preferred to *pound sign* when referring to #.

numbers   In general, spell out zero through ten. But use a numeral when referring to a specific disk drive, key, slot, track, sector, address, byte, or when expressing amounts of memory. Spell out numbers at the beginning of a sentence or when expressing an approximation. When using small and large numbers in the same sentence, use numerals for consistency. Use a comma in numbers of five digits or more. Exception: program line numbers, which never take commas. For example: 1024 and 65,536; but line 4567 and line 43567. In reference to numbers, *larger* and *smaller* are preferred to *higher* and *lower.*

numeric (adj.)   Not *numerical.*

off-line (adj.)   Note hyphenation.

OK   Not *okay* or *O.K.* Try to avoid.

on-line (adj.)   Note hyphenation.

opening display   Preferred to *startup display, splash screen.*

operating system   Not capitalized when used generically.

output (n., adj.)   Never use as a verb. Instead use *write (to), display (on), print (on).*

paddle buttons   Use *buttons on the hand control* or *hand-control buttons.*

page   A unit of contiguous bytes of memory on an even address boundary. Memory pages come in 256-byte chunks. Display pages come in two sizes: 1024 bytes for low-resolution graphics and text and 8192 bytes for high-resolution graphics. See *page one*.

page one, zero page, Page 1, Page 2   The first two are *memory pages*, the second two are *display pages*. See *memory pages, display pages*.

P.A.L.   Acronym for *Phased Alternate Lines*, the European color standard. Use periods to distinguish from *PAL unit*.

parentheses (plural), *parenthesis* (sing.)

parts, volumes   Use Arabic numerals for volumes: Volume 1, Volume 2. Use Roman numerals for parts: Part I, Part II. A part indicates a difference in subject matter and thus takes a subtitle. In specific references, the subtitle is italicized.

A volume is necessitated by page length and does not take a subtitle. In specific references, *Volume* is not italicized. A colon should be used to separate the title from the subtitle when you reference both of them. An em dash should be used to separate Part I from the subtitle. Please remember this publishing standard for future manuals.

Pascal   Note capitalization.

pathname   One word.

P-code   Note capitalization and hyphenation. See *P-machine*.

peripheral card   Use instead of *accessory card*. More specific: *controller card, interface card*. Never *peripheral* (n.).

peripheral device   Or *accessory*. Never *peripheral* (n.).

peripheral slot   Use *expansion slot*.

Phillips-head screw   Note hyphenation. Hyphenate same as *hexagonal-head screw*.

Phillips-head screwdriver   Note hyphenation and spelling.

plug   Not *male connector*. See *connector*.

plurals   When forming the plural of an acronym without periods, do not add an apostrophe before the *s*. This is not the same as forming the plural of a letter, figure, character, or symbol. For example: ICs, RAMs, ROMs; but *p*'s, 6's, 1980's, +'s.

P-machine   Note capitalization and hyphenation. Stands for *pseudo-machine*. The P-machine is a software generated device that executes P-code as its machine language.

pound sterling sign   Use to refer to this symbol: £.

power cable   Use *power cord.*

power-on light   Note hyphenation.

press   Especially appropriate when what users type does not appear on the display. For example: Press CONTROL-Q and then J to quit. See *enter, type.*

print head   Two words.

print wheel   Two words.

printout   Not *print out.*

procedure   A routine that can be activated (or called) from any point in a program and that returns control to the point of call upon completion.

processor   A component of the computer. For instance, the *6502.* See *central processor.*

product names   Capitalize, no quotation marks. For example: Graphics Tablet, Quick File, RPS, Apple Writer.

program   Single, self-contained piece of software. You exit from a program; you do not quit a program, exit a program, or leave a program. (But you can use *quit* in the sense of stopping what you are doing.)

program disk   Use *system disk.*

program listings   Set in computer voice. Any zeros in program listings should have slashes.

program names   Do not use computer voice. Use all caps to agree with catalog (directory) listing. Not to be confused with the product name. For example: The Quick File program is named SYSTEM.STARTUP. See *product names, program listings.*

prompt (adj.)   Try to avoid. Reference to *the prompt character* (]) is occasionally necessary.

prompt (n.)   A reminder.

prompt (v.)   Acceptable to use: The system is *prompting* you for information.

protect   Preferred to *lock.* You remove protection, not unlock or unprotect. You may have to mention *lock/unlock* to agree with software.

quotation marks   Periods and commas go within quotation marks. If necessary for clarity, periods and commas can go outside: AN$ = "1". Semicolons and colons usually go outside quotation marks. A quote is what someone has said. So it's *quotation marks,* not *quote marks.*

Continued

Because we use italics, quotation marks are rarely necessary. Use them for cross references to other sections of manual and direct quotations. Do not use after *called, so-called, known as,* or *termed.* See *italics.*

radio-frequency (RF) modulator Note hyphenation. Use *RF modulator* only after first reference.

random-access memory Note hyphenation. Use *RAM* only after first reference.

raster Use restrictively for a display made up of parallel lines. See *bit-map, dot matrix.*

re- (prefix) Usually no hyphen, even when it creates a double vowel, as in *reenter.*

read-only memory Note hyphenation. Use *ROM* only after first reference.

RESET The key. Use in reference to Apple IIe (word *key* unnecessary). Use *RESET button* in Apple III references. In both instances, use keycaps for *RESET.*

RIGHT-ARROW The key. Replaced with icon and keycapped when typeset. Word *key* unnecessary. When referring to more than one of the arrow keys, *arrow* is not capitalized. In manuals that do not use keycaps, use *Right-Arrow key.*

right-side (adj.) Note hyphenation. Also, *right-side up.*

rigid disk Not *hard disk.* See *mass storage device.*

routine Portion of a program that accomplishes some specific task.

sector-size (adj.), sector size (n.)

SHIFT Not *shift key.* Word *key* unnecessary in manuals that use keycaps.

signaled, signaling Not *signalled, signalling.*

silicon chip Don't use without first introducing *integrated circuit. Chip* acceptable for casual references thereafter.

since Use *because* when expressing a cause and effect relationship. Reserve *since* for reference to time.

single letters Italicize a letter when it is used as a letter. Use *'s* to form plural: *l*'s, *p*'s and *q*'s.

slashes Slash zeros in the computer voice font to agree with the display.

sleeve Use *envelope.* See *envelope, jacket.*

slot 6 Not capitalized. Same as *drive 1, sector 15, line 5.*

so-called (adj.)   Note hyphenation.

socket   Not *female connector*. See *connector*.

software   A generic term for all programs. See *firmware*.

SPACE bar   Not *space bar* or *spacebar*. Use keycaps for SPACE when typeset.

space character   Not *blank* or *blank character*. Acceptable to use *space* for subsequent references.

splash screen   Use *opening display*.

spreadsheet   Not *spread sheet*.

start up (v.), *startup* (adj.) Not *boot*.

statement   A unit of a program in a high-level language specifying an action for the computer to perform, typically corresponding to several instructions of machine language. See *command, instruction, line*.

step   Don't capitalize even in specific references: step 1, steps 1 and 2.

stop   A general term meaning to cause a process (command, program) to cease. See *suspend, cancel, halt*.

subroutine   Procedure that performs some task without returning a value.

SuperPILOT   Note capitalization. Programmed Inquiry, Learning, Or Teaching. A language designed so that teachers can create computer lessons without learning all the details of a full-fledged programming language.

suspend   To stop a process in such a way that it can later be resumed at the point of suspension. See *stop, cancel, halt*.

symbol   Don't use to mean character, letter, or digit. You don't type a symbol. You can use *symbol* in generic sense: the dollar sign symbol ($). See *character*.

system   Broad term that includes peripheral devices or accessories (including software). See *computer*.

system disk   Preferred to *program disk*.

system software   Not *systems software*. Provides access to basic resources and capabilities of the system—includes operating systems, device drivers, and language processors (interpreters and compilers).

tables of contents   There are two kinds of TOC: the main one at the beginning of a manual, and another at the beginning of a chapter, including all levels of headings.

telecommunications   Takes a singular verb.

television set   Not *television receiver, television,* or *TV.* A display device. *TV set* acceptable for subsequent references. See *video monitor.*

text   Use only to refer to information represented in the form of ASCII-coded or EBCDIC-coded characters.

text file   Two words.

that, which   *That* is used to introduce a restrictive clause (a group of words that restricts a general subject to a more specific one). *Which* is used to introduce a nonrestrictive clause (a group of words that provides additional information, which is often descriptive, but if removed from the sentence does not alter the meaning of the sentence). The rule of thumb is that when a comma can be inserted, the word is *which.*

this   Avoid using to refer to general ideas. Replace with a specific phrase.

titled   Not *entitled.*

titles   Keep titles of chapters and sections short and be descriptive. Try to avoid computer voice and keycaps. See *capitalization, computer voice, keycaps.*

tool kit   Not *toolkit.*

toward   Not *towards.*

trial and error   Takes singular verb.

troubleshooting (n.) *troubleshoot* (v.)   One word.

type   Use when what users type will appear on the display. Use *press* for instructions about keys and combination keystrokes. For example: Press RESET and press CONTROL-S. Not type RESET or type CONTROL-S. See *enter, press.*

UP-ARROW   The key. Replaced with an icon and keycapped when typeset. Word *key* unnecessary. When referring to more than one of the arrow keys, *arrow* is not capitalized. In manuals that do not use keycaps, use *Up-Arrow key.*

uppercase (n., adj.)   Not *upper case* or *upper-case. Uppercase and lowercase characters* preferred to *upper- and lowercase characters.*

upper-left corner   Not *upper left-hand corner.* Use to indicate the home position.

users group   No apostrophe.

variable   Place where a value can be stored. The value it contains is its *contents.*

versus   Not *vs.*

video cable   Not *video cord* or *monitor cable*.

video connector   Use *video jack*.

video jack   Not *video connector*.

video monitor   Not *television monitor* or *TV monitor*. A display device. Acceptable to use *monitor* after the first reference. See *television set*.

video switch   A switch on the international Apple IIe that alternates between black-and-white and color.

viewport   One word.

volumes, parts   See *parts, volumes*.

volume name   Two words. May use as one word in syntax references to avoid confusion. In specific references, use all caps to agree with directory listings: The volume named PERSONNEL. See *filename*.

warm start (n.), *warm-start* (adj.)   Never *warmstart*.

which, that   See *that, which*.

whir   Not *whirr*. But *whirring*.

words as words   When a word is used not to represent the thing or idea it usually represents, but merely the word itself, it should be italicized. Also, italics or boldface should be used after *term* or *word* when a definition is being given.

work file   Two words.

wraparound (n., adj.) *wrap around* (v.)

write-enable notch   Not *write-protect notch*. Note hyphenation.

write-protected (adj.) Note hyphenation. Do not hyphenate when used as a verb or predicate adjective: A write-protect tab is used to write protect a disk. See *copy-protected*.

write-protect tab   Note hyphenation.

zero character   Use *null character* ($00), unless you're really writing about the zero character (ASCII $30).

zero page   See *page one*.

zeros   Not *zeroes*. Slash only those zeros set in computer voice.

Zip code   Note capitalization.

For Further Reading

Here are some books I think provide good reading for any technical writer. No, they're not manuals. You will probably read enough of those during the day. These books will help you form your style, tighten your organization, and brighten your mind.

Auden, W. H. *The Dyer's Hand.* 1962.
Barthelme, Donald. *City Life.* 1970.
Buddha. *The Diamond Sutra.* Translated by A. F. Price and Wong Mou-Lam. 1969.
Colette. *My Apprenticeships.* Translated by Helen Beauclerk. 1957.
Cummings, e. e. *I, or Six Non-Lectures.* 1962.
De Bono, Edward. *Future Positive.* 1979.
Freud, Sigmund. *The Interpretation of Dreams.* Translated by A. A. Brill. 1913.
Hall, Edward T. *The Hidden Dimension.* 1966.
Hemingway, Ernest. *The Moveable Feast.* 1964.
James, William. *The Varieties of Religious Experience.* 1902.
Maugham, W. Somerset. *The Summing Up.* 1963.
Montherlant, Henry de. *Selected Essays.* Translated by John Weightman. 1961.
Morris, Wright. *Ceremony in Lone Tree.* 1960.
Neng, Hui. *Sutra.* Translated by A. F. Price and Wong Mou-Lam. 1969.
Pound, Ezra. *ABC of Reading.* 1934.
Sandburg, Carl. *Abraham Lincoln.* 1939.
Schrank, Robert. *Ten Thousand Working Days.* 1978.
Shah, Idries. *Learning How to Learn.* 1978.
Skillin, Marjorie, and Robert Gay. *Words Into Type.* 1974.
Strunk, William, Jr., and E. B. White. *The Elements of Style.* 1959.
Thoreau, Henry David. *A Plea for Captain John Brown.* 1859.
    Walden. 1854.
Thurber, James. *Alarms and Diversions.* 1957.
Twain, Mark. *Roughing It.* 1872.
Tzu, Lao. *Tao Te Ching.* Translated by D. C. Lau. 1963.
University of Chicago Press. *The Chicago Manual of Style.* 1982.
Williams, William Carlos. *The Autobiography.* 1951.

Glossary

This glossary covers only technical writing terms. For other computer terms, please consult a dictionary or encyclopedia.

Access   Ability to get to a topic. Some manuals make it easy to find a subject, no matter how obscure. They have tables of contents, a glossary, an index, a guide to the manual.

Accuracy   Precision in your descriptions of the program. What users expect, but rarely get.

Active Verbs   Verbs that describe an action—not a state of being. (Leave that to the passive.) Active verbs make your writing clearer.

Addendum   Something that has to be added to your manual— a slip-in.

Alpha Draft   Your first complete draft, based on the alpha software. Should have the right tone and organization and, if possible, include all its parts. You can expect to make drastic changes as the software changes.

Appendixes   A good place to put information that does not really fit in a chapter, such as tables and summaries of key codes.

Asides   Fun and human. If you're afraid that your side comments might get distracting, find a way to signal serious readers that they can skip these passages.

Audiences   The various people who will be reading your manuals. Find out as much as you can about them.

Authoring Language   A program that lets you create tutorials that run on the computer. Most are designed for teachers who want to set up one-paragraph lectures followed by quizzes.

Bad Manuals   Myriad manuals can go bad in hundreds of ways, ending up unreadable, unusable, and ugly.

Beta Draft   Your second draft. Very close to perfect, you hope. Should match the beta software. Language should be correct and up to standards. All sections should be written. From now on, you hope the software won't change, so all you'll have to do is make small wording changes.

Bibliography   A list of useful articles, periodicals, and books with information about what's in them, who they're for, and where to find them.

CAI Computer-Assisted Instruction. A tutorial that appears on the computer—not on paper.

Camera-Ready Copy Pages made up so that the printer can photograph them to make printing plates.

Change Pages Pages that have been changed to send out to users who are supposed to take out the old, bad pages, and replace them with the new, good pages. Of course, most change pages end up in the wastebasket.

Clarity A sentence is clear when it draws no attention to itself. It just says what it has to. It seems transparent, letting the reader look directly at the subject.

Code What programmers write. They keep busy by coding the program. Also, the secret formula users must type in. Hopefully, you can provide a table of translations for these.

Completeness Inclusion of all the information users need—not everything you ever heard about the product.

Computer-Assisted Instruction Instruction that does not rely on paper: usually a tutorial on a disk.

Consistency When you do the same thing in the same way, over and over, you are consistent. You should be consistent in applying the standards of English and your department, in making cross-references, setting up your layout, using terms, and organizing your manual.

Cookbook Format A way of presenting procedures, step by step, as in a recipe. More general than a tutorial; takes into account all possibilities, where a tutorial sticks to one.

Corrections Changes you make from your first draft on. You hear that the program has been modified, so you have to correct what you say. You may think you have stopped making corrections when the manual is printed. Not so. You still have a chance to send out an errata sheet to apologize for and correct any mistakes you printed.

Critical Path The path to the product's release. The project leader will always tell you that your manual is on the critical path—slowing everything else down. Then, as you reach your final draft, the program begins to miss all its deadlines. Often, you're finished and the program still isn't. At that point, the programmers promise that from now on any changes to the program will make it match the manual. (This is known as documentation-driven programming.) A critical-path diagram shows what you need to receive before you can produce each draft—what you depend on and, in some cases, who is depending on you.

Cross-References References from one part of the manual to another part, or to another manual in a series. For example: "See Chapter 10, Customizing, for more information."

Data Dictionary   A list of every type of information that the program will use. Developed for programmers, the data dictionary can be very helpful, since it defines what's allowed in every field.

Data-Processing Group   The division that creates and maintains various programs for use by a company.

Deadline   An awful term, like mortgage, suggesting you'll die if you don't hand in your manual on time. Why not use *milestone* or *delivery date* instead?

Definitions   Crucial. But tough to write. Include a few examples. Try to give the gist of your definition in one sentence. Only after that should you go into exceptions.

Design Phase   The period during which people are figuring out what the program will do and how it will do it.

Design Team   The team of systems analysts who outline the way a program will look to the users—and to the programmers who will have to create it.

Developer Handbook   A manual for people who are going to be developing products to work with the one you're describing. Developers are often programmers in another company.

Document Design   A description of the manual you intend to write. Includes a summary of the main topics you will cover, a draft of your table of contents, and a sketch of the audiences you will serve.

Editing   The systematic application of standards to a manual. The editor clears up murky passages, straightens out organizational tangles, and ensures that the manual is consistent with other manuals from your group and with itself.

End User   The person who actually uses an application program, such as an inventory or word processing package.

Errata Sheet   Bad Latin for a sheet that admits the errors you made in your manual and offers humble corrections.

Error Messages   Provide clear information on how to correct the error or back out of trouble. But don't call them that. Call them system messages or help messages. List them in alphabetical or numerical order.

Examples   Yes, by all means! But separate them from the running text so people who don't need them can skip them.

Figures   Illustrations or diagrams. Plan these when you are writing—not afterward.

Final Draft   You hope it's your last draft. Should be ready to be looked over by an editor or supervisor who should only find a few typos and violations of standards. Matches final software, you hope.

Flowcharts Diagrams showing how information is supposed to flow through the program. Useful to you, but a bit obscure for most users.

Footnotes Little notes at the bottom of the pages or at the end of a chapter or manual; state the source of your quotation or expand on the trivial details of the topic. Avoid them. They smell of scholarship.

Format Arrangement. This term is applied to various subjects—the spelling of a word, the word processing codes that position text on the printed page, the way a two-column tutorial looks on the page.

Forms A predetermined layout into which users must enter data. Provide samples of empty—and filled-in—forms. If users have to enter information in a particular format, show that, too.

Functional Specifications A list of the functions the program will someday, maybe, perform. A good clue to the original intentions of the designers. Not to be relied on as an accurate description of the final product.

Functions What the program can do. Describe these in your reference sections, offering, at a minimum, a definition, an explanation, an example, a step-by-step procedure, and any necessary warnings.

Galleys Sheets of paper as long as your arm, carrying the text for your manual, which has not yet been carved into individual pages.

Glossary Definitions of key terms. This is an entry in the glossary for this book.

Grammar The description of the most common ways we arrange words into sentences. Not a bunch of rules. Most of what people call grammar is a set of prejudices inherited from rigid high school teachers.

Guide to the Manual A quick introduction to the manual from the point of view of the user. Should use sentences like: "To find out how to create a memo, turn to Chapter 5, Creating a Memo."

Headings The titles and subtitles of chapters, sections, subsections, and sub-subsections. Similar to newspaper headlines. Make your headings active—full of verbs. Don't have too many sizes, though. That gets confusing. People use headings as a way to browse for facts they forgot.

Humor Jokes, silliness, odd perspectives, a light-hearted attitude. I'm for it. But lots of people hate it in their manuals. Slip it into the less formal areas—examples or tutorials. Stress your sympathy with the reader.

Icons Small images representing key subjects. Helpful for indicating where people should go (to a certain disk, for instance), where the problem could be (a video monitor), or what you are about to talk about (a miniature spreadsheet).

Images Drawings, photographs, diagrams. Any illustrations are gratefully accepted by readers. Plan these early—as you write your alpha draft.

Implementation Phase The period during which programmers are actually writing the program. They are implementing the ideas outlined in the design.

Index A list of important topics in your manual, with page references. Make sure you have included all possible synonyms. Indent subtopics.

Input Forms The form someone has to fill out when putting information into the program. Provide these with full explanation of the terms and the rules for filling them out.

Installation Procedures A description of the way to install computer equipment or a computer program.

Internal Documentation Information for—and often by—programmers. It's internal, because they keep it close to their chests.

Jargon Technical language used in a context where it is not needed. It tends to confuse people who are inexperienced in that field.

Laser Printing A form of photocopying. Very sharp, since the original image is created with a laser.

Layout The way you arrange various elements on the page, putting chapter titles here, running text there, and page numbers over here.

Lead Analyst The head honcho. Leads the other systems analysts and programmers in designing and creating the program.

Maintenance Phase The almost endless period during which programmers fix the program and change it to suit new requirements.

Manual A book explaining how to use a computer, its attached hardware, or its programs.

Marketing Figuring out who the product is for, what they want, and how to sell it to them.

Menus A list of options that users can select. On the top line, put the title of the menu; on the bottom, put a prompt and a place to enter the choice. Don't make the menus too complicated.

Migrate To move a program from one computer to another, from one "environment" to another. (An enviroment includes the computer, all its attached equipment, its related programs, and its managers.) Used this way: "Let's migrate this program to the Macintosh."

MIS Management Information Systems. In many companies, the group that creates and maintains in-house programs.

Novice Users Beginners. People who are not familiar with the program— or with computers in general.

Offset Printing A cheap but fast way of making fairly sharp copies.

On-line On the computer. An on-line tutorial can be reached from within the program while someone is using it.

Organization The first way to make your subject clear. Organize around the tasks the reader wants to do using the program.

Overview A general introduction placed before a chapter or section to prepare readers for the main ideas to be covered there.

Page Count   Your first estimate is always too low. The number of pages in your manual *should* reflect the amount of detail you think necessary—not the department budget.

Page Proofs   These come from your typesetter and show what your final printed pages will look like. You may look at several versions of these before getting them right.

Point of View   Depends on who's looking at the subject. Old-fashioned manuals tended to take the point of view of the programmers, and fell into sections like this: INPUT, PROCESSING, OUTPUT, USER ERRORS. You should adopt the users' point of view and organize your manual around the tasks users really want to accomplish.

Programming Team   The programmers who are busy writing the program. Often led by a systems analyst.

Project Manager   The person who is in charge of getting the program written.

Project Team   The group working on this program. Includes the programming team, the project manager, you, plus marketing people, hardware people, and representatives of the users.

Proprietary Information   Secrets that are the property of your company. Find out what's proprietary and steer clear of it.

Quick Fix   A small correction, often pasted onto the boards the printer uses, to create a new version of the manual.

Quick-Reference Card   A summary of key information presented in tables and lists. Often designed to be pulled out of the manual and placed on the keyboard. Make it handy.

Reader-Response Card   An appeal to the readers to tell you what confused them, what pleased them, what they want you to change.

Reference Material   Material documenting every aspect of a program or computer hardware from the point of view of the user.

Release Date   The date on which the program—and your manual—will supposedly be released to the world. Even when you know this is crazy, you may have to keep your mouth shut and act as if it were realistic, until the program slips so badly that even the project manager has to change the release date.

Reports   The information put out by a program, regularly or on demand. Often arranged in a standard format. In your manual, you should provide samples of typical reports produced by the program, with explanations of every field, error messages, and any other information that the program provides.

Request for a Project   The signal to start designing a program. A request may come from the users or from a marketing person who wants a product to sell. The description of the project in the request can give you a vague idea of what was wanted originally. (Not to be confused with the resulting product.)

Reviewer   Anyone who looks over a manual to make comments on style, organization, and consistency.

Revision   A substantial rewriting of an earlier manual. Much more than a quick fix.

Rewriting   Any time you go back to your text and make changes, you are rewriting. If you start with major issues of organization, you'll simplify the task of changing the wording.

Sample Files   Electronic files, produced using the program you are documenting, given to users so they can practice in your tutorial without having to type for half an hour before starting the training. You create these so that users won't have to. Then, in your tutorial, they can manipulate data without having to start from scratch.

Schedule   A list of dates on which you agree to deliver various drafts of your manual.

Screen Shots   A representation of the display users will see on the screen. Don't use a photograph for this—too fuzzy. Reproduce the text and the graphics as they appear, then shade it with a gray background to suggest the screen itself. Use lots of these to reassure the readers that they're in the right place.

Series   A collection of related manuals. If you get a chance, design the series so it divides the information according to the main tasks people want the program for and then subdivides by level of experience. Strive for a consistent layout. Use interlocking tables of contents, indexes, and glossaries.

Setup Procedures   The way to set up a piece of hardware or get a program ready to use.

Specifications   A list of functions that everyone agrees should be in the program. A good source of information about what the program might be. Of course, by the time you get to your alpha draft, the original specifications have long been out of date. (There are also technical specifications, telling the programmers how to create the program).

Stages of a Manual   When you sketch out what topics you'll cover, who you're writing for, and what your table of contents will be, that's the first stage, known as document design. Your first complete draft is the alpha draft; then comes the beta draft, the final draft, an edited draft, and perhaps typeset and printed versions after that.

Standards   The accepted way of handling grammar, spelling, format, and terminology. Developed by the writers, editors, and supervisors as a team.

Status Report   A regular report on your progress. Also, an emergency report that warns of trouble or delay. Every time the program schedule slips, your schedule slips. That's when you should send out a memo with a report on your status and your revised schedule.

Storyboarding   A way of sketching out each step of your tutorial as if it were another frame. Helps you to make sure that you have not left out any steps.

Story Line   A tutorial should have a story line to help people learn the functions in a realistic context.

Summary   A digest of the material you have just covered. Usually in the form of a table or short list. Helpful for people who have just read the section (it's a brief review) and for people who are flipping through the book for a quick refresher.

Systems Analyst   Someone who can figure out the systems we use to get our work done, and—sometimes—sketch out a computer program that will do the same thing—for only a few million dollars more. Often leads a programming team. Good at explaining why the program has not appeared on time.

Tables   Information arranged in rows and columns. Helpful for readers who want to scan information and quickly emerge with one fact.

Talking Down   Contempt for the reader. Shown in a tendency to use baby talk in tutorials.

Technical Manuals   Manuals written for technicians, repair people, programmers—anyone but the actual users.

Technical Specifications   A description of the program in terms that programmers understand. Also, a brief digest of key features in a program or computer for an audience that understands jargon.

Technical Writer   A writer about technical subjects—scientific instruments, engineering projects, or computer projects. The term is not limited to people who document computer hardware and software.

Techno-Babble   Jargon on top of jargon.

Testing a Manual   Making sure that the manual achieves its instructional objectives.

Time to Write   There's never enough. You've probably agreed to an unrealistically fast schedule, and the prople who provide you with information have probably missed some of their deadlines. That's why you can never wait until you're in the mood. It's always time to write.

Troubleshooting   A series of typical problems followed by solutions. A helpful section, if you can manage it.

Truth   You can test it. If the program does what you say it will, that paragraph is true. Examples of untruth: pretending a design flaw is really an interesting new feature or pretending you are telling readers how to hook up their printers when you know you don't know how.

Tutorial   A series of step-by-step exercises introducing users to the basics of a program.

Typesetting   The process of turning your text into type for a printer to photograph and turn into printing plates.

Update   A manual or brochure that brings an older manual up to date. Perhaps the program has changed; perhaps the way people can use it has changed. Also, the period during which programmers bring the program up to date.

User Friendly   Manuals that make sense to the people who have to use them, provide enough information, and allow quick searches are user friendly.

User Interface   The way a program presents itself to its users. You should work with the team to make the user interface of the program friendly.

Users   The people who will use the program you are writing about. Remember: they're all different.

White Space   You can always use more. Let your text breathe. Plenty of white space on the page helps people zoom in on different parts and skip the rest.

Index

ABC of Reading 265
about 154-5
Abraham Lincoln 265
access 9, 52–3, 135, 267
accessory card 243, 250
accessory slot 243
accuracy 5, 45, 92, 135–6, 267
acronym 66, 121–2, 124, 140, 243
active verbs 65–6, 267
addendum 26, 267
address, geographical 243
address, memory 119, 243
affect 244, 249
afterward 11, 243
Alarms and Diversions 265
alignment in images 186
allow 244, 250
all right 244
alphabetizing 139, 140, 244
alpha draft 17, 21, 267
alpha software 16–7
American National Standards Institute
    (ANSI) 244
American Standard Code for Information
    Interchange (ASCII) 127, 172–3, 244
and so forth 250
anger 25, 54, 83, 111, 122, 159, 233–4
ANSI 243–4
anxiety 33-4, 84, 91, 93, 103, 111, 122, 159
any time 244
A Plea for Captain John Brown 265
appendixes 199, 244, 267
Apple at Work 101, 103, 105
Apple Business BASIC 117–8
Apple Computer, Inc. xvii, 243, 247
AppleFile 99, 107
Apple II Computer 89
Apple IIe Computer 46, 89, 103, 247
Apple III Computer 70, 71, 89, 247
Apple III Owner's Manual 196, 204
Apple III+ Computer 196, 204

Apple Presents the Apple IIe 103
Apple Speller III 85–7, 176–86
Apple Writer 82, 99, 102, 104
Applesoft Tutorial 209
application software 244, 247
arithmetic expressions 117–8
arrow keys 104, 169, 244
articles 244
as 244
ASCII character sets 127, 172–3, 243,
    244, 246
asides 53, 78, 80, 91, 103, 168, 267
assembly language 138–9, 244
Auden, W.H. 265
audiences
    different 8, 32, 57, 267
    interests 32–3, 51–2, 136–8
    levels 57, 79
    questions about 6, 31–5
    research about 34, 57, 196
    their goals 32, 136–8
authoring language 100
Autobiography 265
auto-repeat 244

back panel 244, 248
backplane 244
backspace 244, 248
backup disks 244
backward 244
ball-point pen 245, 250
Barthelme, Donald 265
BASIC 66, 113, 117–9, 243, 245
baud rate 32, 245
Beauclerk, Helen 265
because 153–4, 245, 249
Beeler, Meg 209–12, 214, 216
Beginners All-Purpose Symbolic
    Instruction Code (BASIC) 66, 113,
    117–9, 245
beginnings 65–72, 80–2, 102

beta draft 17, 22, 24, 27, 196, 267
beta software 17, 24
beta testing 24
bibliography 125, 267
big words 149
bitmap 245, 249
black-and-white 245
blank 245
blinking cursor 245, 251
block moves 147
bloodless writing 155–6
board 245
Boolean logic 245
boot 32, 70, 79, 147, 245
braces 245, 248
breaks 91, 104
Bruce and James 171
Buddha 265
bugs 8, 17, 22, 45
built-in disk drive 245–6, 248
bulleted lists 69, 73, 81, 117, 127,
    151, 168
business graphics 69, 106
Butah, Jon 99, 101–2, 104–7
buttons 245

CAI (Computer-Assisted Instruction) 31,
    55–6, 99–107, 268
call 253
callouts 245–6
camera-ready art 268
can 245
cancel 245
capitalization 243–63
captions 246, 250
card 245–6
caret 246
catalog 150–1, 246
category 44, 46–7
cathode ray tube 247
central processor 246
Ceremony in Lone Tree 265
change pages 17, 268
changes to the program 17, 22, 25,
    46–7, 92
chapters 21, 246
chapter overviews 72–3
chapter summaries 115–7
chapter titles 65–7, 71–2, 169
character 246–7
checklist 125–8, 288
chip 246
circumflex 246

City Life 265
clarity 5–6, 8, 45–6, 268
cliches 150
CLS 113
Cochran, Rani 196, 201, 203–4
code (lines of computer program) 268
code file 246, 250
codes 40, 44, 66–7, 93, 105, 119–23,
    129, 140
cold start 246
Colette 265
color in images 168, 187
column 84–5, 246
command 40, 66, 84, 89, 111, 113, 125–7,
    152, 174, 234, 246–7
command names 247
communications packages 43, 114, 247
company 247–8
completeness 9, 45–6, 111–2, 127–8,
    135–6, 268
complex sentences 255–6
computer 18, 31–2, 34, 55–6, 99–101, 247
computer voice 247
computer-assisted instruction 55–6,
    97–107, 268
configuration 43, 199
confusion 6, 40, 77–9, 83–5, 107, 113
connector 247, 257
consistency 57–8, 66, 113, 225–6, 268
console 247
constant 247
contents, tables of 18, 21, 54–5, 65–7,
    71–2, 79, 136, 169, 213,
    215, 261
context 78, 112
contrasts 151–2
control-character 247
control key 244, 247
controller card 243, 246, 247
controlling 247
conventions 40, 102, 118–9, 127
conversions 127
cookbook format 112–3, 268
coprocessor 247
copy-protection 247
copyright 169
corporation 247–8
corrections 17–23, 25–6, 121,
    195–205, 268
covers 168
CP/M 248
CPU 246, 248
critical path 24, 26, 268
cross-references 5, 57, 93–4, 120, 226, 268

CRT 247
Cummings, e.e. 265
curly brackets 245, 248
cursor 73, 81, 84, 91, 104, 126
customizing the program 43, 67, 112
cutout 248

dark-on-light 248, 253
dashes 248
data 248, 253
data base 46–7, 72–3, 81, 84, 104–5, 248
data dictionary 44, 269
data file 248, 250
data processing groups 7, 15–8, 24–7,
    40–3, 46–7, 100, 269
DB-9 connector 248
dead hand 148
deadlines 19–26, 269
dealer 248
DeBono, Edward 265
decision tables 44
default 91–2, 248
definitions 5, 6, 46–7, 72–3, 81–2, 85, 120,
    123–4, 127, 213–5, 269
DEL character 248
delete keys 86, 248
design phase 15, 269
design team 6, 15, 26, 46–7, 269
designing
    layout 168–9, 225
    the document 20–1, 46–7
desktop 248
detail in images 186
developer handbook 26, 269
developing the product 15–26, 43–7
device name 124, 248
Diamond Sutra 265
diagrams 21, 43, 68, 72, 80–1, 86–8, 93–4,
    104, 115–6, 168, 171–86
Dieli, Mary 213–4
different 248
directory 248
Disambiguator 234
disclaimers 169
disdain 6
disk controller card 247
disk names 82, 89, 249
Disk Operating System 249
diskette 248-9
disks 32, 70, 77, 79, 82–3, 86–9, 92–3,
    104, 107, 114, 123–4, 137–9, 176–86,
    248–9
display 85, 99–100, 120, 122, 156, 169,
    247, 249, 257

display device 249
display pages 249
document design 20–1, 45, 269
DOS-formatted 249
dot matrix 6, 172–3, 245, 249
double check 249
doubt 33–4, 45, 84, 91, 111, 122
DOWN-ARROW 249
drawings 21, 68, 72, 80–1, 86-8, 93–4, 104,
    115–6, 126
drive 70, 79, 82–3, 86–7, 89, 93, 104, 114,
    123, 249
due to 249
dummy data 120–1
Dyer's Hand 265

e.g. 249
EBCDIC 243, 249
edge connector 247
edited draft 23
editors 23, 269
effect 244, 249
Eisenberg, J.D. 103
electromagnetic interference 249
electronic worksheet 70
Elements of Style 265
11-pin connector 257
embed 249
EMI 249
enable 250
end 89–90, 93–4, 106–7, 125–8
end user 269
engineer 8, 16, 25–6, 41, 46
enhancements to the program 17, 22–3, 25
ensure 250, 253
enter 250, 253
entitled 250
envelope 250
equal sign 250
equipment needed 33, 43, 70, 79, 187
errata sheets 6, 26, 201, 269
error messages 33, 44, 83, 91, 102, 105,
    122–3, 234–6, 269
error trapping 105
ESC 79, 83, 90, 250
escaping 79, 83, 239
Espinosa, Sue 78
estimating your time 18–26
etc. 250
examples 112–5, 117, 124, 127, 249, 269
exchange 72
exit 79, 83
expansion slot 243, 250
explanations 5, 85, 102, 111–4, 120–125

Extended Binary-Coded-Decimal
  Interchange Code (EBCDIC) 243, 249

fanfold paper 171, 250
felt-tip pen 250
female connector 247, 250
fewer 250, 254
field 46–7, 117, 121–2, 127
figures 21, 43, 68, 72, 80–1, 86–8, 93–4,
  104, 115–6, 168, 250, 269
filename 248, 250
files 44, 72, 77, 81–2, 92, 114, 116, 127,
  148, 250
file types 250
filling 72
final draft 17, 22–4, 47, 269
final software 17, 24
finish 251
firmware 251
first page proofs 23
flashing cursor 245, 251
flexible disk 251 (*see* Disks)
floppy disk 251 (*see* Disks)
flowcharts 43, 80–1, 93–4, 116, 270
focus groups 41
following 251
footnotes 125, 168, 270
format
  of a book 21–3, 68, 270
  of input 120
  of records 115
  of reports 73
  of summaries 115
  of tutorials 184–5
formatting a volume 82–3
forms 119–20, 150–1, 270
formulas 44
fractional spacing 147
Freud, Sigmund 265
functional specifications 20, 43–7, 270
function keys 253
functions, how to describe 7, 8, 16–8,
  21–2, 25, 39–40, 54, 65–6, 69, 71–3,
  77–9, 101, 106, 112–6, 125–7, 270
Future Positive 265

galleys 23, 270
game controller 251
GAME I/O 251
game paddle 251
Gay, Robert 265
getting started on the manual 16–21,
  31–57
giant checklist 288

glossary 53, 123–4, 270
glosses, marginal definitions 168
grammar 21–3, 270
graphics 21, 43, 68, 72, 80–1, 86–8, 93–4,
  104, 115–6, 251
gray 251
green-phosphor 251
grey 251
grounded outlet 251
guessing 105
guide to the manual 20–1, 57, 67–8, 270

Hall, Edward T. 265
halt 245, 251
hand control 245, 251
handy reference card 53, 93, 125–8
hard disk drives 32, 251
hardware engineer 16
headings 45, 56, 58, 65–7, 71–2, 79, 119,
  168, 270
Hecht, Nancy 170, 187
help 46–7, 84, 100–2, 105
Hemingway, Ernest 265
hex 252
hexadecimal 140, 252
hexagonal-head screw 252
Hidden Dimension 265
high bit 252
high resolution 246, 249, 252
highlighted 252
Huber, John 25–6
Hui Neng 265
humor 159–63, 270
hyphenation 145, 243–51, 252, 253–63

I 154
I, or Six Non-Lectures 265
i.e. 252
IBM Personal Computer 54–5, 68, 83, 86,
  117, 172–3
icons 168, 270
ICs 252
identifier 252
IEEE 243, 252
illustrations 21, 43, 68, 72, 80–1, 86–8,
  93–4, 104, 115–6, 167–87
images 167–87, 270
  describing for artists 186–7
imbed 252
implementation phase 15–7, 270
inconsistency 57–8, 66, 113, 225–6, 268
index 5, 21, 53, 56, 135–41, 215, 252, 271
  keywords 21, 136–8
  punctuating 137–9

references 137–9
revising 140
sorting 139–40
subdivisions 137
synonyms 137–8
informality 162
information 253
ing phrases 66
initializing 83
in order to 253
input 33, 40, 44, 51–2, 68, 120, 253
input forms 120–1, 271
insert 71–2, 84, 86–7
installation procedures 42–3, 52, 70, 271
Institute of Electrical and Electronics
    Engineers (IEEE) 243, 252
instruction 246, 253
instruction sets 127
insure 250, 253
interface card 243, 246, 253
internal disk drive 245, 253
internal documentation 43, 271
International Standards Organization (ISO)
    243, 253
Interpretation of Dreams 265
interrupt 253
introduction 21, 53, 56, 69–73, 146
inventory programs 33, 121–2
inverted 252–3
invoke 253
ISO 243, 253
italics 253
Its Its 148

jack 247
jacket 250, 253
James, William 265
jargon 5, 6, 32, 42, 44, 46–7, 53, 73, 81–2,
    85, 120, 123–4, 127, 147, 160–1,
    236, 271
jokes 159–63, 215
justifying text 147

key terms 127, 168
key words 66, 127, 135–40, 247, 254
keyboard 86, 99–100, 104, 156
keycaps 247, 249, 253, 254
keypress 253
keys 250, 253
keystrokes 79, 83, 84–8, 90, 104, 105,
    114–6, 126, 234, 254
kilobyte 254
Korman, Henry 86, 176–86
Krinkow, Miss 153–5

labels 252, 254
Lao Tzu 265
laser printing 271
Lau, D.C. 265
lay 254
layout 21–3, 68, 119–20, 167–9, 271
lead analyst 16, 42, 271
learning 29–35, 37–47
Learning How to Learn 265
leaving 79, 83, 93, 107
Leeman, Dick 202
LEFT-ARROW 254
length 21
Leo Logolover 104
less 250, 254
letters as letters 254
level of audience 21, 29–35, 40–1, 51–2,
    57, 65, 67–8, 70, 79
lie 254
Liedtka, Leslie 223–6
light bulb 254
light-on-dark 253–4
like 244, 254
limitations 127
line 254
line feed 254
line numbers 254
lists
    examples 69, 73, 81, 117, 127,
        151, 168
    style 255–6
Living Videotext, Inc. 89
load 253
lock 256
logical devices 67
logical expressions 117–8
Logo 99, 104, 256
long words 149
look of a manual 167–8
low bit 256
lowercase 235, 256

machine language 256
macro commands 255–6
Mail List Manager 87–8
main logic board 256
main memory 246, 256
maintenance of a program 17, 271
male 247, 256
managers 15–8, 23–7, 31, 42, 167, 201
Mantis, Connie 196–7
manuals
    bad 5, 267
    edited draft 23

manuals (*Continued*)
  friendly 5–9
  guide to 20–1, 57, 67–8, 270
  hostile 5–7
  minimal 56, 271
  organization of 51–8, 65–74, 111–31
  printed 23
  reasons for bad ones 6, 19, 25–6, 31
  in series, 57–8
  technical 43
  typeset versions 23
manufacturing 26–7
marginal glosses 168, 224
margins 137, 167
marketing 7, 15–6, 26–7, 40–1, 271
mass storage device 256
Maugham, W. Somerset 265
may 154, 245, 256
Meade, Susan 45–7
mechanicalness 152–3
media 99–100
memo 24, 198–200
memory 250
memory address 256
memory location 119, 140, 256
memory pages 249, 256
menus 101, 139, 162, 173–5, 234,
  237–9, 271
might 154
migrating a program 18, 271
Miller, Peggy 79–82
MIS 271
mistakes 79, 83, 85, 91, 99–100, 105,
  122–3
modem 146
modem eliminator 256
modes 256
monitor cable 257
Monitor program 257
Montherlant, Henry de 265
Morris, Wright 265
motherboard 257
Mou-Lam, Wong 265
Moveable Feast 265
moving text 55
My Apprenticeships 265

name 252, 257
Name plate 257
New York *Times* 168
New Yorker 159
9-pin connector 248, 257
non (prefix) 257
noun clumps 145–6

novice users 7, 31–5, 52–7, 65–71,
  77–107, 271
now 155
null character 257
number sign 257
numbered lists 83, 114, 168
numbers 257
numeric 257

off–line 257
offset printing 23, 271
OK 257
Olson, Kris 34
omissions 45–6, 224
online tutorial 55–6, 99–107, 257, 271
One Bite Intro 145–7
Opening display 257
operating systems 257
operations 26–7
optimism in scheduling 25
options 54, 78, 148, 237–9 (*see also*
  Functions)
optional 40
organization 51–8, 224–5, 271
  of references 111–3
outline 20–1, 51–8, 71, 111–3
output 40, 44, 120–2, 257
overviews 53, 69–73, 146–7, 271
ownership of the printer 67

P.A.L. 258
P–code 258
P–machine 258
paddle buttons 245, 257
page layout 167–9, 258
page count, estimating 18–21, 272
page proofs 23, 272
paper for manuals 168
parallel interface card 253
parallels 151
parentheses 258
Parker, Dorothy 159
parts 258
Pascal 172, 174, 202, 258
Pascal Editor 71–2, 175
passives 147–8
patches 17
pathname 258
Peachtree Software Incorporated 247
peripheral 243, 246, 250, 258
Personal Computer Age 125
perspective in images 187
Phased Alternate Lines (P.A.L.) 258
Phillips head 258

pictures 21, 43, 68, 72, 80–1, 86–8, 93–4,
    104, 115–6
plates 23
plug 247, 258
plurals 258
point of view 8–9, 31–5, 51–3, 272
porting a program 18
Pound, Ezra 265
pound sterling 258
power cable 259
power–on light 259
prefaces 146–7, 169 (*see also*
    Introductions, Overviews)
press 23, 250, 254, 259
Price, A.F. 265
print head 259
print wheel 259
printer 23, 167
printer controller card 247
printing 167–8
printout 259
procedures 53, 112–3, 259
processor 259
product names 259
program
    benefits 69–71
    definition of 259
    design 15
    disk 259
    error messages in 122–3
    forms for input to 119–20
    functions 112–3
    implementing 15–7
    limits 71
    listings 259
    maintenance 17
    migrating 18
    output 120–2
    questions about 34–5
    reports 120–2
    request for 15
    researching 39–47
    specifications 45
    stages 20–3
    tutorial 99–107
    update 17
programmers 42, 51–2, 100–5
programming team 15–26, 40–3, 272
project manager 15–26, 40–3, 272
project team 15–26, 40–3, 272
prompt 259
proprietary 272
protect 259
pseudo-machine 258

punctuating in index 139–40
puns 161–2
purpose of images 186

Quick File 46–7, 70, 72–3, 81, 139
quick fixes 17, 22, 201, 203, 272
quick reference card 53, 66, 125–8, 169,
    215, 272
QuickStart 54–5, 82–3
quitting 85, 93, 107, 239
quotation marks 259

radio-frequency modulator 260
random-access memory 260
Rasmussen, Roy 227
raster 245, 249, 260
re- (prefix) 260
read-only memory 260
reader response card 199–200, 272
readers 6, 8, 21, 32–5, 51–2, 57, 70, 79, 91,
    99–100, 112–3, 117, 123–6, 135–8
recipe format 112–3
records 139
Reed, Don 41
reference material 45, 52–5, 57, 65–73,
    111–31, 272
reference
    online 56
    testing 209, 213–4
    index 136–9
relational expressions 117
relationships in images 186
release date 17, 25–6, 272
reports, 40, 44, 73, 114, 120–2, 150–1
    samples 121–2, 137, 272
request for a project 15, 43, 272
required 40, 43–5, 119–20
RESET 260
restrictions 127
returns 88, 102, 104–5, 169
review meetings 196–7
reviewers of your manual 22,
    195–205, 273
reviewing someone else's manual 223–9
revising 22–3, 167–8, 195–205, 273
    index 140
    style 145–56
rewriting 22–3, 195–205
rewriting the program 233–40
Rezeau, Laurel 224
RF modulator 260
RIGHT-ARROW 260
right-side 260
rigid disk 251, 260

rote drill 100

Roughing It 265

routine 35, 66, 260

rules 44, 127, 153–5

run 121

running heads 169

running text 169

runts 146–7

sample files in tutorials 77, 92, 273

sample reports 121–2

sample screens 85, 102–4

Sandburg, Carl 265

saving 68, 73, 77, 81, 92

scheduling 6, 15–27, 273

Schrank, Robert 265

screen shots 85, 102–4, 169, 249, 273

scrolling 172

sector size 260

security 44

Selected Essays 265

Sensible Speller 69

series 57–8, 151, 273 (*see also* Lists)

set–up procedures 39, 43–4, 52, 273

Shah, Idries 265

SHIFT 260

signal 260

silicon chip 260

since 260

single letters 260

Skillin, Marjorie 265

slashes 260

sleeve 250, 260

slot 247, 260

so-called 260

socket 247, 250, 260

soft switches 119

software (*see* Programs)

Software Guild 69

Software Publishing Corporation 247

sorting an index 139–40

SOS 250

sound in computer-assisted instruction 104

SOUND statement 117

source file 250

SPACE bar 261

space character 235, 245, 261

special keys 86, 169

specifications 15, 20, 43–5, 273

spelling 22–3, 69, 87, 176–86

splash screen 257, 261

spreadsheet 70, 82, 261

stages of a project 15–8, 20–4, 273

standards 135–8, 225, 273

start up 32, 40, 43–4, 52, 70, 77, 86–7, 89, 148, 257, 261

statement 246, 254, 261

status reports 26, 273

step 75–93, 102–3, 112–3, 213, 261

stop 83–5, 93, 107, 245, 261

storyboarding tutorials 78, 274

story line 78, 101, 103, 274

strikeover 147

Strunk, William, Jr. 265

style 145–56, 198, 224–6

stylesheet 243–63

subdivided entries 137

subroutine 66

subscripts 169

summaries 53, 69–73, 89–90, 106, 115–7, 169, 274

Summing Up 265

SuperPILOT 261

superscripts 169

supervisors 15–8, 23–7, 31, 42, 167, 201

suspend 245, 261

Sutra 265

symbol 246, 261

sympathy 162–3

synonyms 138

syntax 127, 255–6

system 247, 259, 261

System Utilities Training Pack 79–81

systems analyst 15, 274

tables 117–9, 153, 169, 250, 274

tables of contents 18, 21, 54–5, 65–7, 71–2, 79, 136, 169, 213, 215, 261

talking 19–20, 25–6, 34–5, 39–42

talking down 274

Tao Te Ching 265

tasks 32, 51–2, 57, 113–4

team 15–22, 24–7, 41–3, 46–7, 195–201

technical manuals 45, 274

technical specifications 45, 274

technical writing 274

techno-babble 5, 274

telecommunications 261

television set 249, 261

Ten Thousand Working Days 265

testing 92, 209–17

  preparing for 210–2

  reference manuals 209, 213–4, 274

  tutorials 92, 210

  who and what 210–1

text copying 55, 65–6, 68, 71–3, 86, 113, 126, 147

text file 62

text in images 187
that 262
then 155
ThinkTank 89
this 262
Thompson, Jon 161, 225–7
Thoreau, Henry 265
Thurber, James 265
time to write 15, 20–2, 274
titled 250, 262
titles 67–9, 169, 246, 262
Tognazzini, Bruce 103, 233–9
tool kit 262
toward 262
trademarks 169
trailing off 150–1
translations 122–3
trial and error 105, 262
troubleshooting 122–4, 262, 274
truth 8, 274
turn on 250
tutorials 53–6, 77–95, 275
   on the computer 55–6, 99–107
   testing 92
Twain, Mark 265
25-pin connector 257
two-column format for tutorials 84, 169
type 23, 169, 250, 253, 254, 262
typeface 168–9
typeset version 23, 67, 275
typing errors—in tutorials 83, 105

University of Chicago 265
UP-ARROW 262
update 17, 199–202, 275
uppercase 235, 262
user 8, 32–5, 51–2, 57, 79, 211, 262
user friendliness 7, 275
User Interface Guidelines 233
user-hostile 7
Utilities 79–82, 200

van Nouhuys, Dirk 25
variable 262
variations 78, 88–9, 111–3
Varieties of Religious Experience 265

vendor 7
verifying the manual 92, 209–217
video 262–3
video monitor 99–101, 247, 249
viewport 263
VisiCalc III 70, 82
VisiCorp 54–5, 68, 82–3, 90, 93–4,
   116, 175
VisiLink 90, 116, 175
VisiWord 54–5, 68, 82–3, 94
visual design 167, 189
visual language 170
Voltaire 99
volume name 248, 250, 263
volumes 81–3, 258, 263

Walden 265
warm start 263
warnings 91, 105, 122–3, 169
Watson, Allen 41, 45–6, 163
Weal, Elizabeth 101, 103, 105
whazzats 147
which 262, 263
whir 263
White, E.B. 162, 265
white space 168, 275
Williams, William Carlos 265
word processing package 55, 65–6, 68,
   71–3, 89, 113, 126, 147, 176–89
wordplay 161–2
Words into Type 243, 265
words as words 263
Wordvision 171
work file 250, 263
wraparound 263
write-enable notch 248, 263
write-protected 247, 263
write to 257

zap 72
zero character 247, 263
zero page 258, 263
zeros 147, 160, 263
zip code 263
Zussman, John 171

THE GIANT CHECKLIST
From *How to Write a Computer Manual*

The Benjamin/Cummings Publishing Company

Menlo Park, California · Reading, Massachusetts
London · Amsterdam · Don Mills, Ontario · Sydney

When your manual is truly friendly, it:

☐ Recognizes that readers are different—from you and from each other.

☐ Assumes that readers want to learn and grow.

☐ Tells the truth.

☐ Follows an order that makes sense to users—not the programmer.

☐ Makes the product—and what users have to do—clear.

☐ Takes the long view, with plenty of introductions, overviews, and summaries.

☐ Teaches how to use the product.

☐ Speeds up a user's access to the material.

☐ Offers full details.

☐ Has been checked again and again for accuracy and completeness.

In developing your schedule:

☐ Recognize that most schedules—including your own—exaggerate.

☐ Figure out how many pages your manual may have and multiply that by the number of hours it takes to do a page.

☐ See if you have that many hours available. If not, consult with your supervisor and the team.

☐ Set deadlines for document design; alpha, beta, and final drafts; plus edited, typeset, and printed versions.

☐ Figure out what you need when—and tell the other members of the team.

In describing your audiences:

☐ Get specific.

☐ Distinguish between audiences.

☐ Keep the focus on their goals—not yours.

☐ Remember they're smart.

☐ Organize topics around what they want to know.

☐ Imagine their questions—and figure out how to answer them.

☐ Conduct research—reading and interviewing.

In gathering information about the product, make sure that you:

☐ Ask all the questions real users might have—plus plenty of your own.

☐ Talk with everyone—potential users, marketing people, programmers.

☐ Become a member of the team.

☐ Read whatever you can get ahold of, particularly the specifications.

☐ Write to find out what you don't know. Then find out.

☐ Participate in developing the program.

In general, when organizing your manual:

☐ Follow the readers' interests, not the programmers'.

☐ Include sections that will speed up readers' access to information.

☐ Distinguish clearly between tutorial and reference material and between what should be done on paper and what should be done on the computer.

☐ Figure out the minimum needed.

☐ Make a series look consistent in these areas: cross-reference, guidance, audience, tasks, standards, length, and titles.

Your tables of contents should:

☐ Offer enough information so readers can find major and minor sections using the main table of contents.

☐ Appear at the front of complicated chapters, so readers can find out what is within the minor sections.

☐ Correlate sections with headings on top of pages, so readers can flip to them without knowing the exact page number.

☐ Use active verbs, not abstract nouns.

☐ Arrange material in the order readers think about it—not in the order programmers think about it.

☐ Use consistent phrasing.

Your guide to the manual should:

☐ Anticipate the main reasons readers might want to open the manual and direct them to the right spot for each.

☐ Not talk too long.

☐ Highlight major sections. (A quick outline of the manual from the users' point of view.)

☐ Offer page numbers or chapter numbers, so readers can turn to them quickly.

Your overviews should:

☐ Answer most of my initial questions about the topic—at least in a general way.

☐ Promise further information—and announce what subjects you will discuss in the rest of the chapter.

☐ Do not go into details before having established general principles.

☐ Put the most important ideas first—why readers should read the chapter, what this part of the product will do.

☐ Start positively.

☐ Show how this chapter flows out of the last one and leads into the ᵡt one.

In writing your tutorials you should:

☐ Anticipate every move—every possible move.

☐ Be alert to whatever might puzzle beginners.

☐ Tell people how to use which parts.

☐ Carve the material into digestible sections.

☐ Introduce each section.

☐ Divide each section into a series of short steps.

☐ Show people how to get out.

☐ Separate what readers should do from what it means.

☐ Put in lots of displays and pictures.

☐ Define any unfamiliar terms the first time you use them.

☐ Anticipate the main variations of equipment configuration.

☐ Summarize.

☐ Don't rush. And give readers some breaks along the way.

☐ Allay anxiety.

☐ Test, revise, test, revise, test.

☐ Tell people what to do next.

Your computer-assisted instruction should:

☐ Focus on the basics.

☐ Show a menu up front and let people go back there any time.

☐ Explain what you're about to do on the tutorial.

☐ Make every segment short.

☐ Keep the tone light.

☐ Play foreground information off against a background to show how the product actually looks.

☐ Keep a rhythm going between lecture and activity.

☐ Encourage guessing.

☐ Catch readers' errors without making them feel bad.

☐ Do the boring stuff.

☐ Give people some elbowroom.

☐ Sum it up.

☐ Point out the next step.

Your reference material, in general:

☐ Puts the common before the unusual.

☐ Establishes a context before giving the details.

☐ Is organized around what people want to do.

☐ Avoids repetition and "go to's."

☐ Gets people going fast, without a lot of reading.

☐ Provides some sections focused on the tasks that users want to do as part of their job—not just the functions of the program.

For each function, provide the following:

☐ Definition.

☐ Explanation.

☐ Example.

☐ ￢tions and warnings.

☐ Step-by-step procedure, if needed.

Helpful summaries:

☐ Concentrate on the main point (what users most want to know about the subject).

☐ Give bare-bones instructions and minimal explanations.

☐ Do not start with exceptions.

☐ Stand off from the regular text in plenty of white space.

☐ Rely on drawings.

☐ Appear in the same format throughout.

Readable tables:

☐ Use visual cues to distinguish rows and columns in complex or crowded tables.

☐ Present similar material in the same way.

☐ Have clear introductions, headings, labels, and footnotes, explaining what all those numbers mean.

Forms for input:

☐ Correspond clearly to the fields on the screen.

☐ Tell what each field name means. Distinguish it from similar ones.

☐ Define what the program will or will not accept. Show all permissible codes in the correct format.

☐ Key all explanations to the fields on the form.

☐ Show how the program may respond.

☐ Warn readers about possible surprises and confusions.

☐ Show a filled-in version.

Sample reports:

☐ Show part of each section.

☐ Key explanations to each field.

☐ Include all possible codes, error messages, and administrative data.

Program messages:

☐ Aren't called error messages.

☐ Include all messages in one list. (How would a beginner know which type this one is?)

☐ Tell users what to do about it. If there's an applicable rule, say what it is.

☐ Translate any jargon.

☐ Tell readers where to go for further information.

Glossary entries:

☐ Include every term introduced in the manual.

☐ Do not have lockjaw.

☐ Do not simply repeat stock phrases.

☐ Give examples when they might help.

☐ Refer to other entries, but give the gist of those entries so people don't have to keep flipping back and forth.

☐ Include some advice.

Your section on further reading:

☐ Lists only the most helpful books and magazines.

☐ Explains who the book's for and what readers can expect to get out of it.

☐ Warns readers about the level of difficulty.

☐ Provides a way to get the material—a publisher, address, price, perhaps even a phone number.

Quick-reference cards:

☐ Arrange material by functions.

☐ Include material someone would need but might not easily recall.

☐ Stick to tables and lists.

☐ Fit related material into the same fold.

Your index should:

☐ Include every topic treated in a major or minor heading.

☐ Include every special term, abbreviation, code, and acronym in the manual.

☐ Include synonyms—words readers might think of before remembering your term for the subject.

☐ Use indentations to show subordinate topics.

☐ Give all the information here, rather than telling people to "See also . . . ."

☐ Include only the key page numbers—for the useful pages.

☐ Appear in alphabetical order.

A friendly style:

☐ Breaks up all those noun clumps.

☐ Organizes the material in a forward time sequence.

☐ Allows your introductions to grow so they aren't runts.

☐ Defines unfamiliar terms.

☐ Replaces passive verbs with a name and an act.

☐ Replaces anonymous *it* with a person—and an active verb.

☐ Omits long words when you don't need them.

☐ Cuts cliches.

☐ Revises sentences so they don't trail off.

☐ Keeps each item parallel in a series.

☐ Completes any contrast with its second half.

☐ Doesn't get too mechanical, rigid, and repetitive.

☐ Doesn't fake good cheer.

☐ Shows all your senses are alive—in the writing.

Your humor:

☐ Uses reversal of perspective.

☐ Allows some admissions—such as the fact that you, too, find some of these terms irritating.

☐ Keeps all wordplay accessible—not academic.

☐ Appears in the more informal and optional sections, such as examples and introductions—not in reference material.

☐ Shows your sympathy for the readers.

In designing a look for your manual, you need to decide on each of these things:

☐ Reproduction Method

☐ Paper

☐ Page Size and Shape

☐ Typeface

- [ ] White Space
- [ ] Color
- [ ] Covers

In designing the layout, decide on the position, typesize, and font for each element:

- [ ] Asides
- [ ] Figures
- [ ] Headings
- [ ] Icons
- [ ] Key terms
- [ ] Lists
- [ ] Marginal glosses
- [ ] Prefatory material
- [ ] Running heads
- [ ] Running text
- [ ] Sample screens
- [ ] Special keys
- [ ] Subscripts and superscripts
- [ ] Summaries and quick-reference cards
- [ ] Tables of Contents
- [ ] Tables
- [ ] Text that the readers must type
- [ ] Titles

- ☐ Tutorial text
- ☐ Warnings

Your images should answer key questions, such as:

- ☐ Where is it?
- ☐ What is it?
- ☐ How does it work?
- ☐ Why?
- ☐ What's on that level?
- ☐ And below that?
- ☐ What's the big picture?
- ☐ What are the steps involved?

In describing an illustration you want in the manual, be sure to tell the artists what you want in these terms:

- ☐ Relationships
- ☐ Alignment
- ☐ Scale
- ☐ Detail
- ☐ Purpose
- ☐ Text
- ☐ Equipment Needed
- ☐ Perspective
- ☐ Color

In revising your work:

☐ Ask for comments—and listen.

☐ Call a review meeting to get outstanding issues resolved.

☐ Take the long view first: work on structure before you tinker with details.

☐ Check back with reviewers.

☐ Plan for future updates and revisions.

☐ Read what all the real users say.

☐ Make quick fixes—this week.

☐ Send out errata sheets or change pages as you go.

☐ Call an update an update.

☐ Recognize when rewriting means writing it all new.

☐ Talk to anyone who can help.

In testing the manual:

☐ Get started early.

☐ Decide exactly what you want to test.

☐ Set up a schedule.

☐ Recruit some people who are like your target audiences.

☐ Figure out how many people you'll watch at once.

☐ Calculate what equipment you'll need.

☐ Calm down.

☐ Begin by asking for their help in spotting your mistakes. Encourage them to speak up.

☐ Set up some problems to be solved using the reference sections.

☐ Watch what they do.

☐ Ask what's going on, what they think, why they pause.

☐ Make plenty of notes.

☐ Hold a general discussion at the end.

☐ Congratulate yourself.

☐ Repeat until your manual is perfect.

In reviewing someone else's manual, make sure that the style is:

☐ Free of jargon.

☐ Not too fast or slow.

☐ Appropriate in tone, without sudden changes.

☐ Active, not passive.

☐ Alive with variety, not monotonous.

Make sure that the organization:

☐ Makes sense.

☐ Accomodates the needs of different users.

☐ Makes clear why one section follows another.

☐ Puts first things first.

☐ Leaves nothing out.

Assure consistency so that:

☐ The same term is used for the same object throughout.

☐ The manual matches the program and is accurate.

- [ ] The manual never violates company standards or the standards of English.

- [ ] Similar sections are organized the same way.

- [ ] Style and tone do not vary from one part to another.

- [ ] The table of contents matches the actual titles and headings.

And as you write comments for the writer:

- [ ] Note anything strange, even if you don't know what to do about it.

- [ ] Be specific.

- [ ] Show sympathy and respect for the writer.

- [ ] Sum up what you like and what you recommend.

In softening up the software:

- [ ] Work with the programmer to make the program easy to learn and easy to use.

- [ ] Reduce the number of menus and levels.

- [ ] Help users guess.

- [ ] Don't lead users astray.

- [ ] Don't make users feel stupid.

- [ ] Eliminate jargon.

- [ ] Provide help along the way.

- [ ] Make all the menus look the same.

- [ ] Group activities the way users think of them.

- [ ] Provide examples.

- [ ] Help people escape.